I0130580

Routledge Revivals

Young People's Understanding of Society

First published in 1991, this book represents the first wide-ranging review of young people's understanding of the social world and the functioning of society. Taking a social cognitive view of adolescence, it focuses on the processes by which young people learn to understand other people's thoughts, emotions, intentions and behaviour. Concentrating on the social world of politics, economics, work, gender and religion, the authors cover such issues as: politics and government; work and unemployment; law and legislative matters; religion; marriage and the family; social class; and racial and ethnic differences. This work will be of interest to students of sociology and psychology.

Young People's Understanding of Society

Adrian Furnham and Barrie Stacey

Routledge
Taylor & Francis Group

First published in 1991
by Routledge

This edition first published in 2016 by Routledge
2 Park Square, Milton Park, Abingdon, Oxon, OX14 4RN
and by Routledge
711 Third Avenue, New York, NY 10017

Routledge is an imprint of the Taylor & Francis Group, an informa business

© 1991 Adrian Furnham and Barrie Stacey

The right of Adrian Furnham and Barrie Stacey to be identified as authors of
this work has been asserted by him in accordance with sections 77 and 78 of the
Copyright, Designs and Patents Act 1988.

All rights reserved. No part of this book may be reprinted or reproduced or
utilised in any form or by any electronic, mechanical, or other means, now
known or hereafter invented, including photocopying and recording, or in any
information storage or retrieval system, without permission in writing from the
publishers.

Publisher's Note
The publisher has gone to great lengths to ensure the quality of this reprint but
points out that some imperfections in the original copies may be apparent.

Disclaimer
The publisher has made every effort to trace copyright holders and welcomes
correspondence from those they have been unable to contact.

A Library of Congress record exists under LC control number: 90040790

ISBN 13: 978-1-138-64198-3 (hbk)
ISBN 13: 978-1-315-63012-0 (ebk)
ISBN 13: 978-1-138-64212-6 (pbk)

Young people's understanding of society

Adrian Furnham
and
Barrie Stacey

ROUTLEDGE

London and New York

First published 1991
by Routledge
11 New Fetter Lane, London EC4P 4EE

Simultaneously published in the USA and Canada
by Routledge
a division of Routledge, Chapman and Hall, Inc.
29 West 35th Street, New York, NY 10001

© 1991 Adrian Furnham and Barrie Stacey

Typeset by
Michael Mepham, Frome, Somerset, BA11 2HH
Printed in Great Britain by Biddles Ltd, Guildford
and King's Lynn.

All rights reserved. No part of this book may be reprinted or
reproduced or utilized in any form or by any electronic,
mechanical, or other means, now known or hereafter invented,
including photocopying and recording, or in any information
storage or retrieval system, without permission in writing from
the publishers.

British Library Cataloguing in Publication Data

Furnham, Adrian 1953 –
   Young people's understanding of society. – (Adolescence
and society).
   1. Adolescents. Social development
   I. Title II. Stacey, Barrie III. Series
   305.2355

Library of Congress Cataloging in Publication Data

Furnham, Adrian.
   Young people's understanding of society / Adrian
Furnham, Barrie Stacey.
   p. cm. – (Adolescence and society)
   Includes bibliographical references and index.
   1. Social sciences—Study and teaching. 2. Socialization.
   I. Stacey, Furnham.   II. Title.   III. Series.
   H62.F86   1991
   305.23—dc20   91–40790
                                           CIP

ISBN 0–415–01708–4
ISBN 0–415–01709–2 (pbk)

Youth is a time when the conventions are rightly misunderstood; they are either blindly obeyed, or blindly challenged.

Paul Valéry

The old believe everything; the middle-aged suspect everything; the young know everything.

Oscar Wilde

Youth is a blunder; Manhood a struggle; Old Age a regret.

Benjamin Disraeli

The young have aspirations that never come to pass, the old have reminiscences of what never happened.

H. H. Munro

Youth would be an ideal state if it came a little later in life.

Lord Asquith

Think before you speak. Read before you think. This will give you something to think about that you didn't make up yourself – a wise move at any age, but most especially at seventeen, when you are in the greatest danger of coming to annoying conclusions.

F. Labowitz

When I was a boy of fourteen my father was so ignorant I could hardly stand to have the old man around. But when I got to be twenty-one, I was astonished at how much he had learned in seven years.

Mark Twain

Youth, which is forgiven everything, forgives itself nothing: age, which forgives itself anything, is forgiven nothing.

George Bernard Shaw

There are only two lasting bequests we can give our offspring. One is roots, the other wings.

(Anonymous)

Adolescence: A stage between infancy and adultery.

(Anonymous)

Contents

Contents

Figures and tables

Preface

This book is about the world of grown-ups as perceived and understood by young people. During the mid 1970s and through the 1980s researchers in a variety of disciplines expressed greater interest in how young people (children and adolescents) come to perceive and understand the social world. Political scientists became interested in the political socialization of the young and economic psychologists in how and when young people grasp economic concepts. Psychologists and sociologists did a considerable amount of work on youth employment and unemployment, an issue which dominated the 1980s. Issues of sex-role socialization, gender issues and sexuality among young people attracted a great deal of research and popular attention in the 1980s as did young people's beliefs and behaviours concerning race, colour and discrimination. Social sciences in law and religion continued research into young people's understanding of these often difficult to comprehend abstract systems. Also, research continued apace regarding children's and adolescents' conceptions of social class, justice and inequality in their society.

We have attempted in this book to give a comprehensive and critical account of the research on the above topics. Like all reviews it has been a difficult task, not least because the literature, so uneven in quality, is so widely scattered. We have also attempted where possible to trace themes and issues common to all areas of research, and to evaluate theories which attempt to explain growth and development.

Being separated by 12,000 or so miles makes writing together difficult but we have both found it a rewarding experience. We have Lee Drew to thank for her efficient word-processing of the various drafts of our chapters.

Adrian Furnham
Barrie Stacey

Chapter one

Introduction to the issues

Introduction

All societies socialize their young, although they do it, to some extent, in their own way and with varying degrees of effectiveness. For society, socialization enables accommodation of sorts to be reached between young new members and the ongoing social order. For the individual, it means social development towards adult status and adult involvement in the economy, politics, community affairs, the legal system, the social class structure and so forth. Socialization, taking in family upbringing and school education, is never complete or finished; and for some young people it follows an anti-social, deviant or criminal direction.

Compared to a great deal of research that has been done on young people's understanding of the functioning of the *physical* world, there is a comparative dearth of research on how they understand the *social* world. Researchers from a large number of disciplines including anthropology, economics, psychology, psychiatry and sociology have been more interested in how young people come to understand principles of arithmetic, geometry and physics than those of politics, economics and law.

This book attempts to remedy this imbalance. It concentrates on young people's understandings of various issues like politics and government (Chapter 2); economics and trade (Chapter 3); the world of work and employment (Chapter 4); the institution of marriage and the family (Chapter 5); religion and other spiritual matters (Chapter 6); the nature of racial and ethnic differences (Chapter 7); legal and legislative issues (Chapter 8); the nature of social class and social stratification (Chapter 9). The general focus is on young people – children and adolescents, roughly from the ages of 5 to 19. But the sharpest focus is on adolescence, the transitional period between childhood and adulthood. Different disciplines have tended to use different terms for describing this transition: biologists often use pubescence; lawyers juvenile; journalists teenage; and psychologists adolescence. Some of these terms have acquired pejorative associations and, although used interchangeably through this book where appropriate, they are all meant to imply young people.

Adolescents get a mixed press, probably as they always have done. They are often portrayed in the mass media as difficult or obnoxious in some way or other, when not as actually criminal. Various empirical studies in America and Britain have shown that the most newsworthy aspects of young people appear to be either as perpetrators of crime or else as victims of injury (Porteous and Colston, 1980). Falchikov (1986) found from an analysis of twenty-one British newspapers that victimization and criminal activity tended to be over-emphasized, whilst sport and unemployment are under-emphasized, and that much reporting is actually misleading. According to the British press in the mid-1980s a typical adolescent is criminally inclined, unemployed, sporting, and the likely victim of various crimes and accidents!

Biologists' view of adolescence has emphasized it as a period of physical and sexual maturation. Psychoanalysts and neo-psychoanalysts have tended to focus on adolescent anxieties and search for identity, whilst sociologists have focused on the social environment as the determinant of adolescent development. Anthropologists have looked at how cultural patterns shape the experience of young people, whilst psychologists tend to examine the intellectual, emotional, social and moral development of young people.

This book will take a social-cognitive view of adolescence. In doing so, it is concerned with the processes by which young people conceptualize and learn to understand others (their thoughts, emotions, intentions, social behaviour) and the society in which they live. These processes are also related to the behaviour of young people. Some researchers have questioned whether knowledge of the social world and knowledge of the physical world are gained in the same way. Knowledge about the physical world is predominantly factual and objective and is gained through discovery, exploration, first-hand experience, observation, teaching and trial-and-error. But social knowledge is more arbitrary – determined by social, economic and cultural definitions, expectations and requirements. Young people acquire some social knowledge by direct instructions from adults (parents and teachers) and other (often older) children; by observing the behaviour of adults and other young people; and by experiencing approval (and disapproval) for appropriate (and inappropriate) behaviour. 'Because social rules are less uniform, less specific, and more situation-dependent than physical phenomena, they are less predictable and more complicated to understand' (Rice, 1984). The young always remain to some extent operators who apply their own notions to get what they want or can out of circumstances; and rules and norms may be subservient to their desires.

The young person's view of society then is often partial, imperfect and fragmented. The development of social knowledge and understanding may or may not mirror the development in the understanding of the physical world. An intellectually superior young person may be socially inept and social problem-solving skills may be learnt or taught independently from intellectual skills. In each chapter, this book will attempt to offer a critique of the research and theorizing over a wide range of specific topics.

Common themes

Various theories may be detected in the chapters of this book despite the fact that they cover such different areas. Four themes are most consistent:

the *stages* (steps or phases) that children and adolescents go through in the acquisition of social knowledge (attitudes, beliefs, concepts, ideologies);

the major individual, social and cultural *determinants* of the change, development and growth of social knowledge;

the coherence, consistency, *extent* and *structure* of the social knowledge acquired by young people at various ages in various cultures;

the many ways of *imparting* social knowledge to young people.

In addition, the chapters reflect a recurring concern about whether society and its institutions are preparing the young adequately for the modern economy, labour market and way of life, and for coping with the rate of change. Within society this concern is frequently directed at school education and often enough linked with both teenage unemployment and allegedly inadequate job performance, and also with teenage involvement in drugs, sex problems, vandalism, violence and crime. The conventional employment or higher education of the young after leaving school is an expectation of society, the family and the young themselves. Consumerism is widely endorsed and actively promoted among the young by business interests, but it attracts far less concern than that directed at unemployment and other teenage problems (which are often not seen as problems among adults). Lack of money-management and consumer skills are not equated with lack of employment or employment skills and lack of capacity to deal with common youth problems.

Stage-wise theories in growth

What characterizes a great deal of developmental psychology is the idea that the development of a process or the 'unfolding' of a skill can be

3

described in terms of a specific number of identifiable stages. In science description, taxonomy usually precedes description, explanation and so it is in developmental psychology.

A recurring pattern of theorizing and research often appears. Firstly, through observations and experiments researchers posit a series of developmental stages children and adolescents go through in acquiring a full understanding of a concept or the mastery of a skill. Secondly, it soon becomes noticeable from the work of different researchers that there are competing stage-wise explorations such that one researcher may have four stages and another six or even eight. Although there is broad agreement as to the age at which noticeable change occurs, there remains debate as to the precise nature of the stages. Unless the stage-wise development is theory driven and the stages linked to more general developmental trends, a pluralistic view may preside so that there is no agreement about the number, length, etc., of the stages.

Even if there is broad agreement as to the number of identifiable, psychologically coherent and meaningful stages in the development of a concept, stage-wise theories have a number of specific problems. Firstly, the theories are descriptive rather than explanatory, for what is considered is how, rather than when, a young person moves from one stage to another; that is, what precipitates the jump from one stage to another. Secondly, there is the problem of the 'clearness' of the jump and how long is the period between the full relinquishing of the beliefs and behaviours at one stage for the beliefs and behaviours of the next. Thirdly, there is the problem of whether the order of the stages is invariant and whether all stages must be passed through or some are skipped by individuals. Most stage-wise theories implicitly rather than explicitly assume that all individuals pass through the various stages linearly from beginning to end, not considering whether all individuals necessarily reach the final stage or indeed if they may sometimes regress to a previous stage rather than move to the next.

Piaget's famous stage-wise theory has not been without its critics. They have been critical of his 'clinical' methods of research; stages proposed that are not rigidly coupled with chronological age; the change proposed from one stage to another being neither sudden nor all embracing; and the consistency of the stages being a function of the regularity of a culture's child-rearing patterns rather than some in-built and inevitable sequence of development.

The following chapters contain many stage-wise formulations, most highly specific to a single concept or idea. Sometimes researchers look at a whole area and develop stage-wise conceptions. Consider, for instance, the detailed and specific stage-wise formulation by Furth (1980) of how children come to understand the economic world.

Stage I: personalistic elaborations and absence of interpretative system

General criteria: Children fail to recognize the basic functions of money and confuse personal and societal roles, neither of which they understand. In contact with societal events they either do not see a need for explanation of what they observe or, when they do, they associate personal experiences in playful elaborations, largely unconstrained by logical or functional exigencies. The dominant context in which they think about social events, personal or societal, is their own psychological reactions.

Specific criterion: Money is freely available. Money transactions are a simple exchange of money or an empty ritual without precise meaning. Change received after payment for goods is considered a primary source for obtaining money.

Stage II: understanding of first-order societal functions

General criteria: Children understand the basic function of money as a special instrument of exchange in transactions they observe, but not much more beyond that. In familiar instances they distinguish realistically the acquisition of a societal from a personal role. Their images beyond the experienced social events, lacking an interpretative system, are playful and person-centred. The images engender in children's minds a static social order, thereby avoiding possible cognitive conflict.

Specific criterion: Money is paid in exchange for goods bought. Change is understood, but not what happens with the money paid to the shopkeeper. The shopkeeper's payment for goods received is either ignored, denied or, when affirmed, not clearly related to the customer's payment.

Stage III: part-systems in conflict

General criteria: Children construct functional part-systems, through which they interpret societal events beyond first-order observations. These differ from the playful images of Stage II in being 'functional', i.e. adapted to the actual societal system. However, the systems are incomplete, hence 'part-systems', and thereby lead invariably to cognitive conflict of which the children may be more or less aware. This is another contrast with Stage II thinking where conflict is very largely absent. They understand qualitatively – not quantitatively – the mechanism of buying and selling and of a paid job. They do not adequately take into account differences in scale between personal and societal events, such as differences in time scale, in monetary expenditure, in the network of conditions surrounding the particular event. One manifestation of cognitive imbalance is children's adoption of so-called compromise solutions together with one-sided (or partial) direction of reasoning. By means of this they tend to diminish given cognitive problems and camouflage the incompleteness of their part-systems.

Specific criterion: The shopkeeper's buying of goods is recognized as logically obligatory and as deriving from the customer's payments. However, the variety of conditions in the shop's transactions is not taken into account or co-ordinated, particularly the notion of profit necessary for the personal expenditure of the shop-owner.

Stage IV: a concrete-systematic framework

General criteria: Children understand the basic mechanism of monetary transactions and can move from personal possession of money to its societal use and vice versa. They recognize the money base of societal roles, including the function of the government. They take into account individual differences between people and differences in societal roles according to context and need of the community. Generally, they appreciate differences in scale between personal and societal events. The children have eliminated the major inconsistencies and conflicts found in Stage III and the playful images of earlier stages. Nevertheless, their understanding of the political system and governmental functions is still quite vague and their thinking about the general needs of a societal community, its historical traditions and cultural symbols is concrete and therefore unsystematic and principally on an affective-emotional level.

Specific criterion: The children understand that the shop-owner buys for less and sells for more. From this simple mechanism derives the money needed to run the shop as well as the money for the shop-owner's personal expenses.

It may well be that general stage-wise theories are too insensitive for describing the manifold and subtle changes that occur in a particular developmental process, while an extensive description of the stages that young people pass through in the development of an understanding of a concept does not generalize to all concepts.

Major determinants of development

A fundamentally important question in this whole area concerns what are the precipitating factors in the development of understanding about society. Traditionally these have been classified as heredity vs. learning; biological maturation vs. experience; internal vs. external.

Because they are concerned with the development of social knowledge, rather than the acquisition of physical knowledge or skills, most researchers in the field have under-emphasized the role of any possible hereditary or biological factors in the development of social knowledge. However, whilst it is freely acknowledged that young people need to be intellectually capable of thinking about certain complex, subtle and abstract ideas and beliefs, these ideas are not the consequence exclusively or even primarily of biological development. If indeed that were the case, people all over the world living in quite different societies (urban vs. rural; capitalist vs. socialist; democratic vs. authoritarian), would show similar beliefs and understanding about society, which is manifestly not the case. Hence these ideas and beliefs must be learnt. However, much of the socialization process is *intended*, everywhere, to foster acceptance of the existing social order and of its values, an adaptation to its requirements and rejection of alternatives.

There are many ways of classifying leading environmental influences on the development of young people's understanding of society. For instance, one might talk about primary socializing agents like family, peers and the school, or secondary agents like the physical environment, the economy, the media and indeed the culture as a whole.

The most powerful primary socialization agent is probably the family, which is unique in terms of its individual members' backgrounds and the dynamic relationship between individuals. The family members all constantly contact, assess and evaluate the outside world which is daily brought into the home. Families tend to interpret the social world in specific characteristic ways. Since family life offers opportunities for major social experiences and contacts with societal institutions, its power to influence the future of its young cannot be overlooked. The life-courses of some offer much more scope opportunity and satisfaction than those of others. Early and indeed later family-based experiences represent prototypes for the learned interpersonal relationships and attitudes towards other individuals and groups. Child-rearing techniques, be they restrictive vs. permissive, warm vs. cold, friendly vs. hostile, calm and detached vs. anxious and emotional, may have long-lasting cognitive and emotional consequences.

A second powerful source of ideas and experiences is the young person's peers, especially during the teen years. Adolescence involves changes in social development and the nature of peer relationships. The peer group increases in size and complexity, with adolescents spending and enjoying more time with chosen peers. Peer groups are, next to parents and relatives, the most significant individuals in the young person's life. Depending on their shared activities and sociometric make-up, peer groups can expose young people to a range of experiences, institutions and concepts that parents and relatives do not. The power of peers to shape

7

young people's perspectives is manifest in parents' concerns about their young mixing with the 'wrong crowd'. Naturally, once a youngster learns to identify with individuals of his/her own age, parental identifications and outlooks lose some of their original strength.

A third major socializing agent is the school, be it kindergarten, primary or secondary (high). For in most industrial countries practically all children are in school for ten to twelve years, regardless of motivation or ability. There are many academic reports as well as personal reminiscences that demonstrate the role of the school in contributing to the educational development of the young. The young may be influenced by specific teachers; by specific school subjects; by being introduced to peers; by being exposed to new ideas or by being required to live a particular institutional routine. These experiences may or may not follow the explicit desires of the school; indeed, young people may acquire beliefs and behaviours precisely antithetical to the school's explicit objectives. Finally, the school is also important because it frequently prescribes, recommends and encourages specific 'after-school contacts' which themselves act as socializing agents for young people. From a societal perspective, school education visibly plays a predominantly conservative role in social development.

Fourthly, there are other societal factors that are likely to influence a young person's understanding of society. These include the socio-economic structure of the young person's environment and exposure to the mass media especially television. The physical and social environment is important because of the range of experience open to young people. Hence a cut-off rural environment compared to an urban inner-city environment exposes young people to a quite different set of people, institutions and experiences which help shape their ideas. However, the mass media can bring into people's homes and lives experiences they might otherwise not observe. Major socialization is produced by the operation of the politico-economic system itself, and is enhanced further by the ethos, the ideology and the goals which it generates.

Determinants of the development of young people's understanding of society are numerous. Each chapter in this book will consider what they are and how they operate to shape beliefs. Inevitably the factors are differentially important in shaping understanding of different issues.

The construction of the social world

Over the past decade or so there has been a growing research interest in how children come to understand the social world; how they make sense of institutions and how they eventually become socially competent. Bruner and Haste (1987) have argued that there has been a 'quiet revol-

child experiences
concepts in social
practice and
social negotiation
of meaning;
brings own level
of complexity to
the encounter

INTRA-INDIVIDUAL

child learns, through media, parents,
teachers and peers, the normative
justifications, legitimations and
frameworks for making sense; brings to
this understanding own level of cognitive
complexity which mediates the extent of
understanding

INTERPERSONAL

SOCIO-HISTORICAL

co-ordinated peer action and
interaction with teachers filters the
socio-historical framework and this
discourse is itself defined by social
and cultural practice; meaning and
justification generated at the
interpersonal level – e.g. in periods
of rapid social change – may alter
broader social representations

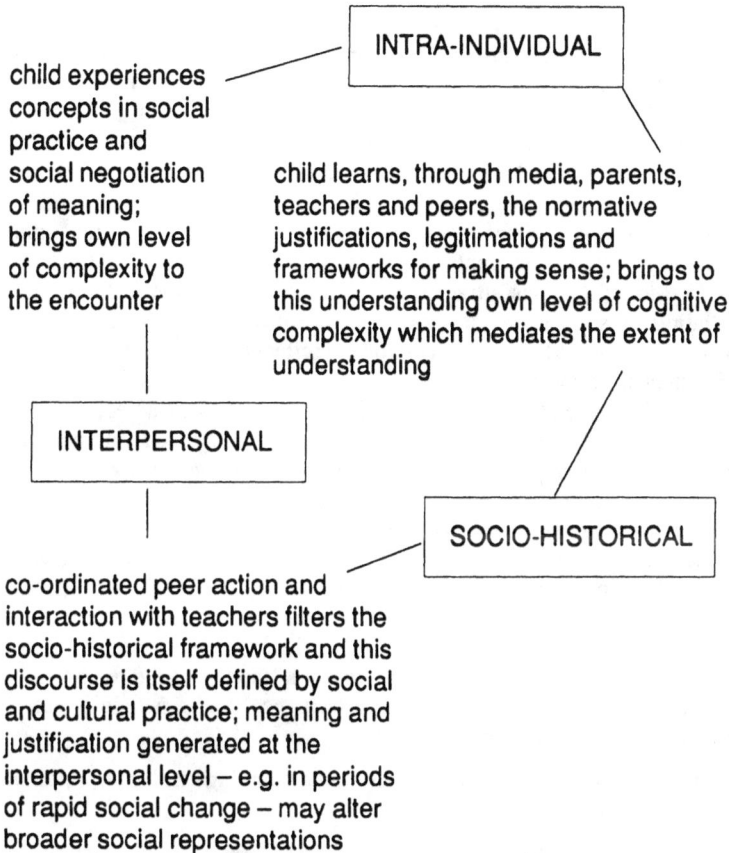

Figure 1.1 A model of the relationship between the intra-individual, the
interpersonal and the socio-historical

ution' taking place in developmental psychology from the idea of a
solitary problem solver to that of a social being situated in, and drawing
from, a particular cultural and historical context. They also stress the role
of language which eases the child into a particular cultural-social world:
'its metaphors, its kinds of explanations, its categories, and its way of
interpreting and evaluating events. These are not *invented* by the child;
they are the common currency of the culture, the framework that determines the boundaries of the child's concepts' (1987: 2). Children learn,

in other words, the commonsense knowledge which is available in their culture and hence the shared representations of the world. Social experience in a particular culture shapes the perceptions and conceptions of that child and the frameworks, schemas and 'scripts' which are transmitted to the child. Bruner and Haste (1987) claim to trace three themes in relation to discourse: scaffolding (the child's struggle to make sense of experience), negotiation of meaning (a dialectical relation to the parents and the family's construction of the world) and the transfer of cultural representations (through accounts, stories, symbols, representations, etc.).

One topic that has attracted a good deal of attention is the understanding of sex differences and the quite different roles of men and women. Lloyd (1987) noted that mothers reflect their own representation of gender in the way they respond to children as young as 6 months by the toys they give them, and through language, such as the adjectives used to describe behaviour, and the whole style of linguistic interactions. Parents, particularly mothers, in their own behaviour and use of symbols reveal their conceptions of gender. By showing these in a whole range of behaviours, mothers shape and scaffold the child's interpretation of their experience and this ensures that boys have a quite different framework for interpreting experience than girls. By only just after their first year, boys and girls show noticeably different behaviours. Effectively, they operate within the different representational schemes provided for them.

Haste (1987) has attempted to represent a 'model' of the relationship between three worlds that interact to influence young people's understanding of society (see Figure 1.1):

Inter-person: social interaction where understandings and interpretation of meanings are negotiated;

Socio-historical: association with the cultural mores, symbols, metaphors and codes for action.

It (the socio-historical domain) delineates the scope and boundaries for the generation of rules and their justifications. It is a resource for the rules for conducting *interpersonal* interaction, as well as for how one should engage in *intrapersonal* reflection upon rules and order. A two-way process is involved; the child's interpretations of the socio-historical resource depend on the level of cognitive complexity. In our interactions with children we unconsciously manipulate the interaction between cultural resources and individual levels of complexity; we present to them particular messages, particular frameworks within which to make sense of the world, but we adjust the level of that message to the child's level of comprehension. So the child learns two things: the *content* of the message (which will endure) and the appropriate *structure* for conceptualizing it, which we as parents or teachers

Table 1.1   Major changes in social-conventional concepts

	Approximate Ages
1. *Convention as descriptive of social uniformity.* Convention viewed as descriptive of uniformities in behaviour. Convention is not conceived as part of structure or functions of social interaction. Conventional uniformities are descriptive of what is assumed to exist. Convention maintained to avoid violation of empirical uniformities.	6–7
2. *Negation of convention as descriptive social uniformity.* Empirical uniformity not a sufficient basis for maintaining conventions. Conventional acts regarded as arbitrary. Convention is not conceived as part of structure or function of social interaction.	8–9
3. *Convention as affirmation of rule system; early concrete conception of social system.* Convention seen as arbitrary and changeable. Adherence to convention based on concrete rules and authoritative expectations. Conception of conventional acts not co-ordinated with conception of rule.	10–11
4. *Negation of convention as part of rule system.* Convention now seen as arbitrary and changeable regardless of rule. Evaluation of rule pertaining to conventional act is co-ordinated with evaluation of the act. Conventions are nothing but social expectations.	12–13
5. *Convention as mediated by social system.* The emergence of systematic concepts of social structure. Convention as normative regulation in system with uniformity, fixed roles and static hierarchical organization.	14–16
6. *Negation of convention as societal standards.* Convention regarded as codified societal standards. Uniformity in convention is not considered to serve the function of maintaining social system. Conventions are nothing but societal standards that exist through habitual use.	17–18
7. *Convention as co-ordination of social interactions.* Conventions as uniformities that are functional in co-ordinating social interactions. Shared knowledge, in the form of conventions, among members of social groups facilitates interaction and operation of the system.	19–25

11

have presented as a scaffold for understanding, but which we expect to change with increasing maturity.

(Haste, 1987: 176)

Like others, Haste draws on the work of Turiel (1983) who established a sequence of stages of development within the framework of conventional reasoning (see Table 1.1).

As Haste (1987) notes, Turiel's (1983) stages illustrate the operation of a socio-historical dimension at the level of individual reasoning. An important distinction is made between moral rules that transcend local conditions and conventional rules which are realistic. Children first acquire a knowledge of the differences between these two rules, then learn to recognize and to reproduce the distinction in terms of the kinds of justification given for the rules in different domains.

Both Haste (1987) and Turiel (1983) look at the development of social knowledge in general, paying particular attention to moral rules. Others have examined how relationships (child–child and child–adult) provide major sources of understanding, each serving distinct developmental functions. For instance, Youniss and Volpe (1978) list ten points that are axioms for their model in which social understanding is determined by socialization and self-construction:

1. Children enter social life seeking order among the events that they experience. They look primarily to interpersonal interactions, episodes in which they exchange actions and reactions with other persons.

2. Children cannot find order in the particular details of interactions, which are, in fact, variable sequences that are freely composed and not scripted. They can, however, discover order in *general forms* of exchanging behaviour.

3. Procedures of exchange depend on both persons in the interaction. Each can bring his or her respective ideas about exchange to an encounter. If the persons continue to interact together for any amount of time, they will have to reach some agreement about procedures, which will guide them in subsequent interactions.

4. There are several general procedures of interaction that social scientists have identified. In the first, someone with controlling power imposes a procedure on the child. The child, who attempts to get along with this more powerful person, eventually adopts the appropriate part in this procedure.

5. The most likely person to interact with children in this matter is the adult. Adults are seen as persons who participate in society at large and know from experience about several procedures of exchange, and they

bring their children examples of these exchanges. When children construct conceptions of exchanges they experience with adults, they are making self-constructions that simultaneously take account of the concepts held by other persons in society.

6. This process is one way to describe the construction of thought and the socialization of thought. Procedures of unilateral constraint show the way in which thought is achieved by the individual through collaboration with other persons. It demonstrates why 'social cognition' is self-constructed and societally determined.

7. Another procedure important to children's lives is represented by situations in which neither the child nor the other person has unilateral rights of imposition. It applies to cases when two persons are on equal footing, for example, peers and friends. They discover procedures together by making them up through reciprocal exchange. Their collaboration is based on cooperation or coconstruction, in contrast to unilateral imposition.

8. Still, as equals, each person brings to the other a version of social reality. Each, of course, is also participating with several different persons, who are also members of a society. Constructions discovered from interactions with equals who function by reciprocity thus add further to the socialization of thought.

9. Although as developmental psychologists we focus on the child's constructions, we have to recognize that the other in these interactions is also constructing concepts of exchange. It takes two persons to compose exchanges. Even when children seem to be adopting an adult's version of an exchange, they do so from their own understanding, which may differ somewhat from the adult's. In turn, children's conceptions may influence the adult's, and so on throughout their interactive life together.

10. Development, in this model, pertains to discovering exchanges, conceptualizing them as interpersonal relations, and continuing to organize relations with respect to each other and to their application to social reality.

(Youniss and Volpe, 1978: 4–5)

Work on the general development of social cognition has moved forward extensively over the past decade and there seems to be a general consensus that young people's conception of the social world can be understood in terms of a 'knowledge system' different from, but clearly related to, that of adults. Development in understanding goes through a series of qualitative transformations with more adaptive and flexible systems replacing earlier ones. More importantly, the knowledge systems or social-world understanding are determined both by children's understanding of and by their response to events. But as youthful knowledge meets the real world, changes occur such that understanding is in some sense determined by the experience of the young. This means the young do influence the functioning of the socialization process; with such influence being on an intra-personal, person-to-person and small group basis rather than on a large group and institutional basis.

However, it is the work of Furth (1980) through his book *The World of Grown-Ups* that is most relevant to the material considered in this book. He has focused on the child's general approach towards making sense of the social world at every age. Furth has attempted to specify explicitly the sort of social knowledge, or understanding about the working of society, that most adults in modern western society take for granted. He presented twelve statements:

(1) Societal institutions function primarily in response to societal not personal needs.

(2) Acquiring a societal role, such as an occupation, implies a constellation of various societal and personal prerequisites.

(3) Not all societal customs are law, nor are personal morality and societal law synonymous.

(4) Compromise, tension and conflict are normal by-products of the limitations inherent in all concrete societal situations.

(5) Societal institutions have an historical origin and are subject to change.

(6) Societal institutions are not concrete in the sense of 'point-at-able' things.

(7) No particular 'I' is at the centre of society.

(8) With some rare exceptions money is a neutral means of exchange for all societal goods and services.

(9) Simple arithmetic requires that in a monetary economy the seller must buy things for less and sell them for more so as to include in the selling price all expenses and personal profit.

(10) Two principal ways of acquiring money are paid work and buying and selling.

(11) Although the country's government has power to print or coin money, it has basically no other way of acquiring money than by

charging its citizens for its goods and services, principally in the indirect form of taxation.

(12) Governmental functions are exercised at different political levels and in a variety of spheres to regulate and assist the interplay of societal institutions.

(Furth, 1980: 4–5)

Although this list is not meant to be comprehensive or exhaustive, it does illustrate the type of self-evident principles that underlie the functioning of social institutions. However, what is important about this example is that few young people's acting, thinking and talking on everyday issues are in accordance with those sort of statements.

To illustrate most clearly the change or development of thinking about society, Furth (1980) compared the thinking about society of a 5–6-year-old, with that of an adult. Thus, a 5–6-year-old's understanding of the social world is:

(1) *Undifferentiated*: All people and societal roles are substantially similar; personal and societal roles and functions are confused.

(2) *Voluntaristic*: Societal events happen according to the personal wish of the individual.

(3) *Rule-bound*: Events happen according to known rules; chance and contingency are not recognized.

(4) *Conflict-free*: A fairy-tale atmosphere of rational perfection and personal happiness prevails along with a quasi-miraculous concordance of personal and societal needs.

(5) *A-historical*: Events are static in their present shape.

(6) *Superficial*: Events are identified in the superficial aspects of particular instances.

(7) *Ego-typical*: Personal experience is the main criterion of the child's thinking.

(8) *Money is personal and concrete*: It is subject to personal fancy.

(9) *Money is a ritual*: Its exchange serves no other societal function.

(10)*Money is freely available*: It is accessible as is any other necessity such as air or food.

(11)*Money is produced like any other good.*

(12)*Government and community have no meaning at all.*

By contrast adult thinking about society has the following characteristics:

(1) The personal–societal distinction is experienced as basic and underlying all other statements; individual differences among people and societal differentiations are recognized.

(2) Differences in making personal and societal decisions are taken for granted, together with personal and societal constraints on choice of actions.

(3) Different types of rules regulating one's conduct and differences between legal statutes, societal customs and personal values are beginning to be understood.

(4) Both personal and societal life are seen as necessarily imperfect and open to tension, compromise and improvement.

(5) Both people and societal institutions are considered as having a life history, but with largely different time scales.

(6) Whilst what is personal can be more readily grasped in particular people and their interrelations, what is essential in societal institutions is no longer placed in concrete instances and appears that much more 'abstract'.

(7) As children come to experience 'self' at the core of what is personal and what it means to be a person, they contrast themselves with other individuals. At the same time they contrast themselves as individuals with the society in which they find themselves (more or less) active participants.

(8–11) The basic functions of monetary use and exchange, of selling with profit, of payment for goods and services, are now firmly accepted and extended to the governmental enterprise.

(12) The community in its historical and political context, and the function of government, is beginning to be understood.

Furth (1980) also specified four hypotheses, very reliant on Piaget, about children's conception of society:

Hypothesis 1. Children's thinking and behaviour are primarily products of their developing minds. From observation of their behaviour the mental frameworks that underlie the behaviour can be inferred.

Hypothesis 2. Children spontaneously apply their available mental frameworks to make sense of what they experience; this is an environmental experience in the sense of a meaningful contact with a particular situation.

16

Hypothesis 3. In doing this, children frequently go beyond existing frameworks, constructing new frameworks: in simpler language, the experience of thinking becomes the occasion for a growth of mind; this is a developmental experience.

Hypothesis 4. Understanding the social world is basically not a different process from understanding the physical world; that is, the area that is often interpreted as being Piaget's primary concern. If this is the case, one would expect that developmental experiences are as crucial in social as in physical understanding and that one could establish developmental landmarks analogous to the stages Piaget postulated for physical thinking.

It seems then that researchers agree that the way young people acquire knowledge of the social world is not systematically different from the way they acquire knowledge of the physical world. That is, it is stage-like and determined both within and without. However, it is quite probably a necessity that knowledge about the physical world is acquired before knowledge or understanding about the social world. Thus, whereas Piagetian research tends to focus on young children (frequently under 10 years old), many studies in this book will focus on teenagers who struggle to make sense of moral issues, economic and political institutions, social stratification, etc.

Some methodological issues

A number of methodological issues need to be considered as they have implications for the kind of data we have on young people's understanding of society.

The first concerns self-report. There are a number of survey-type studies which look at young people's social attitudes (Department of Education and Science, 1983). For instance, Furnham and Gunter (1989) surveyed by questionnaire over 2000 young people in Britain, looking at everything from their knowledge of politics to their attitudes to crime, developing countries, health, religion, school, sex roles and work. Essentially these studies look at attitudes and not necessarily understanding, though most authors attempt to ensure that subjects understand the meaning of the questions they use. Even content-analytic studies of written responses, such as that of Simmons and Wade (1984) which looked at the spontaneous responses of young people, tend to be restricted to attitudes, values and beliefs. It may be argued that attitudes, beliefs and values reflect or underpin understanding and knowledge but that link is frequently very difficult to infer. Hence it seems wiser to examine understanding either through direct questioning about knowledge or through behaviour itself. Though many of the studies mentioned in this book are self-report based (questionnaire or interview), as one may expect when looking at understanding, some also examine behaviour which under certain circumstances can be seen to reflect understanding.

Secondly, it is possible to detect two rather different approaches to young people's understanding: content vs. process. The content approach is dedicated primarily to describing the content and organization of the individual's belief system. That is, one can take a specific issue or idea like economics and describe the beliefs that individuals have about its constituent parts (money, saving, gambling); the relationship between these beliefs; the stability and consistency of these beliefs; the structure of these beliefs and the relationship between these beliefs and behaviour. Essentially, the content approach focuses on the *content* of knowledge about specific issues.

The process approach is less interested in the content of a belief system than in the process of how the belief system arises and how it 'works'. Thus, researchers from this perspective are interested in the aetiology or development of beliefs; the function of those beliefs for the individual; the consequence of belief in behaviour; and the changing and manipulation of those beliefs. Essentially the process approach focuses on the function of knowledge about specific issues. As Furnham (1988) has noted, the content and process approaches are not antithetical but overlapping. Indeed, both will be detected in this book.

Conclusion

Developmental and social psychologists have long been interested in when, how and why young people come to a partial or full understanding of the society in which they live. Though there are some theoretical differences of emphasis, there is some general agreement about how young people move through stages in the acquisition of their knowledge of the institutions and functioning of the social world. What determines this development are factors from within and without – that is, the youngster's present understanding leads him or her to interact with the social world in a particular way and, hence, gain certain experience. Young people construct and test reality in the social world. The remaining chapters of this book examine topic by topic young people's understanding of the complex world in which they live.

Chapter two

Politics and government

Introduction

How much do young people know about the political system and the sort of government they live under? What stages or phases do they go through in the acquisition of this knowledge? What experience or factors are the best determinants of this knowledge? How much do first-time voters understand of the workings of the political system? How can we best educate children about politics and government in order to make them responsible, effective and participating citizens?

Adelson and O'Neil have noted:

> During adolescence the youngster gropes, stumbles, and leaps towards political understanding. Prior to these years the child's sense of the political order is erratic and incomplete – a curious array of sentiments and dogmas, personalized ideas, randomly remembered names and party labels, half-understood platitudes. By the time adolescence has come to an end, the child's mind, much of the time, moves easily within and among the categories of political discourse.
>
> (Adelson and O'Neil, 1966: 295)

However, Jackson (1972) has noted that children develop concepts of political symbols (like the flag) and of political figures as early as 4 years old, showing that development begins in early childhood.

A great deal more research has been done on young people's political attitudes and beliefs than on their political *knowledge* or their *understanding* of the political process at all levels (Jaros and Grant, 1974; Lonky, Reihman and Serlin, 1981). This may be due to the fact that it is assumed that political attitudes are better predictors of political behaviour (i.e. voting) than political knowledge, though all three are, of course, related. Public opinion polls are carried out on a variety of issues throughout the year, but at election times in particular. These rarely focus specifically on young people, presumably because (in many countries) until the age of 18 years they cannot vote. But there are, of course, exceptions. For instance, Cochrane and Billig (1982) reported a large survey of over 1000 British 16-year-olds who seemed rather cynical about the political process. Over half thought that 'politics is a dirty business' and that 'politicians don't care what ordinary people think', while about a third believed that 'real decisions are not made by government, but by the powerful forces which control it'.

Presumably young people's opinions are most keenly sought when they are relatively influential. In countries, like Great Britain, where their relative numbers are decreasing there may be less interest in the political knowledge and habits of young people, while the opposite is true of Hong Kong whose young people are by far in the majority.

Political attitudes

More work has been done on attitudes to and beliefs about politics (and government) than on knowledge among the young. Furnham and Gunter (1983, 1989) have suggested that the extensive psychological and socio-logical research into young people's political attitudes and beliefs can be conveniently divided into four areas: sex difference in socio-political ideology; cross-cultural or cross-national differences in political attitudes and beliefs; the structure of social and political attitudes; and, finally, possible generational and genetic differences in political beliefs and behaviours. The research, published in English, has been done in a wide variety of countries from all five continents.

Sex differences

Studies on sex differences in political beliefs in adults *and* adolescents have revealed fairly consistent findings though not striking differences (Sidanius and Ekehammar, 1980; Furnham, 1985a; Ekehammar, 1985). Males appear to be more interested and engaged in politics than females (Hess and Torney, 1967; Almond and Verba, 1973; Dearden, 1974; Furnham and Gunter, 1983), but when females are interested in politics it tends to be local rather than national politics (Greenstein, 1961). Furthermore, several studies have shown that male adolescents have a greater political knowledge and awareness than females (Dowse and Hughes, 1971; Orum, 1974). Some research on ideological beliefs suggests that females are more conservative than males, though it is unclear why this should be so (Furnham, Johnson and Rawles, 1985). However, recent research by Ekehammar and Sidanius on large adolescent groups in Sweden (Sidanius and Ekehammar, 1980; Ekehammar and Sidanius, 1982) suggests that the opposite is true, namely that women are less conservative with respect to party choice and social attitudes (less punitive, racist and capitalist and egalitarian) but more religious than males. They are also less conservative on women's issues. Similar results were obtained by Furnham (1985a) on a sample of nearly 300 British adolescents and Marjoribanks (1981) on a sample of Australian adolescents. Furthermore, Ekehammar (1985) has also shown that these sex differences occur within party preference groups such that, although ideological profiles for males and females are similar within (and different between) groups, these sex differences remain. In other words, although the pattern of pro- and anti-attitudes is much the same with respect to different issues like the United Nations, apartheid, etc., there are consistent differences between males and females. They explain the different results of various studies in terms of age differences (other studies had a wider range), education differences (not controlled in other studies) and the women's liberation movement. According to Ekehammar *et al*, the available results are not well explained or predicted by biological, Marxist or socialization theories. Therefore, there seem to be some noticeable differences between adolescent male and female political attitudes, though it is far from clear why they occur.

Cross-cultural differences

There have also been a number of studies done on adolescent (mainly school students) political beliefs and attitudes in different countries with people from different socio-political systems. Oppenheim and Torney (1974) investigated the social, political and civic attitudes of over 1300 10- and 14-year-old children from England, Finland, Italy, the Netherlands, New Zealand, Sweden and the United States and found a number of interesting and predictable differences between them. They were interested in what the respondents thought about democratic values and the characteristics of a good citizen and found adolescents have fairly strong and sophisticated views. Many studies using conservatism or F (fascist) scales have yielded informative results. Meade and Whittaker (1967) found Indian and Rhodesian students had the highest F scores, the Americans lowest with the Brazilians, Arabians and Chinese intermediate. Shaver, Hoffman and Richards (1971) found German students to be more dogmatic and authoritarian than American students who were relatively tolerant of groups they disliked. Sidanius, Ekehammar and Ross (1979) compared Swedish and Australian psychology students (of 18–21 years) and found the latter were less punitive and had greater ideological consensus and consistency than the former. Later, Furnham (1985a) compared matched groups of British and South African adolescents on a 49-item socio-political item test. Not unsurprisingly the white South Africans were less in favour of equality and sexual freedom and more in

21

favour of religion. Similarly, Furnham (1985b) found white South African university students more conservative than British students, and they tended to be hostile and unsympathetic to victims of social injustice. However, a large number of studies have been concerned with the generality of the factor structure or organization of socio-political scales in different cultures (Bagley, Wilson and Boshier, 1970). As Furnham and Gunter (1983) observed:

> Not only are these studies few in number but they suffer numerous methodological weaknesses; arbitrary choice of nations; poor sampling and matching; and perhaps most importantly few attempts to relate social and political attitudes to similarities and differences in the political economic systems of the different nations from which the samples were drawn.

Studies comparing political beliefs and attitudes of adolescents from different countries are extremely interesting but very problematic because of issues of matching samples, ensuring that questions have equivalent meaning in different cultures.

Structure of political attitudes

Most studies of the structure of socio-political attitudes have been concerned with testing whether the attitudes of children and adolescents are organized in a similar way (i.e. along the same dimensions, like conservative/radical; capitalist/socialist) to those of adults (Insel and Wilson, 1971). Nias (1973) found four relevant factors in his study of over 400 pre-adolescents: religion, ethnocentrism, punitiveness and sex/hedonism. There is a considerable literature on adults' political beliefs, and some controversial evidence that these can be classified along two dimensions as originally suggested by Eysenck (1951), namely conservative–radical; tender–tough minded (Wilson, 1973; Furnham and Lewis, 1986; Furnham, 1986). Brand (1981) has however considered a rotation of these axes which he labelled hedonism–moralism; authoritarian–humanitarian. However, it remains to be seen whether this structure is appropriate to adolescent political attitudes. Clearly, it will be much easier to measure attitudes when we know the major issues or factors to focus on. It is quite likely that political issues thought important by adolescents are quite different from those of adults but as yet there is very little information for us to go on. Some work has been done in Sweden by Ekehammar and Sidanius (1979), who found that high-school students perceived three underlying dimensions in the eight political parties in that country – left–right, extremity and religiosity, though it is uncertain whether these apply to all countries.

Generational differences

Finally, some studies have attempted to uncover genetic, developmental or generational differences in political beliefs, especially conservatism. Feather (1977) compared the responses of mothers, fathers, sons and daughters on the conservatism scale and found that on 35 out of the 50 items parents were significantly more conservative than their children, whereas the reverse was true for only two items. These inter-generational differences are due, he argues, to life-span changes (the assumption of greater family and economic responsibility) as well as changes in social trends, but it is possible that the parents were more conservative when they were adolescents. Jennings and Niemi (1971) asked parents and their 16- to 18-year-old children to complete identical political questions, with their children also filling it out as they thought their parents might do. Although the correlations varied between 0.05 and 0.60, accuracy of estimation was much greater for political party preference than for actual political belief. Himmelweit and Swift (1971) found that the likelihood that a boy would imitate his father's voting was strong where the father was interested in politics and where their interpersonal relations were good, but not when either of these were poor. Indeed, Himmelweit *et al* (1981) found that half the adolescents in either study chose their parents' party preferences and that this went up 70 per cent if Liberals were omitted. In a genetic developmental study on parental transmission of television watching, preferred entertainments, sports interests and political habits and beliefs, Cavalli-Sforza, Feldman, Cher and Dombusch (1982) found the strongest vertical transmission for religious and political beliefs. All these studies suggest modest social background factors in the family with regard to socio-political beliefs among young people. This is a potentially very interesting area of research: namely, what determines young people's political attitudes, behaviours and beliefs and how they change over time. We know that people probably get more conservative as they get older, but it is certainly not clear what determines how conservative they are in their adolescence or what the most important factors are in determining change in political attitudes over time. Clearly age, cohort/generation and historical trends can all affect the outcome.

Political knowledge

Compared to research on political attitudes, there have been comparatively few studies which have looked at adolescents' knowledge of how the political system works. Dennis and McCrone (1970) found in several countries that by the age of 10 years, primary school children could accurately name the country's main political parties and express a preference for one. This was reported for 80 per cent of British school children

(Himmelweit *et al*, 1981). But knowing the names of politicians is quite different from knowing how parliamentary democracy or local government works.

An exception to this paucity of system research was provided by Stradling (1977). He was commissioned by the Hansard Society, firstly, to produce a reliable estimate of the extent of political knowledge and ignorance in a sample of 4027 British 15- to 16-year-olds which, he believed, could act as a yardstick of political literacy against which to measure the effects of future developments and, secondly, to examine the sources of political information for the mid-teens in our own society. He distinguished between *propositional* or *factual* knowledge and *procedural* or *know-how* knowledge of politics. He aimed specifically to have a multi-dimensional approach which lessened the risk of underestimating the political awareness of young people. The study attempted to discover the determinants of political awareness and found some evidence of sex differences – boys are more politically knowledgeable than girls (particularly on political office-holders and internal affairs) – but no evidence of systematic class differences (though it is uncertain if the very top and bottom of the class structure were well sampled). Stradling also found fairly strong evidence of schooling effects with grammar or selective school boys being more knowledgeable than their comprehensive non-selective cousins, no evidence of a political education effect, but some evidence of an educational aspiration effect (adolescents who leave school once they have attained the legal minimum age are less likely to fare well on this test). Stradling concluded that

> the general lack of political awareness revealed in this report must make depressing reading for anyone who is concerned about the future of our representative democracy and the prospects for greater participation by the public. There is something essentially paradoxical about a democracy in which some eighty to ninety per cent of the future citizens (and the present citizenry) are insufficiently well-informed about local, national and international politics to know not only what is happening but also how they are affected by it and what they can do about it. Most of the political knowledge which they do have is of a rather inert and voyeuristic kind and of little use to them either as political consumers or as political actors.
>
> (Stradling, 1977: 57)

Furnham and Gunter (1983, 1987, 1989) repeated Stradling's study on a smaller population and also attempted to specify various determinants (demographic, media usage, interest) of adolescent political awareness. They found that the level of adolescent knowledge about politics was much the same as before. The best predictor of political knowledge was not media usage but expressed interest in political affairs. There was, however, some indication that those who watch more television news tended to have greater political knowledge than those who say they watch less news.

Specifically Furnham and Gunter (1987, 1989) looked at knowledge of the different political parties, knowledge of political leaders, parliamentary and local political knowledge and knowledge about the public services. Between a fifth and a half of the adolescent respondents were able to identify a political policy with a specific party – e.g. 'Taxes on both people and industries should be cut as soon as possible'; 'The government should take over and run more industries'. The more popular the party, in terms of votes and members in parliament, the more the young people were able to recognize its political creed.

It seemed that potential voters are able to spot their chosen party's policies much more easily than those of any other party. Further, respondents overall were better at identifying the policies of the two main British political parties (Labour and Conservative) than those of the more minor or middle-ground parties. Finally, the three questions where over 50 per cent of the sample were correct in their answers concerned not so much industrial or macro-economic politics as public spending and the issues of privatization and nationalization.

Most young people (95 per cent) could name the Prime Minister and 86 per cent could name the leader of the Opposition. But only about half the sample knew the names of the home and foreign secretaries. These are interesting results that may change with various phenomena like General Elections, scandals or Cabinet changes. In other words, it is likely that respondent knowledge about politicians is closely related to how frequently they appear on the media. Knowledge about British parliamentary procedure was not particularly impressive.

Furthermore, the knowledge of these young people is not particularly impressive as fewer than a *third* of the sample were correct in their answers to *two-thirds* of the questions (questions 1, 2, 3, 4, 5, 7) and on only one question did more than half the sample get the answer correct. It is, however, realistic to point out that these were fairly difficult questions, and that a representative adult sample may not do much better. There were *no* age, class, religious belief or vote preference differences, and only one sex difference, suggesting that none of these demographic factors related directly to political knowledge of this type.

It is informative to note which of the questions were correctly answered and which not. Most of the respondents knew that local politicians cannot overrule parliamentary laws. About 40 per cent knew that an MP does not have to live in his or her constituency. But less than one in five knew that a general election *must* be held every five years or that a backbench MP is any member of parliament who is not a government member. However, it should be pointed out that there is no evidence to suggest that an enfranchised adult population actually knows significantly more than our teenage respondents. Young people's lack of knowledge may, in fact, have little or nothing to do with their ability to understand, or take part in, a parliamentary democracy. On the other hand, the young people seemed relatively well informed on such issues as who was responsible for public services.

Young people in Furnham and Gunter's study appeared to be most familiar with local politics – specifically knowledge of public services, where they could accurately distinguish between governmental, local council and regional board responsibilities. They were also well informed about political leaders, especially the Prime Minister and the leader of the Opposition. Their greatest area of ignorance concerned party political and parliamentary system knowledge, where their knowledge was patchy. There were, for instance, quite large proportions of 'not sure' answers to questions on parliamentary knowledge, as well as ignorance of Liberal Party policy. In other words, although they knew who politicians were, they did not have a very comprehensive or well-informed picture of how the political system actually works. The results tend to suggest, quite logically, that adolescent political knowledge is limited to areas that they have been exposed to, or probably had most experience of.

In Stradling's original report, he provided evidence that not all adults had a much wider knowledge of political practices than the adolescent sample. Yet he concluded:

> In fact it is apparent that they [his sample] lack much of the kind of basic information which the political consumer needs if he is to understand decisions and actions which affect him and if he is to make political choices between actions, policies, parties or candidates. One of the most disturbing findings ... is their ignorance of where the political parties stand on the main issue of the day.
>
> (Stradling, 1977: 23)

It should be pointed out that the majority of respondents in the Furnham and Gunter (1987) study had between two and five years before they were eligible to vote, and it is possible that their knowledge would increase over this period, as their cognitive abilities would advance.

There seems to be little evidence of any major changes over this ten-year period of investigation in young people's understanding or knowledge of politics, which suggests that empirical results are fairly stable over time. However, there is considerable concern about a politically ill-informed electorate. Blumler (1974), for example, suggested that ignorant electors put pressure on governments to adopt ill-conceived and undesirable policies. Some government policies can only be effective if the public understands the necessity for them (for example, not driving while intoxicated and not smoking for health reasons), and a politically ignorant public is all too easily ignored or used. Furnham and Gunter's (1987) results suggest that more attention perhaps needs to be paid to political education in school and community so as to encourage a more politically knowledgeable population. However, this education would need to cover many other, perhaps adolescent-orientated and more important questions than those first put to their respondents regarding their knowledge of politics.

Overall there seem to be comparatively few age, sex and class differences in political knowledge among teenagers in state schools. Stradling (1977) found some evidence of sex differences in knowledge (in favour of boys); a small but significant class effect (middle class knew more than working class); a particular type of school effect (with grammar school children knowing more than secondary modern children); a small educational factor (those leaving at 18 know more than those intending to leave at 16), and a small political education factor (those who had had lessons in politics knew more). Of course, it should be pointed out that some four of these variables are confounded. For instance, middle-class children are more likely to attend grammar schools, stay on until they are 18 years old, and have political education. Furnham and Gunter (1983) provided modest evidence for sex and class differences but found that interest in politics was the strongest determinant of political knowledge. Furnham and Gunter (1987) however observed few sex and class differences, and also surprisingly few age differences among 12–16-year-olds. There was evidence that potential voters for a particular party were able to recognize their party's political agenda better than that of another party. That is, political activity in the young seems to improve knowledge and tolerance.

Why is it, then, that there is fairly strong evidence for sex differences in socio-political beliefs and attitudes, but very little evidence of sex differences in political knowledge? There could be at least two explanations: firstly, that attitudes and knowledge are not well related and not dependent on one another; secondly, that socio-political beliefs and attitudes precede understanding of the workings of the political system. Furnham and Lewis (1986) have found that class attitudes (to money and related issues) are determined before adolescence, but that it is not until early adulthood, when people have some conception of macro-sociological and economic forces, that they can fully understand the economic system. It may well be that political knowledge and understanding are not the same, in that the latter is not well enough comprehended until early adulthood.

However, this begs the question as to what determines political knowledge (and attitudes) if not the conventional demographic variables considered earlier. The answer may be partly tautological, as Furnham and Gunter (1983) have already suggested. Those young people who, for whatever reason, are interested in politics, expose themselves to more political coverage on the media and hence learn more about it. It is not surprising that the sample's knowledge was greatest in terms of individual politicians, as it is frequently through individual personalities that television and newspapers report political events. What we need to know is what makes children or adolescents interested in politics in the first place, and whether (indeed how) their political interests lead to increased political knowledge and behaviour such as voting preference, standing for election or canvassing.

Stages of development

Despite the fact that various researchers in psychology, education and political science have expressed considerable interest in the growth of political knowledge in young people and the determinants of the transition from one stage or phase to another, comparatively little work has been done in this field. An exception is the work of Adelson and O'Neil (1966) who studied 11-, 13-, 15- and 18-year-old Americans in the attempt to see how their sense of community related to their political ideas. They found that before the age of 13, young people use personalized modes of discourse and find it hard to imagine the social consequences of political action. Most young people below 15 years find it difficult to conceive of the community as a whole and tend to conceptualize government in terms of specific and tangible services. They are also pretty insensitive to individual liberties, preferring authoritarian options, and cannot grasp the legitimate claims of the community upon the citizen. It is only near the end of adolescence that young people take into account the long-range effects of political action, and use philosophic principles for making political judgements. They argue that there are five developmental factors or parameters which together bring about growth in political understanding:

the decline of authoritarianism and the realization that authorities may be irrational, presumptuous, whimsical and corrupt;

an increasing grasp of the nature and needs of the community and the understanding of the functions of social institutions;

the absorption of political knowledge and a feeling for the common and prevailing ways of looking at political issues;

the growth of cognitive capacities such as the ability to weigh the relative consequences of actions and the attainment of deductive reasoning;

the birth of orderly and internally consistent political ideology.

They note that the 11-year-old is concrete, egocentric and tied to the present in his political thinking, while 15-year-olds can deal with abstract ideas but have a lack of political information. On the other hand, 18-year-olds are more fluent, knowledgeable, philosophical and ideological. 'Taking our data as a whole, we usually find only moderate differences between 15 and 18. We do find concepts that appear suddenly between 11 and 13, and between 13 and 15, but only rarely do we find an idea substantially represented at 18 which is not also available to a fair number of 15-year-olds' (Adelson and O'Neil, 1966: 305–6). Berti (1988) has recently part replicated this study on 6–15-year-old Italian children. She found conceptions about government changed slowly in 12–13-year-olds, who differed from younger children in the belief that making laws is the job of the whole community, not that of one or several political leaders. Yet 14–15-year-olds spoke spontaneously about conflict, regarded the constitution of the government as the starting point for the establishment of the community, and expressed a general and abstract idea of the function of the law. By and large these results agree with those of Adelson and O'Neil (1966).

In a similar study, using the same population, Adelson, Green and O'Neil (1969) looked at growth in the idea of law. They found that understanding moves from concrete to abstract – a restrictive emphasis is replaced by a stress on the positive aims of law while a conception of amendment is increasingly present in later years, as is an emphasis on the intrapsychic effects of the law.

Younger adolescents rarely imagined on their own that a law is absurd, mistaken or unfair. They assumed authority to be omniscient and benign, hence law to be enacted only for good and sufficient reasons. But if they were conservative with regard to the maintenance of existing law, they were radical with respect to enforcement. In a mood of serene omnipotence they proposed baroque methods for the detection and punishment of 'crime', giving little apparent heed to the gap between the possible triviality of the violation and the Orwellian apparatus needed to control, enforce and punish. By the time a child is 15 – in some cases earlier – a very different tone of discourse is evident. Now it is understood that law is a human product, and that men are fallible; hence, law is to be treated in the same sceptical spirit we treat other artifacts. Though the *institution* of law may be deemed sacred, specific laws are very much in the realm of the secular, subject to disinterested scrutiny. Law invites tempering and tampering, all to the greater good, that good either social or spiritual. Law is a tool of the spirit, not spirit itself.

(Adelson, Green and O'Neil, 1969: 332)

Using teenagers aged 14–19, Furth and McConville (1981) examined adolescent understanding of compromise in political and social awareness. Four aspects of political understanding were examined: the recognition of individual rights; articulation of other viewpoints; the need for reasonable compromise; and the separation of legal from conventional-moral regulations. A clear progression in mature understanding of the conflictual issues was demonstrated with the 18–19-year-old group quite distinct from the 16–17 group, who were closer to the youngest age group. They single out a number of specific aspects of political understanding that develop over this age range. The first is the adolescent's growing recognition of individual rights vis-à-vis those of society, and that awareness of the infringement of rights increased with age. Secondly, older teenagers are able to articulate the viewpoint of other interested groups in society and to recognize and expect organized action on specific issues. Thirdly, teenagers seem to acquire a much greater understanding of the concept of compromise over this period – the idea that to live in society the individual has to relinquish certain rights and others are legally protected by the government. Fourthly, older teenagers are able to distinguish between conventions and legal sanctions.

These four aspects of political understanding are intimately related. Consider the four aspects in their mutual relations: to the individual with certain rights correspond societal interest groups with their rights; to the uniqueness of each individual correspond differences in societal interests and viewpoints; the coordination of these adversary rights and viewpoints entails a practical solution which in the political arena usually takes the form of a rational compromise. Understanding of these three points leads to, and is in turn differentiated by, an understanding of the various sources which establish and justify social rights and obligation: moral, conventional and legal. These four points in mutual interaction make up a basis for societal–political understanding as it develops during adolescence. If the opposing rights of individuals and social groups are not understood or taken into account, there can be no awareness of potential conflict; if there is confusion between the sources of regulations, the compromise solution is inappropriate or limited.

(Furth and McConville, 1981: 424)

Based on his extensive interviews with 119 Australian youngsters from 5 to 16, Connell (1971) devised four stages in the development of political beliefs (see Table 2.1) . He noted:

Up to about the age of 9, politics is not seen by the children as a problematic sphere of life in which sets of choices must be made between possible alternatives. Most of their statements of preference

Table 2.1 Stages in the development of political belief

Interpretations		Stances	
Stage	Characteristics	Stage	Characteristics
1. Intuitive thinking	Confusion of political and non-political material; wild leaps in narrative and argument; fantasy.	1. Politics not problematic	Most judgements *ad hoc*, unqualified, not consistent. A few stable attitudes formed under adult instruction.
2. Primitive realism	Disappearance of fantasy; identification of a distinct political world at a remove from the self; appearance of task pool.		
3. Construction of political order	Division of task pool; expansion of concrete detail about politics; perception of the multiple relationships among political actors.	2. Politics problematic — (i) Isolated stances	(a) Positions taken on issues; preferences expressed ↓
4. Ideological thinking	Use of abstract terms in political argument; conceptions of societies and polities as wholes.	(ii) inter-connected stances — Ideologies	(b) Alternative actions considered and sometimes undertaken.

are *ad hoc*, unqualified, probably highly unstable and not necessarily consistent with each other....This situation is transformed when the children begin to recognize political alternatives and notice opposing policy positions. They are then enabled to, and do, take positions on issues and develop consistent preferences of their own. At first... these preferences are specific to their subject-matter, and isolated from each other. Later they are linked together into coherent sets of opinions. From the combination of such inter-correlated stances with abstract and holistic interpretations, ideology may form. The expression of preferences does not necessarily involve action to realize them. There is further development when the child recognizes himself as a political actor, potential or actual and recognizes his own action as problematic, involving choice among possibilities. This development may follow rapidly on the formation of opinion, or it may be long delayed: we are here dealing with a moveable sequence rather than strict chronological stages, though there is a sense in which we can regard this development as characteristic of late adolescence.

(Connell, 1971:231–2)

Political socialization

Young people acquire political attitudes and knowledge through primary socialization in the family, secondary socialization in the school and continuously from television. The latter may amend, change or reinforce the pattern of political learning acquired in the home in both a dramatic and enduring way. Some have stressed the great importance of early political beliefs in determining adult political behaviours (Hess and Torney, 1967). But this stress on the early years has been challenged (Stacey, 1978).

Palonsky has noted:

The various orientations and definitions (of political socialization) stem from competing ideologies, and there is little likelihood, or desirability, that social educators will agree to a single set of goals for the political education of children.... Other educators contend that the conception of political socialization forces teachers to serve as unwilling agents of social inequity, defending the power and privilege of the few against the claims of many for whom the system is not working. If, as these educators argue, the rules of the game are rigged against those without wealth, power, and representation in the society, the goal of political socialization would not be to have students learn the rules as correct, but to question whether or not the society should be left the way it is, or changed.

(Palonsky, 1987:494–5)

Yet, from either perspective, education which actually helps 'the many for whom the system is not working' to make active use of their resources in their own interests is significant for them.

However, in his comprehensive and critical review of political socialization – defined as all political learning, both formal and informal, deliberate and accidental – Palonsky (1987) has noted some important trends in research findings over the past twenty years. For example, many studies done in the 1970s found the school was considered a strong environmental factor affecting the magnitude and valence of early political attitudes and knowledge learning. This finding, of course, put pressure on educators to be fair and non-partisan (if that was ever possible) in their formal teaching about politics. However, studies also showed, but were unable to explain why, students became increasingly cynical about the political system as they got older.

Research on political socialization has examined such things as explicit and implicit political values in text books and school materials, and the effect of the school climate (progressive, democratic, authoritarian) on political opinions. Hess and Torney (1967) have noted that 'citizenship training', an American euphemism for political socialization, often seems less concerned with education about the state and government than with ensuring obedience to authority, law following and rule obeying in the school.

To a large extent the research on political socialization has treated children and adolescents as passive interpreters of the political information that they receive. But young people seek out political information, and on occasion reject the information that they receive. In this sense, new political meanings may be created by children in particular circumstances. They also carefully select out and subtly change information to fit into their interpretative framework.

It seems that studies into formal and informal political socialization are beginning to realize the importance of the various different factors (formal learning, vicarious learning, direct exposure) that lead to a child's and adult's view of the social and political world.

Conclusion

Though the research has not been extensive, longitudinal or programmatic, there remains a good deal of information on how young people come to understand the world of politics. Through studies of considerably different quality and quantity, certain relatively robust findings seem to emerge on sex differences in political beliefs and knowledge; various cross-national and cross-cultural determinants of political beliefs; the basic underlying factor (conservative–radical) structure of many political beliefs; the extent of young people's knowledge at various ages; and, perhaps most importantly, stages in the growth of understanding about politics.

There remain, however, various problems with research in this area. Palonsky has noted:

The data from one-shot surveys provide portraits of striking detail. However, they are limited in what they tell us about the ways in which individual children develop complex and personal understandings of political events, actors and institutions. Surveys cannot show more than single points in the dynamic process by which political attitudes are constructed. It is not possible to determine if a one-shot survey design has measured a trend or an aberrant moment in the life of a child, or whether the questions asked on one day allow children to report adequately their political realities.

(Palonsky, 1987: 502)

Young people become voters at 18 in some countries and 21 years in others. Given the age distribution of some national populations, particularly of developing countries, the young are a very important numerical political force. It therefore becomes of some considerable applied interest what political attitudes and knowledge young people have; how they are acquired and changed; and most importantly how political beliefs translate into political action whether it is through the ballot box, demonstration or even violence.

Chapter three

Economics and trade

Introduction

It is not until comparatively recently that there has been much research on young people's understanding of economics and trade or their behaviour as consumers (Lea, Tarpy and Webley, 1987; McNeal, 1987). There are a number of good reasons why the topic of economic socialization and education is an important if neglected topic. Firstly, it may be that adult habits of spending, saving, investing, gambling and purchasing are established in childhood or adolescence (Furnham and Lewis, 1986). Secondly, from a teaching perspective it is reasonable to teach economic concepts to children and adolescents on the grounds that their knowledge is not extensive (Ingels and O'Brien, 1985; Leiser, 1983), their buying power is considerable (Davis and Taylor, 1979; Furnham and Thomas, 1984b) and there is accumulating evidence that training at a young age is both possible and effective. Many critical questions remain about children's knowledge of economics. Are there age, experience, gender, class differences? What concepts are acquired early and which later on? Are there definable progressive stages of economic concept development? Have children in capitalist societies been socialized into particular economic concepts? How do economic beliefs affect consumer behaviour in young people?

There appears to be a relative paucity of research on adolescent economic beliefs and values. This is perhaps surprising as there are both practical and theoretical reasons for wanting to know what adolescents know of, and think about, the working of the economy. Two 'practical' reasons seem obvious: firstly, adolescents have considerable buying power – for instance, in America, children spend over $4 billion annually and teenagers spent over $40 billion in 1980; while British 5–16-year-olds had an estimated £780 million to spend in the early 1980s on preferred goods and services – and it is of considerable interest to people in trade how, where and why that money is spent. Secondly, teachers of economics are clearly interested in the way economic concepts are acquired so that they may teach them more effectively at the appropriate age (Kourilsky, 1977; O'Brien and Ingels, 1985, 1987). There are also many interesting *theoretical* questions concerning adolescent understanding and beliefs about the economy (trade, work, consumption, advertising), such as at what age various sophisticated economic concepts are grasped and what socialization experiences determine the extent and structure of economic beliefs. McNeal (1987) in fact listed twenty theses that could guide studies on children as consumers. He also noted the number of agents in the socialization process whereby children learn to become consumers: parents, peers, teachers and business. Visits to stores, advertising, features, functions and packaging for young people's products are all considered.

The acquisition of specific economic concepts

A number of studies have made attempts to trace the development of certain specific economic concepts. They can be classified into three categories: studies on the understanding of *money* (its origins, functions, etc.); research into concepts associated with *exchange* (buying and selling, profit, banking, etc.); children's ideas of the causes of, and morality associated with, the *distribution of economic resources*, including young people's economic values.

Children's ideas of money

To a large extent, the beginning of economic understanding occurs with a child's use of money (Pollis and Gray, 1973; Witryol and Wentworth, 1983). One experiment on the perception of money published in 1947 has led to considerable research from various countries (Hitchcock, Munroe and Munroe, 1976). Bruner and Goodman (1947) argued that values and needs play a very important part in psychophysical perception. Hence the greater the social value of an object, the more it will be susceptible to organization by behavioural determinants (i.e. perceptually accentuated) and the greater the individual need for a socially valued object, the more marked will be the operation of behavioural determinants. Rich and poor 10-year-olds were asked to estimate which of an ascending and descending range of circles of light corresponded to a range of coins. Another control group compared the circle of light with cardboard discs of identical size to the coins. They found, as predicted, that coins (socially valued objects) were judged larger in size than grey discs and that the greater the value of the coin, the greater the deviation of apparent size from actual size. Secondly, they found that poor children overestimated the size of the coins considerably more than did the rich children. This was true with coins present as well as those rated from memory of their sizes.

Replicative studies have been done in different countries (McCurdy, 1956; Dawson, 1975) with different coins (Smith, Fuller and Forrest, 1975) and with poker chips as well as coins (Lambert, Solomon and Watson, 1949). Although there have been some differences in the findings, the effects have been generalizable. Tajfel (1977) noted that about twenty experiments have been done on the 'owner estimation effect' and only two have yielded ambiguously negative results. Nearly all the researchers have found that stimuli salient to the subject in terms of his or her needs and values had effects on subject perceptual judgements of magnitude as well as size, weight, number and brightness.

However, these studies do not tell much about the child's understanding of the origins and functions of money. In an early study with open-ended questions, Sutton (1962) asked eighty-five children randomly chosen from the first to sixth grades (approximately 6 to 12 years old) twelve questions, such as 'How do people get money?', 'What is a bank?', 'Why do people save?' etc. The 1020 answers were categorized into six responses: no replies (1 per cent); *precàtegorical stage* where objects are named but with little understanding of economic meaning (63 per cent); a category of *moral value judgements* – good/bad, right/wrong – irrespective of economic function (18 per cent); two *isolated acts*/factors that are economically significant are juxtaposed (e.g. people save just by saving) (12 per cent); two *acts involving a reciprocity* which cannot be explained by other economic relationships (if you put your money in a bank, you get more back) (5 per cent); and the subjective explanation gives rise to the *objective* – the single act derives its significance from its position in a system of relationships that is no longer conceived in an isolated way (1 per cent). Sutton found that age, intelligence and socio-economic background variables did not significantly discriminate between the children's stages of understanding, yet he argued that external stimuli and experiences were important in understanding the development of economic concepts.

In a large longitudinal study conducted in Italy, Berti and Bombi (1981) attempted to ascertain 3- to 8-year-olds' conceptions of money and its value. Children were shown a variety of coins and notes which they were asked to identify. They were asked what (from chocolate bar to motor car) they could buy with this money and they took part in a shopkeeper game-sequence to determine how much the children would pay for a purchase (as a customer) and give as change (as a shopkeeper). From the work of Strauss (1952) and others, they hypothesized various stages: (i) no awareness of payment (children do not pay in shopping game or recognize money); (ii) obligatory payment (children recognize that the customer must pay but do not discriminate between various kinds of money); (iii) not all types of money can buy everything (children realize that not all money is equivalent since they deny that the proffered money cannot purchase a particular object); (iv) sometimes money is insufficient (children recognize that some things cost more and others less and that certain types of money are not sufficient); and finally (v) the correct use of change (children realize the excessive value of some money with respect to price, and give change). As predicted, they found a clear development sequence in which 'the progression through the first four stages is developed around pre-operational thinking and precisely during that chronological period in which such thinking is dominant. In contrast, the fifth and sixth stages imply the use of logical and arithmetic operations' (Berti and Bombi, 1981: 1182).

In an earlier study, Berti and Bombi (1979) concluded that the idea of payment for work emerges from a hinterland of spontaneous (and erroneous) beliefs developed by children to explain the origin of money. In effect, the concept is only acquired in a verbal way; if a child occasionally notices that his parents (and other adults) take part in extra-domestic activities, this is not defined as work and the child cannot have any direct knowledge of payment. Only when the understanding of work is substantially developed does it support the spontaneous beliefs about the origin of money. It was also established that the link between money and work is initially understood asymmetrically. Children affirm that parents work for earnings but do not understand that there is a need for money which can be obtained through working. This indicated the existence of systems of ideas that are relatively independent, although they possess certain facts in common.

Finally Furnham and Weissman (1986) compared 4–5- and 9–10-year-old British children on their ability to recognize the value of British coins. Whereas the older group were nearly always 100 per cent correct, rarely more than 50 per cent of the younger group made the correct guess. British coins are particularly problematic in that value is not simply or logically related to covarying criteria such as shape, colour, circumference, etc. Nevertheless the results show that by the age of 5 years children are not necessarily familiar with the value of their own currency, let alone understand the origin or function of money.

To a large extent the child's first contact with the economic world is through money – receiving pocket money, watching their parents shopping, buying and in some instances selling goods; giving money in church or the street. Studies in this area have shown that, at an early age, money is imbued with value but that the role of money in the economic system is imperfectly understood. Children have to understand the role and nature of money before they can understand more abstract economic concepts like profit, loss, etc. They need to know such things as the role of money in obligatory payments, the fact that different coins and notes are of different values, that change can be and needs to be given where necessary, etc. Once these concepts are mastered, the development of abstract concepts can occur.

Children's ideas about exchange

A central concept in any economic system is that of exchange: the exchange of money or goods and vice versa (buying and selling); the temporary loaning of money (banking); motives for exchange (profit); price setting, establishing wage levels and inflation.

Central to any economic activity are *buying* and *selling*, yet for the young child these transactions are by no means easy to grasp. Furth (1980) has noted how difficult it is for the child to understand the transaction of goods, particularly a child of 5 or 6 who has not even mastered the number system. The child has to master a number of observed and non-observed transactions. For instance, he/she must understand the origin of money, the function of change, the ownership of goods. Children must also integrate the payment of wages, shop expenses and the shop-owner's money into the system in order to understand the pricing of goods.

For Furth (1980) there appear to be four major stages concerned with the understanding of buying and selling: no understanding, understanding of payment of customers but not of the shopkeeper; understanding and relating of both customer and shopkeeper payment, but not of profit; understanding of all these things, with the idea of profit. Even then it is not certain if and when children understand how goods are priced, the relationship between profit, pricing, sales, etc. Jahoda (1979) conducted two buying/selling studies – one involving role playing and the other semi-structured interviews – in order to investigate 6- to 12-year-olds' conception of *profit*. In the role-playing study, children played the role of shopkeeper and the experimenter those of customers and suppliers (farmers). The critical part of the role play involved the child's realization that the price that one *bought* goods for was different from that one *sold* goods at to the customer. Where the purchasing price was consistently lower than the selling price, the child was credited with an understanding of profit; when the two prices were consistently identical, lack of such understanding was recorded; and a mixture of responses was regarded as transitional. It seemed that it was not until the age of about 11 that most children began to understand the concept of profit. The second more detailed interview study showed the child's development from no grasp of any transaction system to the development of two unconnected transaction systems and finally to one integrated system. Younger (6–9-year-old) children simply described events and made up nonsensical answers on being questioned about profit, whereas older children tried to make sense of economic relationships but failed to arrive at the correct solution.

Jahoda (1983) replicated this study with young African children in Zimbabwe in order to test the hypothesis that, because of their great exposure to salient trading and bartering experiences, African children acquire the concept of profit more rapidly than European children. That is, the stereotypical 'cultural lag' between European and non-European children would be reversed. The results confirmed the hypothesis – being active in trading makes for an earlier grasp of the concept of profit. Indeed the Zimbabwean children were shown to be significantly in advance of British children within the same age range. This would imply that experiential factors have an important part to play in the development of the concept of profit (if not in all areas of economic understanding). Yet Tan and Stacey in a study of the understanding of socio-economic concepts in Malaysian Chinese school children found that the developmental trend was 'highly similar to that found among previous western samples of children studied…but there was also a suggestion that there may be less of a tendency for young Chinese children to refer to an imaginary source of money and to refer to parents or work as a source of money, than western children' (1981: 44). Thus there appears to be conflicting evidence as to the universality of the development of economic concepts. Clearly both maturational and experiential factors are relevant. These studies are not comparable, and the exact amount and type of exposure of the children to the economic world need to be checked. Nevertheless it does seem that economic concepts like profit which are dependent on the understanding of the basic concept of buying and selling may be partly dependent on personal economic experience of shopping.

Jahoda (1981) followed up the study on profit with a study on children's conceptions of *banking* – a complex and often remote economic concept for children and adolescents to grasp. First, 11-, 13-, and 15-year-olds were put through the shop transaction study in order to ascertain whether the subject understood the notion of profit. They were then asked a number of questions about the functions of a bank such as: 'Supposing I put £100 into a bank, and after one year I take the money out again, would I get more, less or the same?' and 'Supposing I borrow £100 from a bank to pay back after one year, would I have to pay back more or less or the same?' The responses of the children fell into six categories: no knowledge of interest (get back the same amount); interest on deposits only (get back more but pay the same); interest on both, but more on deposit; interest the same on deposits and loans; interest higher on loans – not fully understood; interest on loans – fully understood.

The developmental trends were striking and highly significant yet only a quarter of the 14-year-olds fully understood the function of the bank, with no increase for the 15-year-olds.

This study was, in fact, replicated by Jahoda and Woerdenbagch (1982) in Holland. They found that, while primary pupils in both locations overwhelmingly saw the bank as simply a place that keeps money, twice as many of the older Dutch subjects realized that one borrowed money from a bank compared with the older Scottish subjects. However, the authors concluded that the socio-cognitive pattern of development for economic ideas is much the same for all modern industrial societies. Ng (1983) replicated and extended Jahoda's (1981) study with ninety-six children, 6 to 13 years old, from Hong Kong. Although he found much the same developmental trend, a full understanding of the bank emerged at 10 while the idea of profit emerged at 6 years old. Thus for both concepts the Chinese children were more precocious than the Scottish (and Dutch) sample. As in previous studies, Ng examined the dynamics of conflict between schemes in the child. For instance, to induce cognitive conflict the interviewer deliberately asked the child to explain how the bank obtained money to pay its employees, electricity charges, etc., while having the same interest charges on money lent and borrowed. Although the impact of this conflict instruction was not significant, it seemed to be useful in examining economic development. Ng (1983) concluded that Hong Kong children's maturity represents a case of socio-economic reality (partly at least) causing or shaping socio-economic understanding.

More recently Furnham (1989a) looked at 11–16-year-olds, understanding of four exchange-related factors – prices, wages, investments and strikes. They were asked the following twenty questions:

(1) Do you often go to the supermarket by yourself?   Yes   No

(2) What do you think determines the price of each article?

(3) Can the shopkeeper ask as much as he wants to?   Yes   No

If you have answered 'yes', why doesn't he ask more?

(4) What does a shopkeeper do with the money he receives from his customers?

(5) What is inflation?

Is it good or bad?   Good   Bad

Why?

(6) Would you say prices of things in the shops tend to go up or down at the moment?   Up   Stay the same   Down

(7) What are salaries/wages?

(8) Who receives them and who pays them?

(9) What determines how much each person gets?

(10) Who decides how much each person gets?

(11) Where does the money come from?

(12) Suppose a person has plenty of money he doesn't need right now. What can he do with it?

(13) Is there a way of increasing this amount?

(14) How did factories start?

(15) Why were they started?

(16) Is it possible to start a factory today?   Yes   No

If you have answered 'no', why not?

If you have answered 'yes',

  (a) Can anyone start a factory?

  (b) What do you need to start a factory?

(17) Why would anyone want to open a factory?

(18) What is a strike?

(19) Who decides there will be one?

(20) Why do people sometimes strike?

Results showed few sex and class, but predictably many age differences.

The price setting of products was the only real departure from a clear developmental trend, showing the oldest group having the lowest understanding; that is 15–16-year-olds thought that the government or manufacturers decide shop prices rather than shopkeepers. Why this question should show a marked difference from all the others is unclear; however, it is evidence for the existence of part-systems in young people's economic understanding. Whilst having superior or comparable understanding to both 11–12- and 13–14-year-olds in virtually all other areas, in this particular area they have an inferior understanding, confirming that economic understanding is not a global term with all areas progressing equally, but is subdivided into part-systems which, ideally, will eventually merge together and become integrated into one whole system.

In accordance with Berti, Bombi and Lis (1982), recognition of profit was inconsistent. Of 11–12-year-olds, 7 per cent understood profit in shops yet 69 per cent mentioned profit as a motive for starting a factory today, and 20 per cent mentioned profit as an explanation of why factories had been started. The figure for understanding shop profit is consistent with Jahoda's (1979) finding that around 11 is the age where this understanding starts to occur. However, it is clear that different conceptions exist for the three groups, and while the 11–12-year-olds have not yet had to confront any inconsistencies, in 15–16-year-olds this process *has* started to occur.

Few subjects of any age group saw profit as a determinant of shop prices, but increasingly with age subjects saw profit as something shop-keepers take from money they receive. Thus, while the process of profit making was understood, its predetermined nature in the mark up of prices was not appreciated by 15–16-year-olds.

Inflation was not well understood, as Leiser (1983) found, with sub-jects of all ages confusing the causal with the descriptive. Most children said inflation was the rise in prices (a description), yet inflation was the most common reason given for *why* prices go up (a causal inference). However, older children showed wider, more integrated conceptions by being able to accommodate profit and price rises as two separate processes whereas 11–12-year-olds confused them more often. Similarly, older children understood market competition as the limiting factor in shop prices much more than younger children. This inability to comprehend macro-economic phenomena is due to younger children being unable to appreciate the aggregate effect of individuals' actions, according to Leiser (1983). Conceptions are tied to the actions of only one individual, and only when reasoning develops can aggregate effects and macro-economic changes be appreciated.

In the absence of this understanding, younger children tend to view social relations as the result of the constraint and coercion of authority figures (Damon, 1977), and economic transactions will often be seen in terms of moral or legal imperatives (Burris, 1983). Thus 27 per cent of 11–12-year-olds gave moralistic reasons why shopkeepers didn't ask for more money, saying it would be 'unreasonable' or 'too expensive', against 7 per cent of 13–14-year-olds and no 15–16-year-olds.

Understanding of wages as payment for work was high, with virtually all subjects understanding the process by age 13–14. However, younger subjects saw the relationship in much more immediate terms than older subjects. Eleven–12-year-olds tended to see the manager or the till as the origin of wages, whereas 15–16-year-olds primarily saw company profits as the origin. This illustrates well how conceptions organized in terms of part-systems (company profit and exchange of work for money) are linked together to form one system. As the process continues, conceptions become wider and more interlinked and integrated (Furth, 1980).

With increasing age, adolescents understood more of the determinants of income, though even at 15–16 only the minority of subjects mentioned both amount and quality of work as determinants. Burris (1983) found that the numbers mentioning amount of work as an income determinant dropped from age 11, being replaced by different emphases on the type of job. This accords with very young children's inability to distinguish natural and social phenomena (Piaget, 1965), social transactions being seen in physical terms. However, in this study the proportion mentioning quality was highest in 13–14-year-olds and lowest in 11–12-year-olds, somewhat against this trend. Congruent with Burris's (1983) finding though, the proportion mentioning type of work increased steadily up to age 15–16, whereas two-thirds of subjects mentioned it as an income determinant.

Almost all subjects suggested investing 'unneeded' money in banks or shares in order to gain more money, though slightly fewer 11–12-year-olds did so than older subjects. Once again, incomplete integration of conceptions was shown in all age groups, since in the follow-up question only the minority of subjects linked investment to the origin of factories. However, over 80 per cent of 13–14-year-olds mentioned investment as a necessary prerequisite for starting a factory today, and over half of this age group realized there were other things needed too, such as a good idea. Subjects thus did understand investment in factories and some aspects of entrepreneurship in the present and future, but not in the past, a similar finding to that about understanding of profit.

There was a trend for older children to understand industrial relations more fully than younger children, only slightly in defining a strike, but significantly for understanding why people go on strike. Interestingly, 13–14- and 15–16-year-olds emphasized union leaders' roles in decision to strike, whereas 11–12-year-olds emphasized workers' roles, with only a small minority of the older groups putting forward the idea of them both having a role. A possible explanation for this is the high profile given to union leaders in the media; it is generally the union leaders, not workers, who convey strike decisions to the public. As they get older, children have more interest in social events and more access to adult media, and may thus acquire this slant towards union leaders. This could also explain why they understand strikes more fully.

Thus, even for 16-year-olds able to leave school, understanding of economics is poor in many areas. It may be seen as desirable to improve this state of affairs, since, while experience may be important in some areas, it is still not known which economic misconceptions are corrected by maturation and life experience (Fox, 1978). Many studies have shown that children can be taught economic understanding at school, often to levels thought beyond their development capability, by means of role play (Kourilsky and Campbell, 1984), class discussion (Kourilsky, 1977) or just by presenting the correct relevant information (Berti, Bombi and de Bein, 1986).

It may also not be valid to assume similar developmental trends across industrial societies. What it is important to know is how the exposure to *which* economic *activities* (buying, selling, work) at *which age* relates to *which aspect* of economic understanding. Of course it is possible that the direct line of causality from economic activity to understanding is bi-directional, such that a grasp of a concept gives the child the confidence to partake in the activity.

Children's understanding of distribution and ownership

An important economic (and political) concept is that of ownership. Berti, Bombi and Lis (1982) have been particularly interested in children's conceptions of ownership and the means of production. They argued that children pass from an initial stage of complete ignorance about the productive function of means to recognizing that various means have to do with work and money and the production of goods. Finally, when a coherent and comprehensive view of the network of economic exchanges has been formed, the child will understand that the sale of produced goods permits the owner to realize a profit and pay his employees.

Over 120 Italian children were interviewed in order to determine whether the child recognized the existence of an owner for various objects (e.g. a factory, a bus, a farm), who they were and how they became the owner; the existence of agricultural and industrial products of these objects and whose they were; and what advantage the child thought the owner derived from each means of production. From their extensive structured interviews on who owns such things, five distinct levels were distinguished. The owner is the person found in *spatial/temporal contact* with the production means (passengers own buses). The owner is the person who *exercises an appropriate use* of or direct control over the producing means in question (drivers own the bus). The owner is the one who not only directly uses the producing means in question but also *controls its use* by others (the boss owns the bus). The owner is clearly differentiated from the employee, in that they have the *function of giving orders*. The owner is at the *top of the hierarchy* of command, and the boss at an intermediate position between the owner and worker.

The authors also identified five different levels for the perceived ownership of products. These include a stage where the children believe products are owned by anybody, followed by a stage where they are seen to be owned by those closest to them or using them. Yet only at the final level do children realize that products belong to the owner of the means of production and that the employees are compensated for their work by a salary. The results showed further that children's ideas about different production means develop with different speeds but through the same sequences. Furthermore, the parents also had a developmental view of their children in that parents of the youngest children said that they had not been told or asked about jobs and ownership, while the opposite was true for older children.

Economics and trade

The concept of ownership/possession (Furby, 1978a, 1978b, 1978c, 1979, 1980a, 1980b) and the concept of theft and justice (Brown and Lalljee, 1981; Irving and Siegal, 1983; Siegal, 1981) are clearly linked. Although research into the concept of possession began comparatively early (Beaglehole, 1932), it is not until comparatively recently that empirical work on children has taken place. Furby (1980b) has proposed two basic motivations in acquiring possessions – the enhancement of feelings of personal efficacy and control over the environment – though these are influenced by various social and cultural factors. Furby (1978a) has argued that one may take a life-span approach to the meaning and functions of possessions which change throughout the life-span. In children, for instance, possessions become valued because they are a source of constant stimulation and they may become a weapon for controlling interaction with others. In America McGrew (1972) has demonstrated the links between possession and social power in infant-school children, which have been related to the source of conflict (Strayer and Strayer, 1976) and the affirmation and denial of friendship (Corsaro, 1979). Furby (1978a, 1978b, 1978c, 1979, 1980a, 1980b) has demonstrated numerous developmental and socialization patterns in the concept, function and meaning of possessions. The concept of *control* seems the most salient defining characteristic of possession across all ages, though the acquisition process shifts from being passive in young children (10 and under) to being more active in those over 10 years.

With a more active approach to acquisition, there is the development of more powerful affect attached to the objects possessed. It is at this stage (about 11 years or over) that enhancement of personal freedom becomes an important reason for owning possessions. A further factor in young and older adolescents is the implication of power and status which goes with the ownership of certain specific possessions. Thus, from adolescence onwards, possessions enhance feelings of personal security and may become substitutes for unfulfilled desires (Furby, 1978a).

The concept of (private) possession is inextricably linked with the concept of theft. Although Furby (1980b) has looked at cross-cultural differences in the concept of possession and ownership, she has not devoted much attention to the related concept of theft. There has been a sizeable literature on children's understanding of and attitude towards theft and criminal justice (Brown and Lalljee, 1981; Irving and Siegal, 1983). Most of this literature has concentrated on the extent to which children and adolescents use mitigating circumstances to diminish partially the defendant's ability to act in a responsible, law-abiding manner. Using 15–17-year-olds in an open-ended free response paradigm, Brown and Lalljee (1981) found, for most crimes (including theft, breaking and entering), that the subjects could and did provide a number of mitigating circumstances including brain damage, passion, economic need, revenge, provocation and coercion. Irving and Siegal (1983), on the other hand, looked at the mitigating circumstances in children's perceptions of criminal justice for three types of crime: assault, arson and treason. They found that as subjects got older (from 7 to 17 years) they tended to make fewer legal judgements mitigated by a variety of circumstances and more judgements in which these circumstances do not apply. Overall younger subjects tended to be harsher in their judgement; their leniency and perception of mitigating circumstances were highly dependent on the situation.

More recently Furnham and Jones (1987) looked at the relationship between views of possession and of theft. Four groups of children aged 7 to 8, 9 to 10, 12 to 13 and 16 to 17 completed a questionnaire based on the work of Furby (1980a, 1980b) and Irving and Siegal (1983). The results demonstrated that possession concepts become more differentiated with age, focusing more on the importance of positive acquisition, single ownership and social influence. Attitudes towards theft crimes become more harsh even in the face of mitigating circumstances. This increased harshness may be understood in terms of possessions becoming progressively more a part of the self-concept. Thus theft and consequent loss to self lead to empathy with the victim and feelings of retribution for the thief.

Related to the concept of ownership or possession is the concept of distribution of wealth. Psychologists in general have, unlike their many social science colleagues, dedicated little time to poverty – its definition, causes, consequences, etc. (Furnham and Lewis, 1986). Even less has been done with children; hence Siegal (1981) set out to determine children's perceptions and evaluations of adult economic needs. Adolescents aged 13 to 16 were asked to distribute token money to dolls dressed as doctor, shopkeeper, bus driver or waiter, with the question, 'How much money does each need to take care of his children?' They were also asked whether their (unequal) distributions were fair and about the amount of effort required in the various professions. The results showed that the youngest children did not realize that unmet needs exist while older children were divided on the issue of equality – some believed that needs should be met regardless of the bread-winner's occupational efforts while others believed that inequality is fair and that effort and ability should be rewarded irrespective of need.

Winocur and Siegal (1982) predicted that older adolescents would be more likely to base judgements on equal pay for equal work, while younger children would be more likely to advocate that pay should correspond with family needs. Further they hypothesized that, though girls may be more likely to treat male and female workers equally, they would be more conservative in their achievement judgements than boys. Although they found support for the former hypothesis, they did not find it for the latter. Thus, concern for family needs appears to decline with age and objective work outcomes take precedence over need in adolescents' allocation of economic rewards.

Leahy (1981) was specially interested in the development of class concepts (specifically comparisons between rich and poor people) in cognitive developmental terms. Over 700 young people in four age groups (mean 6, 10, 14, 17 years) were interviewed and asked to describe rich and poor people and distinguish between them. These responses were classified into categories of person description, including peripheral (possessions, appearances and behaviour), central (traits and thoughts) and socio-centric (life chances and class consciousness) categories. Lower- and working-class subjects were more likely than upper-middle-class subjects to mention life chances and thoughts in describing the rich and the poor, while upper-middle-class subjects were more likely than subjects from the other classes to mention the traits of the poor. In the older subjects there was an increasing tendency to view classes of rich and poor people as not only differing in their external, observable qualities, but as being different kinds of people. As children get older, they place more emphasis on individual differences in effort, ability and other salient personality traits.

Two models are offered to account for the findings: a cognitive development model and a general functionalist model. In the former model, the results suggest that later adolescence is characterized by an increased awareness of the nature of complex social and economic systems. That is, subjects become more cognitively sophisticated and have more knowledge of the economic system. Hence class differences and economic equality are seen not only in terms of an individual's characteristics but also in terms of their relationship to other classes. According to the second model, socialization results in considerable uniformity among classes and races as to the nature of the social world. This uniformity retains stability in social institutions while also providing a rationale for the unequal distribution of assets.

Furnham (1982a) sought to compare two groups of adolescent school children's (15-year-olds) explanations for poverty. Public or fee-charging school boys (primarily middle class) tended to offer more individualistic explanations for poverty (e.g. lack of thrift and proper money management; no attempt at self-improvement) than comprehensive (primarily working-class) school boys who in turn tended to rate social or structural factors (e.g. failure of industry to provide jobs) as more important. These results have been found with adult samples (Feagin, 1972; Feather, 1974; Furnham, 1982b). Yet it should be pointed out that comprehensive school boys saw both individualistic and fatalistic explanations as relatively unimportant in explaining poverty. That is, the major differences between the groups lay in the importance that they attached to societal explanation.

The estimates of annual incomes of the poor showed interesting results. Public school boys gave higher estimates than comprehensive school boys. By and large the estimates were rather low, in that many people on social security or supplementary benefits earn more money than those estimates. It is known, for instance, that children underestimate both poverty and wealth because of their own experience of money (Danziger, 1958). Presumably adolescents also tend to underestimate, but not to the same extent. Interestingly, more comprehensive school boys estimated the amount in weekly wages than public school boys, who in turn preferred to make estimates in terms of annual amounts. This may reflect what they have learnt from their parents, some of whom are probably paid monthly (middle class) and some weekly (working class). Ideas about relative poverty and wealth appear more developed in adolescence than in early childhood and they necessitate a more global perspective on the distribution of wealth in the society.

Finally, a few studies have attempted to understand how children perceive and understand political and economic *justice*. For instance, Miller and Horn (1955) were interested in children's perceptions of *debt*. Similarly, a few studies have considered adolescents' knowledge of and attitudes towards trade unions (Haire and Morrison, 1957; Patterson and Locksley, 1981) but strictly these studies are related more to socio-legal attitudes than to an understanding of economic issues.

With reference to ideas of economic justice, Siegal and Shwalb (1985) conducted a cross-cultural study of the perception of economic justice among Australian and Japanese adolescents. They were interested in whether concerns for worker ability, effort and productivity (outcome) compensated for family need in the distribution of economic rewards. There were numerous cultural differences, and, as predicted, older Japanese adolescents compared with their Australian counterparts were most willing to allocate a significantly greater income increment to workers with high family needs or lower ability.

Furnham (1987a) replicated this study comparing the beliefs of 15–18-year-old British and South African young people. The study demonstrated a marginal overall nationality difference, with South Africans allocating more money to workers overall than British adolescents. This may be due either to a minor artefact (the fact that the base-rate sum was less realistic for South Africa than Great Britain) but may equally be accounted for by the fact that white South Africans are used to higher salaries than their British counterparts.

As predicted, each of the four worker variables – effort, ability, outcome and race – yielded significant effects. This partly replicates the finding of Siegal and Shwalb (1985), but whereas they used need of workers as the fourth worker characteristic (or equivalent dimension), this study looked at the race of the workers. Overall, the adolescents allocated more money to white than to black workers. This may be due either to actual discrimination on the part of white, middle-class adolescents or to the fact that they are simply reflecting the reality of the economic world as they see it in their respective countries.

These results make more explicable the cultural differences in reward allocation. South African adolescents have been demonstrated to be more conservative in their socio-political attitudes and to hold stronger just world beliefs than comparative British adolescents (Furnham, 1985a, 1985b). Both conservatism and just world beliefs are closely associated with the Protestant work ethic (strong achievement motivation through work) and, indeed, there is evidence that South African students do have high scores on this. Thus it seems that prevailing socio-political norms may influence the development of belief systems (such as just world beliefs, the work ethic, etc.), which in turn influence the perception of economic justice. Siegal and Shwalb argue that 'a particular issue meriting attention is whether youths regard the norms of "equal pay for equal work" or "greater pay for greater need" as social conventions or universal moral rules' (1985: 324). These studies have suggested that neither apply universally and that, whereas some societies are more predisposed to principles of equality of work rewards, others stress individual equity.

Studies on economic distribution and ownership have demonstrated that it is not until early adolescence that children begin to grasp the complexities and interrelatedness of the economic system. They tend to be very simple-minded in their conception of ownership and possession and make punitive judgements for theft which become more tolerant over time. Once again not only are there clear developmental trends but indications that experiential and educational experience affects children's habits and judgements.

It seems that conceptions of money predate those of exchange, which in turn predate conceptions of the distribution of economic phenomena. This, in fact, may be the sequence in which children encounter these phenomena. However, it does seem that the development of these concepts follows much the same developmental sequence from little or no knowledge of the concept; partial knowledge which may be poorly integrated or incorrect in some aspects; patchy knowledge where some aspects are fully understood but not others; to complete knowledge. Yet it certainly is not clear from the studies in this area if indeed the same experiential or maturational factors contribute to the development of each concept in the same way.

Economic values

Recently O'Brien and Ingels (1987) set about developing a valid and reliable instrument to measure young people's attitudes and values with respect to economic issues – the economic values inventory (EVI). This multi-dimensional (8-factor) instrument was shown to be in part related to the adolescents' formal education in economics, whether they had a full-time job, their socio-economic status, their political party identification, their sex, age and race. O'Brien and Ingels' main hypothesis, that formal education in economics would influence students' economic attitudes, was confirmed. Most of the research has been concerned with the development of this scale rather than testing any specific hypothesis; however, it appears to be a robust and reliable instrument suitable for use in any developed capitalist economy.

In their original study O'Brien and Ingels (1985) divided the 44 items into eight subscales which were consistent and which had respectable internal reliabilities. The scales are described thus:

A. *Free enterprise system* (12 items): the respondent asserts the need for hard choices in an economy of limited resources, the importance of saving, the valuable contribution of business to society, the importance of competition for keeping prices low, the importance of freedom of occupational choice.

B. *Trust in business* (5 items): the respondent asserts almost unquestioning trust or faith in businesses as benevolent institutions that provide cheap, trustworthy, reliable goods and services.

C. *Economic alienation and powerlessness* (7 items): the respondent asserts that they feel alienated from their economy and personally powerless in the face of the economic system.

D. *Government role in social welfare* (6 items): in this factor the respondent asserts that the government is responsible for the well-being of the least well-off in society.

E. *Government role in price setting* (2 items): in this short 2-item factor the respondent is against any government involvement in setting prices.

F. *Unions* (3 items): the respondent expresses negative attitudes to powerful unions.

G. *Treatment of workers* (4 items): the respondent expresses the view that most employees and workers in the country receive fair treatment.

Table 3.1 Means (and percentages) from American and British teenagers' views of the economy

	American			British		
	Junior High	Senior High	Mean	Agree (%)	Uncertain (%)	Disagree (%)
1. The unemployed shouldn't blame themselves for their situation: it's the fault of the economic system	3.8	3.8	3.6	53.6	16.5	31.0
2. Resources are always limited, and we must make hard choices about the best way to use them	6.2	6.0	5.8	85.9	3.5	10.7
3. One of the bad things about our economic system is that the person at the bottom gets less help and has less security than in some other systems	5.1	4.9	3.7	58.2	15.2	26.6
4. The average worker today is getting his/her fair share	3.6	3.7	2.8	31.6	24.1	44.3
5. The average worker today is getting less than his/her fair share	4.5	4.6	3.3	48.1	16.9	35.1
6. It's the duty of people to do their jobs the best they can	6.5	6.5	5.0	89.5	4.7	5.9
7. Britain's wealth is far too unequally shared	4.7	4.8	4.3	73.8	7.1	19.1
8. There are few real opportunities for the average person to start a new business in Britain today	4.5	4.0	2.8	32.4	19.7	47.9
9. The poor and the ill have a right to help from the government	5.7	5.8	5.0	88.2	4.7	7.1
10. It is the responsibility of government to take care of people who can't take care of themselves	4.7	4.9	4.8	80.7	12.0	7.2
11. Unions are too powerful	4.3	4.2	4.1	65.4	15.4	19.2
12. We need a way to make incomes more equal in this country	4.9	4.7	3.5	54.4	16.0	28.6
13. Profits are essential to our country's economic health	5.5	6.0	4.8	86.7	6.0	7.2
14. Our society owes much to the contributions of business	4.6	5.2	4.4	76.7	17.8	5.5
15. Being in business means taking unfair advantage of others	2.7	2.5	1.9	21.5	7.6	60.9
16. The way our economic system is set up, nobody has a chance to get ahead any more	3.2	2.6	1.5	11.4	8.9	79.7
17. My freedom to choose my own occupation is very important to me	6.6	6.8	5.6	96.5	0.0	3.6
18. Competition between businesses makes for the lowest prices	5.7	5.8	4.7	86.7	6.7	6.7
19. Businesses could provide more jobs, goods and services if they didn't have to pay so much tax	5.2	4.7	3.4	54.8	14.5	30.7
20. It's foolish to do more than you have to in a job	3.0	2.4	1.2	5.8	4.7	89.6
21. A person who cannot find a job has only himself to blame	3.1	3.3	1.6	8.2	17.6	74.1
22. Most companies don't give employees a fair share of what the company earns	4.8	5.0	3.7	55.9	25.0	19.2

Table 3.1 continued

	American			British		
	Junior High	Senior High	Mean	Agree (%)	Uncertain (%)	Disagree (%)
23. Most companies give their employees a fair share of what the company earns	3.5	3.2	2.2	13.2	25.0	61.7
24. Having the freedom to start my own business really means having the freedom to take advantage of others	2.4	2.3	1.7	14.6	11.0	74.4
25. It's no use worrying about the economy: I can't do anything about it anyway	3.1	2.8	2.4	25.9	16.0	58.0
26. Our economy needs more people who are willing to save for the future	5.6	5.2	3.4	47.1	31.4	21.4
27. A company deserves its profits when they come as a result of doing the best job for less money	5.4	5.6	4.4	73.7	17.1	9.1
28. If workers want higher wages, they must work harder and produce more	5.2	5.0	3.7	59.8	22.0	18.2
29. Companies should only be allowed to charge a government-controlled price for their products	3.6	3.5	2.6	31.0	19.7	49.3
30. Profits are a sign that someone is being taken advantage of	2.6	2.1	1.9	21.0	2.5	76.6
31. Advertising helps consumers to make intelligent choices	4.1	4.0	2.3	26.2	13.1	60.7
32. Most people like their jobs	4.6	3.7	2.8	36.5	16.2	47.3
33. Getting ahead is mostly a matter of luck	2.8	3.0	2.1	14.6	28.0	57.4
34. The situation of the average person is getting worse, not better	4.7	4.7	2.8	36.0	16.0	48.0
35. We'd all be better off if labour unions were stronger	3.6	3.7	1.6	11.8	17.1	71.0
36. If you have a valuable skill, you'll get ahead in our society	5.2	5.4	3.7	63.5	15.5	20.1
37. Taking care of the poor and the sick is the job of families and churches, not the job of government	2.7	2.8	1.5	18.8	18.8	67.3
38. It's not the business of government to control prices	3.8	4.1	2.9	40.0	14.7	45.4
39. Most businesses won't sell products they think are unsafe	4.3	4.3	3.4	51.2	16.2	32.5
40. It should be the duty of the government to be sure that everyone has a secure job and a decent standard of living	4.4	4.3	4.1	70.7	15.0	13.5
41. Government should listen more to what the business community has to say	5.5	5.1	4.2	75.0	19.7	5.2
42. Employers should have the right to hire non-union workers if they want to	5.4	5.2	4.8	83.5	7.6	8.9
43. People who blame other people or 'society' for their economic problems are just copping out	5.0	5.2	4.0	68.0	16.0	16.0
44. Groups of individuals with specialized skills, working together, can produce better products than individuals working alone	5.6	5.2	4.2	71.2	15.1	13.7

H. *Economic status quo* (5 items): the respondent holds the opinion that resources and opportunities are unfairly distributed in the present economic system, and that the status quo should be changed.

Furnham (1987b) examined the economic values of about 100 British young people (16–17- years-old) and compared them with the findings of O'Brien and Ingels (1987) from America.

Table 3.1 shows the means from the American junior high ($n = 452$) and senior high sample ($n = 207$) as well as the mean from this sample which is more comparable in age with the American senior high pupils. Although it is not possible to do any formal comparative analysis, the differences and similarities between the two samples are interesting. On a number of items there were surprisingly few differences in mean scores (e.g. items 1, 2, 10, 11, 40); however, on others there were large differences. There was a mean difference of 1.5 or above on items 6 (the Americans believed more than the British that it is the duty of people to do their jobs the best they can), 21 (the Americans believed more than the British that a person who cannot find a job has only himself to blame), 26 (the Americans believed more than the British that their economy needed more people who were willing to save for the future), 31 (the Americans believed more than the British that advertising helped consumers make intelligent choices), 34 (the Americans believed more than the British that the situation of the average person is getting worse, not better), 35 (the Americans believed more than the British that we'd all be better off if labour unions were stronger) and 36 (the Americans believed more than the British that if you have a valuable skill, you will get ahead).

The differences between the American and British adolescents' beliefs may be attributed to a number of possible causes: the fact that youth unemployment is probably a more salient issue among British youth; more Americans go into higher education than do the British; there are fewer long-term provisions for the long-term unemployed in the USA than in Britain.

What is interesting about the items that most British subjects either agreed or disagreed with (over 75 per cent) was the fact that they were often naive and contradictory. Thus they believed in a welfare state (see item 10 agreed to by over 80 per cent: 'It is the responsibility of the government to take care of people who can't take care of themselves') and appeared equally to believe in free enterprise (e.g. item 42 'Employers should have the right to hire non-union workers if they want to'). It could of course be argued that in a mixed economy such as Britain these statements are not incompatible, yet the overall pattern of results (compare items 1 and 43) shows that the respondents do not follow clearly and unambiguously any one politico-economic line. Furthermore, the results seem also to indicate a relatively poor understanding of the workings of the economy as those items which require some understanding (e.g. 26: the role of saving) had a high percentage of uncertain responses.

However, the main reason for the study was to isolate those independent variables that best discriminated economic values. Very few – amount of pocket money received and political party preference (vote) – appeared to discriminate in logical patterns. This is in accordance with previous studies which have not found many clearly discriminating variables (Marshall and Magruder, 1960; Furnham and Thomas, 1984b). This may be due to the fact that the sample was drawn from a fairly homogeneous socio-economic group. Indeed, O'Brien and Ingels (1985) found socio-economic status one of their most discriminating independent variables (six out of eight factors yielded significant differences). However, whereas O'Brien and Ingels (1985) found vote (political party identification) did not discriminate with their sample (two out of eight factors showed significant differences), the British study found vote the most discriminating variable (five out of eight factors showed significant differences). This may be due to the fact that in Britain – more than America – the political parties are divided on economic issues, and to a limited degree class (socio-economic) differences (Eysenck, 1978). Furthermore, adolescents appear to be fairly interested, knowledgeable and aware of political issues in Britain (Furnham and Gunter, 1983). It is also possible as Jahoda (1983) suggests that experience in the economy speeds up economic socialization and knowledge and that this may account for some of the difference between the two national groups.

Other studies related to young people's economic values concern their beliefs about how public expenditure should be decided. Lewis (1983) asked university student subjects first to estimate then show preferences for public expenditure items. He found the subjects' political preferences clearly affected their preferences about on what services public expenditure should be made.

Furnham (1987b) replicated this finding with young people. Subjects were required to complete the Public Expenditure questionnaire devised by Lewis (1983). This is a brief and simple questionnaire which asks subjects to apportion the total annual budget (in terms of percentages) on seven macro-public expenditure items: Trade and Industry; Social Security; Defence; Education; Health and Welfare; Roads and Housing. However, in Furnham's study subjects were required to do this four times. The results were fairly similar to the findings of Lewis (1983) save the fact that his student sample favoured spending less on social security and more on education than this sample (12 vs. 17 per cent; 22 vs. 19 per cent). Interestingly, the subjects appeared to want to spend most money on trade and industry, closely followed by health and welfare, and finally education.

Certainly, as Lewis (1983) has argued, public expenditure perceptions and preferences can be broadly predicted from social and political attitudes. Furnham (1987b) showed that not as many differences arise in adolescents as in adults (Lewis, 1983) but that predictable patterns do occur. It should be pointed out however that responses to his questionnaire may be relatively unstable as popular debate on such issues as defence strategy, social security (welfare) fraud, education cuts may significantly alter the response pattern of subjects.

The two major public expenditure items that yielded consistent significant differences were (predictably) social security and defence. Whereas conservative voters believed that approximately equal amounts of revenue were, are and should be spent on each, left-wing labour supporters discriminated sharply between them, not unnaturally favouring social welfare over defence. But what is perhaps most interesting is the way subjects of the left *and* right exaggerate the difference between expenditure on these two, underemphasizing the difference in their own preference. This may be seen as a sort of attribution error that may function to confirm one in one's own beliefs. Why this error does not extend to trade and industry (possibly favoured by capitalistic conservatives) and health and welfare (possibly favoured by socialist labour supporters) is unclear.

One of the advantages of asking people to estimate these public expenditure expenses is that one may compare their estimates with the actual sums spent on each item. By-and-large, subjects were reasonably accurate but tended to over estimate the amount spent on defence and roads, and underestimate the amount spent on social security and education. As Lewis (1983) noted in his study, the results tend to suggest that subjects from the 'right' (Conservatives) tend to have a more accurate picture of public expenditure than subjects from the 'left' (Labour).

Certainly the research on young people's economic values remains in its infancy but is both promising and interesting. More importantly, it may well be that the best predictor of economic behaviour is economic values rather than economic knowledge.

Developmental stages in the acquisition of economic concepts

Nearly all the early work in this field was clearly in the tradition of stage theory and attempted to describe the various developmental stages through which children pass in their acquisition of economic knowledge. Nearly all of the studies on children's understanding of economic concepts have looked at more than one concept at a time, yet still tried to specify a general stage-wise process. It may well be that various concepts develop at different stages.

Sutton (1962) has maintained that theory and research on the attainment of economic concepts should attempt to answer five questions. How do children achieve information necessary for isolating and learning a concept? How do children retain the information from encounters so that it may be useful later? How is the retained information transformed so that it may be rendered useful for testing a hypothesis still unformed at the moment of first encountering new information? What are the general features in the growth of economic concepts? To what extent are the concepts of children a cultural product of the environment?

In one of the earliest studies in the field concentrating only on money-related concepts, Strauss (1952) asked 4½–11½-year-olds, seventy-one detailed predetermined questions. From his study he drew up nine different stages or transformations through which children pass as they become acquainted with money. He argued that neither insightful learning, conditioning nor simple rewards can fully account for this cognitive development, though it is not clear from his studies which maturational, experiential or environmental factors provoke a child to move from one stage to the next. Later, Danziger (1958) suggested that the development of general social and economic concepts may follow different paths or stages which may not fall into line with the theoretical model elaborated in connection with physical concepts. Using interviews with children of 5 to 8 years old, he asked them about the meaning of rich and poor, the uses of money, and the position of the boss at work. He codified the various replies into four developmental stages. An initial *precategorical stage* occurs when the child lacks economic categories of thought altogether. At a second *categorical stage*, the child's concepts appear to represent a reality in terms of isolated acts which are explained by a moral or voluntaristic imperative. At the third stage, a child becomes able to *conceptualize relationships* by virtue of the fact that a reciprocity is established between previously isolated acts. Yet these relationships are isolated and not linked systematically. Finally, at the fourth stage, these various isolated *relationships become linked together* to form a system of relations and a broader understanding of the workings of the economic system as a whole. Danziger believed, like Strauss, that the development in the stages of economic understanding is not simply a consequence of internal maturation, but depends on experience with money and economic exchange, a phenomenon clearly demonstrated by Jahoda (1983). This may account for class, regional and national differences in the development of economic understanding and money-related habits (Cummings and Taebel, 1978; Stacey, 1982). However, what is less clear is to what extent formal teaching in economics may accelerate economic understanding (Marshall and Magruder, 1960).

More recently, studies into the development of economic concepts have become more conceptually and methodologically sophisticated, asking more penetrating questions or setting up simple role-play experiments which allow children to demonstrate their economic knowledge. Burris (1983) interviewed thirty 4–5-, 7–8- and 10–12-year-old American children who were chosen to be representative of the distinct and widely accepted Piagetian developmental stages (pre-operational, concrete operations and formal operations). The children were interviewed with regard to six basic concepts: the *commodity* (products exchanged in the market place), *value* (that which governs the production and circulation of a commodity), *exchange* (economic transaction in the market economy), *property* (the nature and ownership of property), *work* (social relations at work) and *income* (payment from work). Within each area the author found qualitatively different types of responses and significant levels of association between types of response and age levels of the children. For instance, when asked why some people get more money than others for the work that they do, the youngest group argued that it was the quantity (they worked harder or longer); the next group said it was the quality of people's work which may be more important, functional or helpful to others; while the oldest group argued that people get paid more because their work requires more skill, training or education. The results suggest that the younger children tend to represent social phenomena in terms of natural or physical categories (value is identified with physical size; income with the physical quantity of labour). Furthermore, the younger children exhibit extreme realism in that they do not understand the conventionality or normativeness associated with social phenomena or institutions – they are accorded the same ontological status as physical laws or objects. Thus it appears that cognitive developmental theory *may* be applicable to understanding the growth of economic ideas and relationships.

In a similar study using eighty-nine Israeli children aged 7 to 15, Leiser (1983) asked children (by interview and questionnaire) questions about prices, salaries, strikes, savings and investments, factories and banks, and the mint. He found that younger children (8 to 9 years) interpret economic transactions from the perspective of free, independent, individual participants having no awareness of the system of economic forces. Older children integrate their economic knowledge, become aware of various conflicts and try to resolve them. For instance, some children believe simultaneously that 'government sets all the prices' and yet 'shopkeepers are free to change them'. Similarly, once children realize the concept of profit on a fair transaction, they are able to resolve the apparent contradiction between 'buying as an exchange of money for something of equivalent value' and 'selling goods as a way of earning a living'. When asked how a shopkeeper would feel about a drop in the price of his goods, all the children realized that there would be diminished profit yet only 25 per cent of the youngest but 75 per cent of the oldest realized that this would probably be accompanied by an increase in sales. When asked what would happen if the economy was suddenly injected with a massive distribution of money, 21 per cent of the younger (8 to 9), 31 per cent of the intermediate group (11 to 12) yet 89 per cent of the oldest group (14 to 15) successfully predicted negative economic consequences (rising prices, shortage of goods, people's unwillingness to work). The more abstract and complex the phenomenon (e. g. inflation, market forces) and, more particularly, the more difficult it is to personify, the less children (even up to the age of 15) understand it. Children, it seems, can understand the motives of individual actors, but not the cumulative or aggregated effect of people's economic actions. It is only when children have some conception or model of the structure and function of society at large that they can begin to comprehend macro-economic changes. What is uncertain, however, is which *adults* have a reasonably comprehensive and thorough understanding of economics (Furnham and Lewis, 1986): that is, to what extent do adults understand more than 14–15-year olds about the workings of the economy?

The work on developmental stages thus shows patterns, if not a well-developed, explicit theory. Whereas some authors appear to favour a cognitive maturational approach, others emphasize the role of economic experiences in the growth of economic concepts. Clearly both are important. The major problems with the research in this area are fourfold. Firstly, studies have usually interviewed a limited number of unrepresentative children or adolescents from a restricted age range. If, as Stacey (1982) suggests, economic concepts develop later than many other social concepts, the age range of subjects needs to be extended. Secondly, studies have concentrated on a restricted range of economic concepts – some have only considered money while more recent studies have investigated a whole range of concepts such as inflation, banking, etc. The precise relationship of these concepts needs to be specified by considering, for instance, which are more central or important than others. Thirdly, nearly all the relevant research consists of self-report studies using interviews. Most Piagetian work is task based (role play, games, etc.) and it may well be that experimental studies on economic concepts would yield clearer, more interesting results. Finally, most of these studies have been conducted in western, industrialized, capitalist countries and, if economic education and experiences are relevant to the development of economic concepts, studies need to be done in third world or socialist countries.

Economic socialization and education

If experiences in the home and marketplace can dramatically affect children's and adolescents' economic understanding, how are children socialized by their parents and what are the effects of this? What experiences or what parental instructions make a difference? Why do parents and schools in western societies usually invest so little effort in economic instruction? Can formal, classroom-based economic education radically improve children's and adolescents' knowledge of the workings of the economy?

Work in this field falls into two major parts: work on pocket money as a means of studying how parents socialize the young into ways of using money, and, secondly, effects of explicit teaching of some economic concepts. Stacey (1982) has divided the research on economic socialization into four different areas: money, possessions, social differentiation and inequality, and socio-economic understanding. He concludes that most early experience of economic socialization appears to revolve around possessions which take on social characteristics. Between the ages of 4 and 6, children seem to acquire monetary understanding by associating money with buying, but it is not until the age of about 10 that the numerical value of money and the functional understanding of money transactions develop. At about the same time children begin to develop ideas of poverty, wealth, income, property and class differences. In early adolescence, teenagers are able to give near-adult explanations of economic events and relationships. Finally, the literature led Stacey to conclude:

> In the first decade of life, the economic socialization of children does not appear to be strongly influenced by their own social backgrounds, with the exception of the children of the very rich and possibly the very poor. In the second decade of life, social differences in the development appear to be more pronounced.
>
> (Stacey, 1982: 172)

Perhaps the most important way in which western parents socialize their children in monetary and economic matters is through their pocket money (allowances) – a weekly or monthly allowance given either unconditionally or for some work. Almost no research has been done in this area, although market research over an eight-year period in Britain has attempted to determine changes in pocket-money patterns which naturally increase, roughly in line with inflation. Girls tended to get less than boys at all ages, and pocket money was often supplemented by part-time jobs, as well as gifts. It is also noted that children's spending power was almost £640 million a year on pocket money alone, and more than £780 million if earnings from jobs and gifts from relatives are included (Walls, 1983).

On the other hand many popular articles have been written in an attempt to guide parents in the economic socialization of their children.

Rarely, if ever, do they present data but are nearly always forceful, moralistic and middle class in their advice. Consider the following:

The allowance should be paid weekly – on the same day of each week – to younger children, and monthly to kids as they approach their teens. The shift to monthly payment is not for your convenience but is for the purpose of encouraging more careful attention to budgeting and planning ahead on the part of your teenager. The important thing is that the payment should represent a predictable source of income that the child can count on.

(Davis and Taylor, 1979)

Fox (1978) has argued that, even by the time children enter school, they already have experience of working, buying, trading, owning, saving, etc. 'Research on children's informal economic learning indicates that early economic instruction in the classroom needs to take into account these unprocessed experiences, economic attitudes and children's cognitive capacities' (Fox, 1978: 137).

The study by Marshall and Magruder (1960) is one of the few that specifically investigated the relationship between parents' money education practices and children's knowledge and use of money. Among the many hypotheses examined were: 'children will have more knowledge of money use if their parents give them an allowance' and 'children will have more knowledge of the use of money if they save money'. They found as predicted that children's knowledge of money related directly to the extensiveness of their experience of money – whether they are given money to spend, if they are given opportunities to earn and save money and their parents' attitudes to and habits of spending money. Thus it seems that socialization and education would have important consequences on a child's or adolescent's understanding of economic affairs. However, they did not find any evidence for a number of their hypotheses. They were: children will have more knowledge of money use if their parents give them an allowance; if children are given allowances, less of the family's money, rather than more, will be taken for children's spending money; if children are given the opportunities to earn money, they will have more knowledge of money use than children lacking this experience; children will have less knowledge of money use if money is used to reward or punish their behaviour; and children will have the attitudes about the importance of money and material things that are expressed by their parents.

In an extensive study of over 700 7-year-olds, Newson and Newson (1976) found that most of their sample could count on a basic sum of pocket money, sometimes calculated on a complicated incentive system. Some children appear to be given more money for the express purpose of allowing the possibility of fining (confiscating); others are given it as a substitute for wages; while some have to work for it. Over 50 per cent of the sample earned money from their parents beyond their regular income but there were no sex or social differences in their practice. They did, however, find occupational class differences in children's unearned income and savings. Middle-class children received less (18p vs. 30p) than working-class children and saved more (90 per cent vs. 48 per cent). That is, 52 per cent of class V children (bottom of the socio-economic scale) always spend their money within the week, whereas only 10 per cent of class I or II children do so (top of the socio-economic scale). The authors conclude:

> Having cash in hand is equated with enjoying the good life: the relationship between money and enjoyment is specific and direct... the working-class child already begins to fall into this traditional pattern of life in his use of pocket money.
>
> (Newson and Newson, 1976: 244)

Furnham and Thomas (1984b) set out to determine age, sex and class differences in the distribution and use of pocket money by testing over 400 7- to 12-year-old British children. Results showed there were many more age than sex or class differences in amounts received. Older children, not surprisingly, received more money, saved more and were more likely to go shopping than younger children. Middle-class children reported more than working-class children that they had to work around the house for their pocket money and tended to let their parents look after the pocket money that they had saved. Overall, however, there were surprisingly few class differences, either because they no longer exist in Britain to the same extent as they did in the past or because the sample was unrepresentative in terms of classes from which the children were sampled or because class differences in economic behaviour appear later in life.

More recently Furnham and Thomas (1984a) investigated adults' perceptions of the economic socialization of children through pocket money. Over 200 British adults completed a questionnaire on their beliefs concerning how much and how often children should be given pocket money, as well as such things as whether they should be encouraged to work for it, save it, etc. The results indicated that females were more willing to treat children as responsible individuals, for instance by negotiating the amount of money to be paid and the various duties that they would be expected to fulfil for it. Overall, as expected, middle-class adults were more in favour of giving children money. Indeed, some working-class respondents did not believe in the system of pocket money at all. A similar class difference was revealed with the question concerning when children should receive their pocket money. Whereas 91 per cent of the middle class believed children should receive it weekly (and 4 per cent thought when they need it), only 79 per cent of working-class adults believed children should receive their pocket money weekly (and 16 per cent when they need it). Furthermore, significantly more working-class adults believed that boys should receive more pocket money than girls.

These class difference findings are in line with previous studies on childhood socialization (Newson and Newson, 1976) and with figures on class differences in general. That is, working-class adults introduce pocket money later and more erratically than middle-class parents. However, the study of Furnham and Thomas (1984a) found far fewer class differences, which may be the result of the fact that a greater range of ages was considered in this study.

Certainly the research on pocket money or allowances seems a most fruitful avenue of research, especially as so many researchers have reported that experience plays such an important part in the understanding of the economic world of children and adolescents. However, looking at economic socialization practices in different countries – socialist and capitalist; pre-industrial, industrial and post-industrial – may reveal equally important findings.

One of the more interesting applications of research on children's acquisition of economic concepts is the teaching of these concepts in school. For instance, there have been studies on the 'kinder-economy' or the 'mini-society' which involve classroom discussions of economic concepts like scarcity, opportunity cost, production, specialization, distribution, exchange and so on, followed by a long-term role play (Kourilsky and Campbell, 1984). Kourilsky (1977), using ninety-six 5- and 6-year-olds, attempted to answer four important questions: Is the child's success in economic decision-making and analysis related to instructional intervention or to increased maturity inherent in the passage of time? To what extent and degree, through instructional intervention, are children able to master concepts that, psychologically, they are too young to learn? What type of school, home and personality variables are predictors of success in economic decision making and analysis? For example, does initiative predict success in economic decision making? What part is played by the parents in their day-to-day discussions with their child of his or her economic activities? What are the parents' attitudes towards the teaching of economic decision making and analytic principles as part of early childhood education?

Her results indicated that the children's understanding of economics was most strongly influenced by the intervention programme even at an early age. From their answers, children appeared to be able to master concepts that developmentally they were considered too young to learn by that age. Yet the analysis showed that parental factors were the best predictors of economic mastery–more so than the cognitive, social or verbal development of the child. Finally, parents seemed very positive about the intervention programme, some even reporting that they found it embarrassing to find that their 5-year-olds knew more about economics than they did!

Certainly the widespread ignorance about economics in children, adolescents and adults suggests the importance and relevance of beginning to teach the subject even in early childhood. There are also practical reasons for teaching economics principles. Firstly, adolescents have considerable buying power, for instance, and it is of considerable interest to people in trade how, where and why that money is spent. Secondly, teachers of economics are clearly interested in the way economic concepts are acquired so that they may teach them more effectively at the appropriate age (Kourilsky, 1977; O'Brien and Ingels, 1985). Indeed there is a *Journal of Economic Education* dedicated specifically to research into the teaching of economics. There are many interesting theoretical questions concerning adolescents' understanding of and beliefs about the economy, such as at what age various sophisticated economic concepts are grasped, gender differences in economic beliefs and attitudes, the effectiveness of teaching by using role plays or 'mini-economies', etc.

Economic socialization occurs in three ways: parental instruction and practices (i.e. giving of pocket money); formal schooling in economics and related topics (politics, sociology, accountancy); and personal experience of the economy by personal shopping, work experience, attention to advertising on the mass media, etc. Clearly all three are important but they are very difficult to separate. What the results in this area do appear to indicate is that, although economic beliefs and understanding appear to develop in systematic stages, the speed of changes as well as the end-point of development can be substantially modified by primary, secondary or tertiary socialization.

Conclusion

The literature on child and adolescent understanding of the economic world is highly diffuse and of varying quality. Most of the research has attempted to describe the stages through which children pass in their understanding of a specific concept. There is, however, a good deal of disagreement about the number of stages, the points of transition and the exact nature of the understanding in each stage. Considerably less work has gone into describing those factors which speed up or slow down the transition from one stage to another or individual differences within the various stages. Social class, exposure to the economic world, parental practices and formal teaching seem the most important determinants of children's economic knowledge and use of money, though there may well be other important determinants, such as their schooling experiences, the amount and type of economic activity in the town or country where they live, etc. The importance of this area cannot be underestimated as it seems possible that habits of using money (spending, saving, gambling, etc.) are established in childhood or at least early adolescence. Studies of children's pocket money suggest that class attitudes towards money are established even before adolescence. This is in accordance with the literature on the Protestant work ethic (Furnham, 1984b) which suggests that early socialization in gratification postponement, internal locus of control and need for achievement leads directly to later performance in the adult world. As yet little or no longitudinal work has been done on children's actual economic behaviour.

Current research in this area has tended to focus on an issue of current concern, namely unemployment (Furnham, 1985b). For instance, studies have looked at schoolchildren's ideas about how to get a job (Furnham, 1984a) as well as their concepts of unemployment (Webley and Wrigley, 1983). Indeed, it is this lack of programmatic research into economic socialization and development that probably accounts for the comparative paucity of real findings in this area. Although there appears to be some consensus in the results from very different studies in this area, many critical questions remain about children's and adolescents' knowledge of the economic world.

Lea, Tarpy and Webley (1987) have made a number of important points regarding the research on young people's economic understanding. The first is that studies that have concentrated too much on cognitive structure and stages of thought have tended to underemphasize the very important roles of content and context in shaping understanding. That is, they do not attempt to analyse or describe how, when and where significant aspects of the child's environment contribute to their understanding. Secondly, economic understanding is intimately linked to political understanding and the grasping of constructs like power, equality and the nature of ideology. Consequently they stress the role of schools, media advertising and parents in the socialization of various economic beliefs and behaviours. They note:

> we should examine the economic world that children are constructing themselves. Bartering, swapping, allocating roles (e.g. in games) and rewards, giving presents to teachers and friends, betting and daring, are all activities that deserve our attention.... The more we learn about the autonomous economic world of childhood, the more developmental economic psychology will be able to inform us about the influence of the economy on the individuals who live within it and the way in which those individuals in turn shape economic structure.
>
> (Lea, Tarpy and Webley, 1987:398–9)

65

Chapter four

Work and employment

Introduction

How much do young people know about the world of work? What stages or phases do they go through in the acquisition of understanding about the nature of employment? Does having a part-time job improve their knowledge about work? How realistic are those about to enter work of what is satisfying work? How can we best educate children and adolescents so that they have appropriate expectations and fulfilling experiences of jobs?

Choosing a vocation and entering the world of work and employment is one of the most important decisions young people ever make. What they are going to do when they 'grow up' is a concern of young people for a very long time, often from about the age of 6 till the late teens when they enter the job market. Their image of, and understanding about, and expectations concerning, work and employment in general shape and in part determine what job they are offered, the nature of their training in that job and ultimately their career employment success. From a surprisingly early age children have relatively sophisticated conceptions of work. But, as Roberts and Dolan (1989) found, children's conceptions are not without contradictions. Children seem to feel that work of 'value' does not necessarily attract 'reward' but nearly all accepted a direct link between working hard at school and getting a good job. There appears to be ever accumulating evidence that work perceptions occur primarily through the direct interactions between adolescents and representatives of society's institutions: parents, peers, employers and teachers. Santilli and Furth (1987) have argued that work understanding is related both to personal intellectual development and to expanding social experiences in the home, school and indeed work-place.

It is the case that the world of work is changing rapidly (Furnham, 1989b). There has been an enormous rise in youth unemployment partly as a function of economic recessions but also because of changes in the nature of jobs themselves. There are few jobs for un- or partly-skilled young people as automation renders jobs unnecessary. There has also been a fundamental change in the nature of the work-force and the skills required to do tasks. Pautler and Lewko (1987) examined the views of work by young people who have experienced adverse economic conditions: an unemployed father and community depression. The latter seemed to shape views more than the former, suggesting that macro- and micro-economic conditions play a very important part in determining young people's expectations of work.

Young people have high occupational aspirations and, though these are revised downwards with age, there remains a strong orientation towards higher-status, white-collar jobs. In a very large study of occupational aspirations done in America, Shapiro and Crowley (1982) found a change in the aspirations of adolescent females away from clerical and service occupations to higher-status, better-paid jobs. Employment aspirations are, of course, strongly influenced by socio-economic factors (better educated middle-class adolescents have higher expectations), social values (like religion and sex-role traditionality) and ethnic status but there is evidence that these factors are having less impact.

Recent studies on attitudes to work and new technology show young people to be highly pragmatic. But, as Breakwell and Fife-Schaw (1987) have found, these attitudes clearly link to psychological factors as well as educational and family background. Gender, self-esteem, social class, belief in the Protestant work ethic all relate to attitudes to new technology.

It seems that young people's attitudes, beliefs and behaviours in the world of work are multi-determined. Demographic factors like social class, ethnicity and education play an important part, with middle-class WASPs having higher aspirations and more successful applications than working-class, black, ethnic minorities. But psychological factors seem to play a very important part. Among the most important determinants of work-related beliefs and behaviours in young people appear to be conservatism (especially with regard to sex-linked behaviours); locus of control (where instrumental beliefs are more adaptive than fatalistic beliefs); the work ethic (which is an index of work motivation and commitment), self-esteem and general mental health.

Attitudes to school, work and employment

For many young people there is an interesting and important transitional process between deciding to leave school and going to work. In most countries this decision is restricted to the statutory legal leaving age and the completion of the final year of schooling. However, many young people in first and third world countries opt to leave school and start working long before they are actually required to do so.

Predictably, students' experiences of, and attitudes to, secondary school are a major reason for leaving. Compared to 'stayers', 'leavers' tend to see the school curriculum as irrelevant, school as boring, discipline as restrictive and teachers as unsupportive. But, as Poole (1983) has noted, it is not only attitudes to school that discriminate between 'stayers' and 'leavers'. Early leavers tend to have low levels of achievement motivation and poor self-esteem, lack emotional stability and display less initiative, reliability and extraversion. Other factors include various social structural variables like sex, ethnicity and geographic attainment; early school achievement in terms of literacy and numeracy; the structure and content of the secondary education system; and the influence of significant others like parents, teachers and peers. More specifically Poole found four quite distinct groups:

Female stayers: These are likely to be students who achieve higher grades, conform to school values; are influenced by their teachers; display high academic achievement motivation; possess high organizational skills and verbal ability; come from high SES families and independent schools; discuss job prospects with their parents; are introverted; and do not rate their chances of success highly.

Male stayers: These are likely to be students who achieve lower grades; do not conform to school values; are not influenced by their teachers; show high academic achievement motivation; possess high organizational skills and verbal ability; come from high SES families and attend independent schools; discuss job prospects with parents; are extroverted, self-interested, fatalistic and rate their chances of success highly.

Female leavers: These are likely to be students who achieve higher grades; conform to school values; are influenced by their teachers; have low academic achievement motivation; display poor organizational skills and low verbal ability; come from lower SES families and state or technical schools; do not frequently discuss their job prospects with parents; are introverted; and do not rate their chances of success highly.

Male leavers: These are likely to be students who achieve lower grades; do not conform to school values; are not influenced by their teachers; have low academic achievement motivation; display poor organizational skills; have lower verbal ability; come from low SES families and attend government high or technical schools; do not discuss their job prospects with parents; are extroverted, self-interested and fatalistic and yet rate their chances of success highly.

(Poole 1983: 168)

But as well as push factors (to leave school) such as stress (Dobson, 1980) and boredom there are also a wide variety of pull factors that attract young people to the world of work. Overall, young people still value schooling: most believe that schools train them in independence and see the instrumental value in schooling. More importantly they believe that an educated person stands a better chance in life than an uneducated person (Poole, 1983).

In a recent British study Furnham and Gunter (1989) were interested in attitudes to school and work. The students tended to see schooling as a valuable experience. For instance, 63 per cent disagreed (particularly females compared to males) that it doesn't really matter how well you do at school. Similarly, 44 per cent disagreed (again more females than males) that education is mostly a waste of time. On the other hand, nearly two-thirds believed that school teaches about different sorts of careers (62 per cent), helps to make you become independent (64 per cent), and that employers pay close attention to examination results (74 per cent). More than half also believed that an educated person stands a better chance in life than an uneducated person (57 per cent) and that schooling helps to avoid dead-end jobs (50 per cent). But more disagreed with the idea that failure in examinations ruins a person's chance in life (42 per cent vs. 35 per cent) and that it is wise to think about next year's school work, rather than concentrate on the present.

There were some noticeable sex and age differences with respect to these questions. Overall, females tended to value schooling more than males. For instance, 70 per cent of females, compared to 57 per cent of males, disagreed with the statement 'it really doesn't matter how well you do at school', while 71 per cent of females, compared to 57 per cent of males, agreed that an educated person stands a better chance in life. There were some very noticeable age differences as well. More younger children thought schools helped you to become more independent than older children (69 per cent vs. 56 per cent) and also that school teaches you about different sorts of careers (68 per cent vs. 53 per cent). Despite their comparative scepticism about the value of schooling, more older than younger respondents (70 per cent vs. 59 per cent) felt that employers paid a lot of attention to school reports and examination results. These findings tended to support those of Poole (1983) who used an Australian sample.

In all, 70 per cent agreed that participation in class is more valuable than teachers explaining everything (78 per cent older; 60 per cent younger); 72 per cent agreed that technical and academic subjects should be taught in the same school (82 per cent older; 59 per cent younger); and 71 per cent agreed that they would learn better if the classes were more interesting (73 per cent vs. 69 per cent). The only item that elicited more disagreement than agreement, particularly among older compared to younger respondents (58 per cent vs. 22 per cent), was that examinations are the only fair test of a student's knowledge.

About two-thirds (64 per cent) agreed that school-children should undertake, in school, projects useful to the community and females agreed with this more than males. Females also agreed more than males (59 per cent vs. 50 per cent) that most of the subjects they take are interesting, though they agreed less often than did males (37 per cent vs. 46 per cent) that to get on at school you must put yourself first. Almost equal numbers believed that teachers are good at getting their ideas across in the class-room, but slightly more agreed than disagreed (41 per cent vs. 29 per cent) that students should not expect teachers to like them. Whilst there were no significant age differences on these questions, there were significant sex differences – females agreed with them less than males did.

The study was also concerned with young people's attitudes to work, the most important aspects of a job and how to get jobs. In all, 85 per cent agreed that after the working day a person should put their job behind them and attempt to enjoy themselves but 64 per cent thought hard work made one a better person. Approximately half of the youth sample agreed with the pro-work ethic statements: 'Wasting time is as bad as wasting money' and 'A good indication of a person's worth is how well they do their job'. Whereas there were fewer than expected sex or class differences on work items there were many age differences with older respondents tending to agree more than young respondents with both pro- and anti-work ethic items. One of the biggest differences was on the somewhat fatalistic item which said people should accept life as it is rather than striving for unreachable goals.

Furnham and Gunter (1989) were particularly interested in the youth sample's perceptions of the major sources of job satisfaction. They were, in order, job security (72 per cent), satisfying work (62 per cent), good working conditions (61 per cent), pleasant work colleagues (56 per cent), career development (53 per cent), salary (39 per cent), responsibility (25 per cent), working hours (22 per cent). This is very much in line with the results obtained from adults which show that job security and intrinsic features in the job are more important than wages or hours.

There was also a range of very interesting age differences. Considering only the responses 'very important', a clear and dramatic pattern arose. Older adolescents, many of whom were in work, rated starting wage and responsibility much *lower* than the younger children, who in turn rated career development, satisfying work, working conditions and job security much higher. It seems that younger children believe extrinsic features of a job are more important than intrinsic features but that as they get older they tend to appreciate intrinsic features, more especially the nature of the work and colleagues at work.

But how does one get a job? Various questions were asked about how does one find a job in times of high unemployment? Is it a matter of luck or chance, or a matter of effort and ability? To what extent does it help to have important or influential people pull strings for one? Most of the questions that concerned effort, ability and qualifications were agreed with by the majority who expressed an opinion: 65 per cent agreed that young people get jobs if they look hard, are confident and have a lot to offer; 50 per cent agreed that people will get a job if well qualified; 48 per cent agreed that smarter young people get work; 52 per cent agreed that young people get work if they look hard and often enough.

Questions referring to chance and luck factors revealed rather mixed answers. For instance, 57 per cent agree that it is mainly luck whether a school leaver gets a job and 52 per cent believed that getting a job is mainly a matter of being in the right place at the right time. But only 32 per cent believed that getting a job depends on *sheer* good luck. There was some agreement that the influence of specific people on the job search was useful: 41 per cent believed those school-leavers who got jobs had people pulling strings for them, while 36 per cent believed that, to get a job, you need someone with influence to put in a good word for you. Young people tended to believe (61 per cent agreed) that unemployment is running so high because the jobs are not there, while 52 per cent believed the government is to blame for young people being out of work.

There were a number of dramatic age differences. Compared to younger respondents, far fewer older respondents believed 'If they had better qualifications most of the unemployed would soon get jobs' (52 per cent vs. 25 per cent); 'Unemployed young people haven't tried hard enough and don't know how to sell themselves' (38 per cent vs. 25 per cent); 'If you miss out on getting work it is because you are not good enough' (30 per cent vs. 15 per cent); 'School leavers are unemployed because older people have taken all the jobs' (51 per cent vs. 39 per cent); 'You can get a job if you are well qualified' (54 per cent vs. 37 per cent) and 'Young people who haven't got work don't really want to work or haven't looked hard enough' (38 per cent vs. 16 per cent). On the other hand, older respondents agreed far more often than did younger respondents with various 'fatalistic' items such as 'Getting a job is mainly a matter of being in the right place at the right time' (79 per cent vs. 35 per cent); 'Unemployment is running so high because the jobs simply are not there' (65 per cent vs. 52 per cent).

Studies such as those above give a valuable insight into young people's beliefs about work. These change over time and differ from country to country (Nevill and Perrotta, 1985). Most studies have considered gender and social class influences on work attitudes and behaviours but others have looked at how such factors as parental aspirations influence their children's beliefs. For instance, Marjoribanks (1986) found that for middle-class adolescents occupational aspirations were related primarily to their attitudes to school and to their parents' early aspirations for them, while working-class adolescents' occupational aspirations were influenced by ability, sibling position in the family, gender and perceptions of parental support.

Certainly we need to know not only the content and structure of young people's attitudes to work and employment but also what determines those attitudes.

Youth unemployment

Since the 1970s when the problem became most acute in nearly every developed country, there have been a number of important studies on youth unemployment from a number of countries: Australia (Gurney, 1981); Britain (Warr, Banks and Ullah, 1985); Sweden (Hammarstrom, Janlert and Theorell, 1988), and the United States (Raelin, 1981). The underlying causes of unemployment are, of course, manifold and include demographic factors (changes in birth rate and an extension of the school career); micro- and macro-economic changes (introduction of new technology, new productivity agreements); as well as educational and training factors (the relevance and perceived appropriateness of education). Changes in youth employment move with greater amplitude than those of adults. Indeed, in Britain it has been calculated that if the unemployment rate for males rises by 1 per cent, the unemployment rate for young males under 20 years excluding school leavers rises by 1.7 per cent (Makeham, 1980). Similarly, there is evidence of crime rates being higher for youth during periods of unemployment compared to periods of employment though the explanation for this is unclear (Farrington *et al*, 1986). There are many implications of such facts, for instance for career education in schools (Watts, 1978). In a review of the work on youth unemployment Furnham (1985b) has divided the literature up into various sections:

Psychological adjustment

Many studies from different countries have tended to show that, compared to school-leavers who have found jobs, unemployed young people tend to be more anxious and depressed, have lower self-esteem and subjective well-being, are less socially adjusted (Stafford, Jackson and Banks, 1980). As Millham, Bullock and Hosie (1978) have noted, unemployment frustrates and delays the transition from child to young adult, increases dependence on the family and maintains poor self-perception.

The problem with nearly all the studies on youth unemployment and psychological adjustment is that one cannot infer cause – only correlation.

That is, it is quite possible that poor psychological adjustment leads to a young person being unemployed, rather than the other way around. Longitudinal studies however do suggest that, compared to the employed, unemployed youth tend to get more depressed, with higher external locus of control scores and lower self-esteem (Patton and Noller, 1984) as well as increased psychosomatic and psychological symptoms, increased alcohol and narcotic abuse and increased use of health care services (Hammarstrom, Janlert and Theorell, 1988).

Banks and Jackson (1982) interviewed two age cohorts of young people up to two and a half years after leaving school to investigate the association between unemployment and risk of minor psychiatric morbidity. They found a positive relationship between unemployment and disturbance after controlling for sex, ethnic group and educational qualifications. Further longitudinal analyses showed that the experience of unemployment was more likely to create increased psychological symptoms, rather than the reverse. More recently, Jackson, Stafford, Banks and Warr (1983) studied longitudinally two cohorts of young people in the first three years of their working lives. They found, as predicted, that psychological distress is higher for the unemployed than for the employed, and that changes in employment status lead to changes in distress score. Furthermore, this relationship is moderated by the person's commitment to work – the more committed suffer more from the experience of unemployment.

More recently Warr, Banks and Ullah (1985) found black unemployed teenagers less distressed and depressed than a comparable group of whites, but there was no difference between the two groups in terms of anxiety, financial strain and concern over being unemployed. Viney (1983) found the psychological reactions of over- and under-20-year-olds to unemployment were significantly different. Younger subjects tended to feel helpless, guilty and a sense of shame. Age proved a better predictor of psychological reactions than sex, length of unemployment or migrant status.

Job interview training

One consequence of mass youth unemployment has been a focusing of attention on job interview skills. Many researchers have become aware of the fact that because of skill deficits on the part of both interviewers and interviewees, potentially able candidates were getting rejected because of their poor social performance in the job interview rather than their inability to actually perform the task. Hood, Lindsay and Brooks (1982) allocated school leavers to either an interview-training or a discussion control group. The interview-training group received a combination of modelling, coaching, role play, feedback and discussion to train both verbal and non-verbal interview skills. Later, the school leavers were assessed using video-taped, role-played interviews which were made at the beginning and the end of each training phase. The trained group showed significant improvements on global as well as specific ratings (question asking and answering, fidgeting, smiling, eye contact, gesture, posture and interest) compared to the control group. The researchers all demonstrated the generalization and maintenance of these treatment effects over time. In conclusion they noted:

> Studies that have been concerned with interview training for various populations of adolescents indicated that such training may have a worthwhile contribution to make in preparing them for seeking employment. In view of the current employment situation, performance in the interview is more critical than ever before and interview training may fulfil a preventive function in interrupting the process of failure in interview, lack of work experience, and further failure in interview, before it becomes entrenched and leads to other psychological problems.
>
> (Hood, Lindsay and Brooks, 1982: 592)

Explanations and expectations about employment and unemployment

Many studies have shown that the expectations young people have of finding a job (as well as their job search behaviour) actually determine whether they find a job or not *and* how they subsequently explain it. Feather (1983) found 14-year-olds' confidence about getting a job was greater among those who have higher generalized internal locus of control, higher self-esteem, and feel less hopeless and depressed. There were however numerous predicted and reliable differences concerning males and females and those at state and independent schools. Subjects from state schools were more likely to endorse the following reasons for unemployment as important compared to those from independent schools: poor appearance; the economic situation in Australia; government's failure to provide jobs; failure of industry to provide jobs; and too many married women in the work-force. Females and state school adolescents, compared to males and independent school attenders, tended to have a negative view of self, pessimism, lack of motivation, tension, reduced performance and feelings of powerlessness.

Research within the framework of attribution theory would, however, lead one to make a number of predictions about school children's expectations about unemployment; and the unemployed themselves tend to make more external attributions for the causes of unemployment, in contrast to those in jobs and unlikely to become unemployed. Furthermore, studies have shown that external attributions are to some extent protective of self-esteem in the context of achievement. Hence, Furnham (1984a) predicted that females more than males and working-class subjects more than middle-class subjects – for whom unemployment is statistically more probable – will be prone to make more external attributions about getting a job. Further, it was suggested that these attributions will also be reflected in the number and type of job-search strategies adopted by young people and the barriers and aids that they consider operate in job-hunting success. In this study, Furnham set out to examine sex and class differences in 240 British school leavers' attributions about unemployment, the most and least useful job-search strategies, and which school course they believed most and least useful in getting a job. The results of the four different parts of this study suggest that, overall, attributions about getting a job are frequently internal (i.e. personal attributes or abilities) rather than environmental or societal factors. Confidence, perseverance and qualifications were all considered to be primary factors responsible for success in finding employment, yet this is moderated by the belief that jobs are not currently available (a fact which is attributed to the government). Yet failure to get a job was rarely attributed to the personal shortcomings of the job-seeker himself. Thus, these results tend to support the well-established attributional finding that success is attributed to internal factors and failure to external factors (Webley and Wrigley, 1983).

Similarly, Doring (1984) looked at the beliefs about employed and unemployed people among 1600 Australian high school students. School leavers vs. school stayers were compared and the former were found to be more inclined to attribute employment status to qualifications, experience and luck. The author however notes a serious concern about students leaving school with naive beliefs about their employment future in a time of increasing youth unemployment. It is not surprising that unemployed adolescents tend to be politically disaffected or left-wing in their voting preferences (Banks and Ullah, 1987).

Attributions about work are clearly important. For instance, Jones (1985) noted that it is often assumed that because young people's qualifications are strongly related to their occupational success, this is accounted for by employers' selection on the basis of attainment. However, surveys tend to indicate that attainment-related attitudes, attributions and related behaviours contribute powerfully to this relationship.

Education and unemployment

A number of researchers, particularly in the area of career and vocational guidance, have been interested in education about the possibility of unemployment rather than employment.

Darcy (1978) has argued that young people need to be educated in all aspects of job-sharing and to be encouraged to have a new definition of work, to include not only paid employment but a variety of other activities. Hence a careers education programme should involve such topics as the mechanics of collecting benefits, the acquisition of job-seeking skills, the experience of unemployment, leisure and community roles and the politics of the right to work. Watts (1978) also considered the implications of school-leaver unemployment for careers education in schools. He argues that careers educators have not seriously dealt with the problem of unemployment because they do not feel competent to tackle it effectively; they are aware of its highly political and emotional overtones; it might deleteriously affect the work ethic within and outside the school; and because the teachers feel instinctively hostile to the concept of preparation for unemployment. A number of possible curricular objectives are listed, including equipping children with employability, survival and leisure skills. Four alternative aims are described, depending whether one is focusing on change in society (to help students see unemployment as a phenomenon resolved by social and political measures); change in the individual (to maximize student chances of finding meaningful employment); status quo in the society (to reinforce student motivation to seek work); and status in the individual (to make students aware of the possibility of unemployment and how best to cope with it). Many of the educational responses and strategies are dependent on whether one believes unemployment to be voluntary (aversion of the will to work), cyclical (cycles of recession and expansion) or structural (a major change in the relationship between capital and labour). These solutions may include a deeper inculcation of the work ethic, job creation schemes, etc. Careers education is seen as the education of central life interests and personal growth and development, rather than the matching of people to (non-existent) jobs.

Job search

Another crucial feature of youth employment and unemployment concerns how people set about trying to get a job. In the United States, Dayton (1981) looked at the way in which young people search for a job. He set out to determine what job-seeking approaches were being used by young people and what factors they found positive and useful (aids) and what negative and worthless (barriers) in a job search. Using a population of

250 young Americans, Dayton found they regarded their own positive personal attributes (personality, flexibility, academic ability) as the most important aids in their job search, and external factors (labour unions, welfare and unemployment insurance, government training programmes) as least important. Employment success and satisfaction were correlated with careful analysis of which job suited them best, the assembling of a placement file, letters of recommendation and a c.v., combined with persistence in the job search.

Furnham (1984a) confirmed these results in Britain by finding that the young people saw their own personal attributes as the greatest aids and external factors as the biggest hindrances. Regarding the various strategies, class and sex differences showed that the middle class tended to rate all job-hunting strategies as more useful than did the working class, and girls showed less faith in following specific job choices than boys. The subjects all stressed the importance of summer and after-school work for experience, but tended to rely on personal contacts rather than direct approaches to employers. It would be interesting to compare these beliefs with those of employers, who may have quite different beliefs concerning which factors make an applicant more employable. The belief in the usefulness of A-level courses revealed that males believed science courses (and English) were the most useful in getting a job, although females tended to opt for arts courses and males for science at A-level. Females also believed that arts courses were more useful than science courses, so providing a rationalization for the choice.

Just as studies on divorce throw light on the psychological nature of marriage, so studies on the unemployed give various insights into the nature of work. Clearly because of its numerous and negative consequences, youth unemployment has attracted considerable research attention.

Knowledge of different occupations

There exists a fairly considerable body of knowledge on young people's perceptions of jobs. Himmelweit, Halsey and Oppenheim (1951) were concerned specifically with adolescents' views about the British class structure and found adolescents were very similar to adults in the ranking of occupations. However, unlike adults, adolescents' ranking tended to be influenced by the social status of the ranker such that, for instance, working-class boys overestimated the prestige of a carpenter and underestimated that of a doctor and business manager. The authors note:

> Considering that those boys were still of school age (13–14 years) and had therefore little personal experience of the 'world of work', the similarity in views between adolescents and adults is striking....This close agreement between the two groups is the more striking since it

is unlikely that the adolescent acquired his knowledge through any kind of explicit teaching or in any systematic way. It suggests rather that class distinctions form so much a part of day-to-day experiences of boys of that age, that when asked to talk about them, they can do so without difficulty.

(Himmelweit, Halsey and Oppenheim, 1951: 171)

Nelson (1963) posed the question of how children of different ages and background compare in their perception of sixteen jobs like bookkeeper, janitor and engineer. He was particularly interested in five individual difference characteristics as they related to the perceptions: age, sex, socio-economic level, intelligence and urban–rural background. The 595 young people (aged 9–18 years) had to recognize, describe and rate these various occupations. Predictably, there were numerous and highly significant age differences – older children were more accurate and discriminating in their perception of the job. However, where there were few sex differences in the description of jobs, there were many in terms of the reactions to jobs, mainly accounted for by the fact that boys exceeded girls in their positive reactions to most jobs. There were few significant class and intelligence differences which indicated that, compared to lower social class and less intelligent groups, higher social class, intelligent subjects were better at describing jobs but tended to be less positive about many jobs (particularly less skilled jobs). There were also some dramatic urban–rural differences which indicated that urban dwellers were less well informed but more positive to a wide range of jobs. Some of the conclusions drawn were as follows:

The groundwork must be laid early if the child is to aspire differently from his peers or parent levels of aspiration. There is probably some bias in the labouring population against the less active occupations, and in the professional level against the occupations requiring heavy work. Early reformation of attitudes may be necessary if distress to the individual is to be avoided when lines are crossed....Negatives are of great importance in occupational decision making; negative responses outnumbered positive responses, nearly 3½ to 1 for all children in the study. Besides limiting the occupations from which choices are made, it is likely that they form points of reference to which newly-encountered occupations are compared....There would seem to be some basis to hypothesize that the occupational choice question may be an encouragement to fantasy. Asking an elementary school child what he wants to be when he grows up is on a par with asking what college he is going to or whom he plans to marry. All of the questions presuppose more information than most young people have at hand. It would appear to be more important to investigate whether the child is involved in the process of narrowing the field and whether the process of narrowing seems appropriate in relation to the child's intelligence, opportunities, and background.

(Nelson, 1963: 753–4)

Where do adolescents acquire occupational knowledge. One source is their parents as they hear them talk about work, visit their work-place and meet their peers. Piotrkowski and Stark (1987) looked specifically at what young people think and feel about the work their parents do. The children's source of knowledge came primarily from work-place visits but also discussions with parents. Also children's assessments of how satisfied they perceived their parents to be were compared with parents' reports of their own satisfaction and the correlation was positive and significant. Children who claimed knowledge about fathers' working conditions such as physical environment, experience of supervisors, job demands, job security were more aware of their fathers' feelings about work. As the authors note, their study points to the family as an important feature in the learning about occupations. But what are the consequences of occupational knowledge?

More recently Taylor (1985) has argued that occupational knowledge may affect school-to-work transitions in at least two quite different ways: knowledge about the types of occupations for which one is qualified may facilitate a more efficient allocation of time and effort in job search and, secondly, specific information about job requirements in a given field of study may help students promote their educational qualifications and attractiveness to employers. In a study of university students Taylor found, as predicted, that occupational knowledge actually predicted job offers. Clearly, occupational knowledge has important consequences for young people and may be behaviourally self-fulfilling. Many studies have noted significant relationship between the amount of occupational knowledge and later vocational adjustment. Research such as this however must have important implications for career counsellors and educators.

A topic that has attracted considerable attention in the area is children and young people's occupational sex typing. Young children, particularly those of pre-school age, express preference for clearly linked sex-typed jobs and attribute sex-linked skills and preferences to men and women. In a typical study Tremaine, Sehan and Busch (1982) asked pre-school and elementary children of a variety of jobs (truck-driver, clerk, nurse, secretary, doctor) who would like the job, who the child would choose to do the job and whether the child would like to do the job him or herself. Although the sex-type attribution and service preference increased with age, each sex showed an own-sex bias. In another study, O'Bryant, Durrett and Pennebaker (1980) asked 11-, 13- and 15-year-olds to rate occupations in terms of respect, salary, education and service to the community.

Both sexes evaluated male-dominated occupations identically and highly, while females rated the female-dominated occupations more highly than did males. Interestingly, all subjects agreed that the male jobs required less education than female jobs despite the fact that male workers receive more money than female workers.

What is the effect of part-time work on young people? What is the consequence of experience in the work-place? Indeed, how willing, able and enthusiastic are young people at the prospect of work? A number of studies have investigated adolescents who work (Ruggiero and Steinberg, 1981; Raelin, 1983). Most studies of the impact of work on adolescent socialization suggest that work has beneficial effects (Hamilton and Crouter, 1980). Comparing 16- and 17-year-olds who did and did not do part-time jobs, Greenberger, Steinberg and Vaux (1981) examined the health and behavioural consequences of job stress and found that workers, especially boys, report fewer somatic symptoms than non-workers. They also found that boys whose work is stressful report fewer somatic and psychological symptoms than boys who did less stressful jobs, yet exposure to job stress is related to alcohol and marijuana use for both boys and girls. Constraints on autonomy adversely affect boys but not girls, while impersonal work settings adversely affected girls but not boys. Findings suggest both costs and benefits to adolescent well-being, the major benefits being the development of skills, again in self-reliance and social understanding.

In a large American survey Borus (1982) was interested in the willingness of the youth of America to accept menial employment in times of high unemployment. He examined various demographic differences and found ethnic (blacks more willing than whites), social class (working class more willing than middle class) and certain sex and regional differences. Overall, the results indicated that 14–17-year-olds in large numbers seemed willing to work for effectively subminimal wages in their desire for work experience.

Clearly a major source of knowledge comes from casual, part-time or even menial jobs that young people do. The exposure to this information shapes their attitudes to the job and jobs in general, which suggests the importance of accurate and salient information at a time when young people are making their job choices.

Vocational choices

For all young people choosing an appropriate career is often a long and arduous process. Career choice is highly unstable and involves a great deal of vacillation (Flanagan, 1973).

There is no shortage of theories that attempt to explain, describe or explore job or vocational choice. Poole (1978) identified nine quite different theories that have been supported at one time or another:

accident theories – job choice is due to adventitious circumstances and fortuitous exposure to certain experiences;

drift theories – by a process of elimination one drifts into jobs on the basis of one's qualifications;

vocational developmental theories – which are based on life-cycle factors and are stage-based;

trait-factor matching theories – where there is an optimal fit, compatibility or congruence between traits and job types and people are guided to, and attracted by these;

self-construct theories – a person selects and rejects an occupation which is consistent with their realistic or unrealistic view of self;

structural opportunity models – class, sex, ethnicity or geographic location means that people are differentially placed in various degrees of social proximity and access to different occupations;

vocational decision-making models – people make rational decisions on the basis of relevant information, probabilistic decisions, value and commitment;

awareness context models – the amount of and context in which one processes occupational information determines choice;

prediction models – based on research which suggests that factors like scholasticism, mathematical and verbal ability predict career choice.

What then are the main factors associated with career interest and vocation? These have been fairly thoroughly investigated and, although the list of factors is agreed upon the rank order, the relationship between factors is far from clear. These include:

Community-of-residence

Studies seem to suggest that young people from small and rural communities have lower aspirations and poorer jobs than adolescents from larger and urban communities. Many factors such as socio-economic class, education, job availability may be responsible for this finding.

Work and employment

Socio-economic class

Working-class young people have lower aspirations and more flexible ambitions in the sense that they are more willing to settle for relatively modest jobs. Middle-class young people seem less compromising and less willing to temper their enthusiasm for a preferred occupation since they feel they can and will succeed in getting it.

Gender

There has been considerable recent research on sex differences in occupational aspiration and choice. Although there is evidence of change in some countries with evidence of females being less willing to accept sex-linked jobs, the evidence remains that young people opt for traditional sex-linked jobs.

Father's occupation

Young people, particularly males, tend to identify with their father's career particularly when that career is prestigious, secure, and highly paid. However, when young people know their father's job is dangerous, poorly paid and with little prospect of advancement, it is usually shunned.

Occupational attractiveness

Young people are often attracted to jobs of glamour and adventure. Although initially attracted to jobs in terms of their importance in the community, young children rapidly use criteria such as psychological rewards and power which they are more and more attracted to.

The secondary socializing agents include the physical environment, the media and culture. The physical environment such as geography, climate and preponderant economy cannot be ignored. Depending on the physical environment, urban vs. rural, tropic vs. temperate, nomadic vs. agrarian, etc., young people are exposed to, or indeed deprived of, different experiences which influence their understanding of the social world. Hence, young Africans from a bartering society may be much more familiar with, and knowledgeable about, economic issues than their European peers who have no such experiences. The ways in which personal needs, drives and emotions are expressed are also related to the physical conditions of the home and the surrounding environment.

The particular socialization experience that leads a young person to make career commitment is clearly made up of many factors, and various theories attempt to explain how career planning takes place. Four relatively distinct views on occupational choice are identifiable:

self-concept development ideas emphasize that vocational choice results from a series of changes in self-concept;

cognitive-social growth ideas see occupational choice as a matter of lifelong decision-making in which the individual optimizes a balance between his preferences and the requirements of a job;

life-style orientation sees occupational choice as an attempt to implement one's personality style in the context of work;

a career education approach asserts that vocational choice is a simple function of joint career and vocational experiences.

There is no shortage of 'theories' of vocational choice and among the best known are those of Ginzberg (1972), Super (1957) and Holland (1959). Ginzberg (1972) argues that vocational choice is a developmental process made up of three stages: *fantasy* stage (up to 11 years and no regard to ability, training, opportunities associated with jobs), *tentative* stage (11–18 years and divided into the *interest* period where choices are based on likes; *capacity* period where choice is based on personal abilities; *value* period where choice is based on values and morals; and *transition* period where peers, schools and parents influence choice) and the *realistic* stage (which has periods of exploration, crystallization and specification). It is a stage-wise theory with the limitations of that approach.

Super (1957) in a more dynamic theory proposed, rather than stages, certain vocational tasks through which each individual must pass:

Crystallization (14–18 years)	where ideas about work are related to self-concept
Specification (18–20 years)	where preferences are narrowed
Implementation (21–24 years)	where training takes place
Stabilization (25–35 years)	where there is a settling down
Consolidation (35 years and over)	with advancement, and status attainment.

Holland (1959), on the other hand, has a best-fit theory which focuses on the fit or misfit between personality types and environment for job types. It is perhaps the most sophisticated of the theories in this area and has attracted the most research.

Suffice it to say that the work on vocational choice is rather list-like. There is a plethora of theories, approaches and factors thought to be important in vocational choice but no consensus on the status of these

Table 4.1   Stages of vocational development

Age	Stage of vocational development
5–10	Identification with a worker: father, mother, other significant people
	Concept of working becomes an essential part of the ego ideal
10–15	Acquiring the basic habits of industry
	Learning to organize one's time and energy to get chores and school work done
	Learning to put work ahead of play in appropriate situations
15–25	Acquiring identity as a worker in the occupational structure
	Choosing and preparing for an occupation
	Getting work experience as a basis for occupational choice and for assurance of economic independence
25–40	Becoming a productive person
	Mastering the skills of one's occupation
	Moving up the ladder within one's occupation

theories or the respective importance of the many factors thought to influence vocational choice.

Stage-wise theories

Just as in other areas of adolescent development so there has been research on developmental stages in attitudes to, or beliefs about, work. Furth (1980) examined the beliefs of 5–11-year-olds on occupations by classifying responses to the question: 'What kind of a person is a doctor/teacher, etc.?' He identified four discrete stages in the understanding of occupations: playful, functional, part-systematic and concrete systems.

Certainly one may predict that stage-wise theories of occupational preference and understanding are linked to Piagetian stages of cognitive development and to a lesser extent Kohlbergian stages of moral development. Studies have shown developmental trends in career perceptions. For instance, Borgen and Young (1982) found clear age trends in the ways 12–18-year-olds think about jobs. Younger children perceive careers primarily in terms of work-related activities and behaviours, while older adolescents focus more on aptitudes, interests and abilities involved in the occupation; on steps for entry into, progress through and exiting from an occupation as well as career outcomes like salary and fringe benefits. The authors point out that all occupational information is not of equal value to young people of different ages. At certain ages children and adolescents cannot process all aspects of career information and hence it behoves educators to provide information salient to the cognitive understanding and needs of the child.

For many theorists vocational choice is seen as a developmental task. For instance Havighurst (1972) proposed a four-stage model as set out in Table 4.1.

The stage-wise theories in this area suffer the drawbacks of all other similar theories. They are rigid with respect to exact sequence, nature and timing of stages and thus may be too artificial and contrived. Further, there is little or no consensus about the number of stages, the points of change or, more importantly, which factors promote change from one stage to another. This is no doubt due to the fact there is little longitudinal data but only cross-sectional studies from which temporal patterns are inferred.

Conclusion

This chapter has been concerned with young people's understanding of the world at work. Various themes have emerged from the various topics considered. The first is that a very wide range of demographic, psychological and sociological factors appear to determine work-related beliefs, behaviours and understandings. Among the more important demographic factors are ethnicity, education and social class while the psychological factors include abilities, intelligence but also social beliefs and values. Sociological factors include the family, school and the media (Young, 1983). The relative importance of these factors appears to change with the particular beliefs and behaviours being considered however, and there is little agreement on *which* factors are important, *when* or even *why*.

Secondly, with various caveats, it appears that work is generally beneficial for young people. Certainly their career is one of their major concerns (Evans and Poole, 1987) and there is abundant evidence that unemployment leads to a deterioration in physical and mental health. Other researchers have attempted to specify precisely the psychological effects on health, and it is clearly the case that unemployment affects young people as much as, if not more than, mature adults.

Thirdly, knowledge of the world of work and the nature of careers develops over time from simple minded to sophisticated. Though young people seem to remain ignorant of various aspects of jobs, they retain strong preferences. Again, these choices are multi-determined. Whereas the psychological literature in this field appears to have focused on individual choices, the sociological literature has been mainly concerned with restrictions on choice.

Many of these findings are relevant for how we educate young people about the world of work: the role of trade unions (Sultana, 1988); the changing status and values of young adults in modern society (Husen, 1987); the provision of vocational guidance needs (Cherry and Gear, 1987).

Chapter five

Sex and gender

Introduction

From the moment of conception, the fertilized ovum is destined to mature into a female or male, given normal genetic determination of sex. Though the sex of an unborn human may be a matter of interest and speculation within a family, once the birth is over the sex of the baby has to be accepted. Gender is a permanent human characteristic and, until the recent past, there existed in society relatively stable notions of appropriate sex-role behaviour for the different social classes. Traditional notions of sex differences and sex roles have been challenged in various ways throughout this century, most notably by feminists and by the labour demands of war and its aftermath. In recent years some of these challenges have both stimulated and been reinforced by developmental research on sex, gender and sexuality (Hargreaves and Colley, 1987).

In the process of becoming adult women or men, young people are affected by the gender expectation pressures, constraints, biases and demands of society, and also their own personality characteristics and abilities influence their interactions with the social environment. The young partly socialize themselves in their gender identity and sex roles as they develop during the pre-adult years, selecting from their experiences and accommodating and assimilating that material. This developmental sequence of interacting events has a natural beginning at birth, though female–male differentiation takes place during foetal development. Cultural-social differences between the sexes are maintained in part through sex roles allocated in the family, school, mass media, religion, sports, recreation, economy, and in everyday life. There is scarcely an area of social life untouched by sex typing.

Traditional commonsense views about sex differences reflect specific behavioural gender differences, especially views that the sexes differ fundamentally in non-biological ways and that these differences entail female deficiencies. The commonsense emphasis on sex differences is related typically to biological differences in reproduction. Furthermore,

87

as extensive cross-cultural research has shown, sex-trait stereotypes are common across all western countries, even those with fairly significant cultural diversity (Williams and Best, 1982). Such differences are used to support assertions about a wide range of non-biological differences between the sexes, and about the greater desirability of the qualities ascribed to males. They contribute to justification of inequalities in opportunities between the sexes and to the respective unequal places of the sexes in society. As Black has noted: 'To survey, evaluate, and distil the empirical evidence regarding psychological sex differences at a time of intense, polarized debate on the issues of equality of the sexes and changing sex roles is an awesome responsibility' (1976: 283).

This chapter is concerned with young people's understanding of the concepts of sex and gender. Firstly, sex differentiation will be considered; then socialization of the young in family, school and society; adolescent sexuality; and, finally, conclusions will be drawn. The chapter will also be concerned with the manner in which children and adolescents construe sex, gender and sex roles, and their perspectives on marriage and family life.

At several points reference will be made to a major cross-national study of 'children's sexual thinking', broadly defined, which has been reported by Goldman and Goldman (1982). Among other issues, they were concerned with how children perceive sex differences in babies and adolescents, children's sex preferences in terms of personal identity and choice of friends, children's views on why people get married and how children perceive differences between their fathers and mothers as representative of differences between females and males generally. The study was based upon interviews with nearly 1000 young people aged 5 to 15 years from sixty co-educational schools in Australia, England, North America and Sweden. All these young people were living in a traditional two-parent family and had at least one younger sibling. Sweden was deliberately introduced into the study as a contrast to other nations because of the different approach to sex education it has adopted, with compulsory sex education in school from the age of 8 years. The research remains among the most comprehensive on young people's perception and understanding of sex and gender.

Sex differentiation

Sex differences and sex roles have generated a good deal of public discussion and argument, with politicians, economists, religious leaders and feminists being prominent among the protagonists (Hargreaves and Colley, 1987). Arguments about the relative importance of biological and social differences between the sexes, sex-typed patterns of behaviour,

Table 5.1 Sex differentiation

Characteristic	Male	Female	Comment
Genetic sex	XY	XX	Sex is determined by whether the father's sperm cell contains an X or a Y chromosome, though the process sometimes goes awry
Gonadal sex	Testes	Ovaries	
Hormonal sex	Testicular hormones	Ovarian hormones	These hormones operate before and after birth; at puberty to produce secondary sex characteristics
Genital sex	External genitalia and internal accessory organs	External genitalia and internal accessory organs	
Gender identity	I am a male	I am a female	The basic sense of one's sexual identity; of being a girl or boy, woman or man, female or male
Masculinity/ femininity	Feeling of degree of maleness	Feeling of degree of femaleness	It involves interests, attitudes, fantasies, ways of moving, behaving and speaking
Sex role*			Standards and expectations of a particular structure and social milieu appropriate to one sex or other in all its aspects including sexuality and reproduction
Sexual preference or orientation			Whether one desires and is aroused by members of one's own sex or the opposite sex or both sexes
Anomalies	Many	Many	Incongruity between two or more aspects of sex differentiation

*The term 'sex role' is often used to embrace the several facets of sex differentiation, that is as an all-embracing term. The term 'gender role' is coming into use to refer to the cultural and social phenomena.

socialization into sex roles, the contribution of women to society at large as well as to the family and home, sex-role stereotypes and inequalities in opportunities for the sexes are a recurring part of the on-going public and academic debate. This debate has undoubtedly had a major impact on developmental research. The results of this research challenge some of the views currently in circulation, and indicate that sex differentiation, gender and sex-role development are more complex than many people believe. In the conclusion to their seminal work Maccoby and Jacklin wrote: 'We suggest that societies have the option of minimizing, rather than maximizing, sex differences through their socialization practices.... In our view, social institutions and social practices are not merely reflections of the biologically inevitable. A variety of social institutions are viable within the framework set by biology. It is up to human beings to select those that foster the life styles they most value' (1974: 374).

There is now agreement among developmental researchers that a number of factors are involved in sex differentiation. The terms in Table 5.1 reflect trends in current scientific usage. The term *sex* refers to cases where the distinction made involves biological criteria or considerations. However, some writers restrict it to purely biological phenomena. The term *gender* refers to cases where the distinction is made on the basis of non-biological criteria or considerations; that is, to purely cultural-social phenomena. Given that physical differences between the sexes have great significance in social life, and that physical sex differences and sexuality are loaded with cultural meanings, the phenomena of sex, gender and sexuality are deeply intertwined. From a developmental perspective, the importance of sex differences in physical characteristics, development, reproductive function and life expectancy, and of sexual behaviour, especially with reference to puberty and adolescence, means the wide embrace of the term 'sex role' is highly useful.

In general, a young person adopts a gender identity and sex role compatible with her or his biology, the particular attributes of the gender identity and sex role being congruent with the standards and expectations of the social environment in which she or he grows up. But there are cases in which two or more aspects of sex differentiation are in discord. Transsexuals, for example, have a gender identity contrary to their biological sex, and have difficulty in living the biologically congruent sex role. Another example is the testicular feminizing syndrome which occurs in genetic males with a particular biochemical defect. Individuals with this syndrome appear female at birth, have feminine bodies and develop secondary sex characteristics at puberty. Most develop a female identity and sex-role behaviour. There are other clinically recognized syndromes where there is incongruity between two or more aspects of a person's sex differentiation (Archer and Lloyd, 1985). While discussing physical sex differences, Archer and Lloyd observe: 'at birth the human genitals provide the crucial signal for deciding which of two very different life experiences the child will be exposed to, as a boy or girl.... The importance of this initial signal is perhaps only realized when one considers the anxiety and distress of parents of a baby born with ambiguous genitals' (1985: 84). Young and old alike respond differently to boys and girls from birth as a function of perceived sex and gender cues.

Studies of children whose sex was wrongly assigned at birth, usually because of genital malformation, have provided evidence of the force of sex assignment upon the development of gender identity and sex role (Money and Ehrhardt, 1972). Biological females who have been reared as males follow male patterns of development and, likewise, biological males reared as females follow female patterns of development. The impact of sex assignment and associated cultural factors can thus modify the degree to which biological factors influence development. Although the biology of sex differentiation is undoubtedly of great importance, so-called 'sex errors of the body' have proved informative about the enormous impact of psychological and social factors of gender and sex-role development. Gender identity is established in childhood and assumes further greater significance in adolescent development. Typically, of course, the biological, psychological and social aspects of sex differentiation, gender and role development are inseparable and positively reinforce each other. In this sense, Freud's much quoted statement that 'anatomy is destiny' is apposite.

Gender is one of the most fundamental categorical distinctions in all human societies. Gender identity is a basic organizer of experience, facilitating rapid information processing and actions. Nearly everybody automatically classifies the people they meet as female or male and responds accordingly. Children have to establish their own gender and to accept its constancy. Society and its institutions exert great pressure on the young to do this and to adopt an appropriate sex role. Gender identity is especially potent in our lives because it is central to the way we think about and evaluate ourselves.

Knowledge of gender has been demonstrated in infants and young children by the use of a variety of research techniques (Archer and Lloyd, 1985; Henshall and McGuire, 1986; Katz, 1983). Observations of play among the young, for example, have consistently yielded evidence of a gender relationship to play with toys, objects, language and materials, to rough-and-tumble play and to fantasy play. Young people's understanding of gender reflects developmental changes in language, knowledge, thought and play. Estimates of the extent of children's gender knowledge vary somewhat with the nature of the means used to assess it. But it seems that gender identity appears between 1 and 3 years, and is firmly established by 4 to 8 years. Most 5-year-olds are capable of understanding genital differences and their relationship to gender. Around 6 to 8, the child will come to realize that sex and gender remain constant, irrespective of changes such as height, body shape, hair style or clothes. The attainment of gender identity is an important gain because it establishes an enduring *schema* around which child, adolescent and adult can elaborate knowledge of sex and gender.

According to Bem (1981) a schema is a cognitive structure or network of associations that organizes and guides an individual's perception of the world. A schema alerts the person to certain kinds information and facilitates memory for, and recall of, gender schema-relevant information. Gender is a schema or cognitive structure for processing and organizing information about sex differences. It is a basic organizing principle for every human culture and operates in similar ways. Gender-schematic processing involves perceiving the world in masculine–feminine terms where other schema are possible. In the course of development, children learn the contents of their society's gender schema, that is, the network of associations linked with being male or female. These are then applied to the self, with the gender schema of that culture or subculture becoming a prescriptive standard or guide for children and young people evaluating themselves in terms of the extent to which they match the standard. Sex typing results and the child's self-esteem becomes heavily dependent on it.

There is considerable evidence for the role of gender schema in information processing. Bem and her colleagues have described several studies which demonstrate that sex-typed individuals, generally defined in terms of scores on the Bem Sex Role Inventory, do have a greater readiness to process information in gender terms than do non-sex-typed individuals. Thus, sex-typed individuals (i.e. masculine and feminine) show a greater clustering of words on that basis and a greater readiness to decide, on the basis of gender, which personal attributes are associated with their self-concept than do non-sex-typed individuals. In addition, there is evidence that children and young people more readily take in information that fits their gender schema, that they transform counter-stereotypical information to fit gender schema, and that they recall behaviour fitting their sex stereotypes better than they do counter-stereo-typical behaviour (Furnham and Singh, 1986).

Children and young people possess knowledge about gender-appropri-ate characteristics and behaviour from an early age. There is rapid learning of what is gender-appropriate in many areas of life, including play, use of toys, domestic roles, television material, sports and occupations. In their analysis of gender development, Henshall and McGuire note 'Children are developing in an environment in which behaviour has meaning and intention, and they are learning, not only what people do, but also why they do it' (1986:149). As children come to regard themselves as boys and girls, they display a strong tendency to value their own sex and gender positively, and to devalue aspects of the 'other' group. In general, boys tend to be more intolerant than girls of the opposite sex and of the principle of sexual equality. They display an identification with and preference for their own gender. In late childhood and adolescence, girls tend to have more conflict about their gender identity than do boys. In general, children develop gender identity by learning first what sex they are; which gender category they are in; gender relevant beliefs, attitudes and behaviour; and by assuming the 'other' gender type is different in many ways. Boys and girls are equally aware of the behaviour of each gender, and this suggests that such knowledge is based upon their experience of the social world. Parents as gender models to be imitated are probably less important than they were believed to be in the past.

In their cross-national study, Goldman and Goldman (1982) explored the sex preferences and gender perceptions of their young subjects. When asked to choose the sex they preferred for themselves, the great majority of the subjects chose their own sex; but girls were more likely to choose the opposite sex than boys (13 per cent compared with 6 per cent). At all ages girls gave predominantly female sex and gender reasons for wishing to be girls; whereas boys gave predominantly recreational reasons, and male teenagers a variety of reasons, with vocational reasons becoming more important at age 15. Girls who stated vocational reasons other than home duties for their choice tended to prefer to be male. When asked to choose a friend in terms of sex, most of the subjects chose their own sex; but heterosexual choice became more frequent in the teen years. Reasons given for own-sex preference as a friend fell mainly into two gender categories – identity of interests or activities and identity of feelings, with feelings as a basis of friendship dominating the older female subjects' choices. Considerable aversion to the opposite sex was expressed by high proportions of both sexes. This aversion declined as heterosexual interest began to develop. A minority of both sexes expressed strong aversion to their own sex – about 5 per cent of the males and 10 per cent of the females. The researchers found that the young people they studied established their gender-identity and sex-typing notions by 7, with aversion to the opposite sex increasing sharply about the same time. They expressed concern about the malaise of inter-sex hostility in society and concluded 'It would appear to us that early education is needed in home, school and society stressing the commonality of sexes, and appreciating and accepting sex differences' (Goldman and Goldman, 1982: 190).

Goldman and Goldman (1982) also explored children's perception of biological and anatomical sex differences in babies and adolescents. A progression from unrealistic to realistic recognition of sex differences in babies with increasing age was observed, with the young in Sweden being more 'realistic' than the young in other countries. The same progression from unrealistic to realistic recognition was observed for pubertal differences, with the young in Sweden again being more realistic. Their pre-teen subjects made widespread use of sexual and anatomical pseudonyms in discussion; for example, more than sixty pseudonyms were used for 'penis' and more than forty for 'vagina'. The Goldmans regard such heavy reliance on pseudonyms in the pre-teen years as indicative of both ignorance and embarrassment. What emerged as the most important finding in this part of their study is the invalidity of the psychoanalytic hypothesis of a sexual latency period in later childhood. With increasing age children display an increasing interest in sexuality and wish to acquire more sex information. The latency period hypothesis has been used to support the view of primary school children as non-sexual beings. The Goldmans found no linguistic, cognitive or development barriers which prevent children perceiving sex differences realistically from an early age.

During the recent past, reviews of research on psychological differences between the sexes in childhood and adolescence have tended to stress the lack of important differences, leaving aside sex-typed roles, interests and activities. The more substantiated differences between the sexes are small divergences with considerable overlap between the sexes, and most females and males fall within the common range. Overt physical violence is a more pronounced male characteristic among teenagers (and adults), as is violent crime, though low-level aggressive behaviour shows a less pronounced sex difference. However, as Archer and Lloyd (1985) argue, the young are programmed to look at the social world in terms of categorical differences, with social representations of sex and gender providing a readily available set of materials for this programme to act upon.

Sex-role and gender attitudes and knowledge

What do young people think about sex differences? What are their beliefs about the roles of men and women? In their cross-national study, Goldman and Goldman (1982) investigated how young people perceive the differences between their fathers and mothers as representatives of the two sexes. Though such perceptions were found to change with increasing age and social experience, some clear trends were evident. In the procreation and care of children, sex distinctions were clearly made by boys and girls in all countries. Roles involving child care and rearing were overwhelmingly seen as female. Roles involving authority and leadership in the family were seen as male. With reterence to household duties, in general mothers were allocated the tasks inside the home, and fathers the tasks outside the home. With reference to paid employment, mothers were allocated lower status occupations and fathers higher status occupations. Fathers were more likely to be seen in a leisure role than mothers. The boys and girls made little reference to roles in the family shared by both parents, except where father takes over in an emergency. Overall, females and males in the different countries viewed fathers and mothers in terms of traditional sex roles which they related directly to their perceptions of sex differences. According to the Goldmans, the results of their study do not augur well for current family and educational approaches to sex roles and human relationships directed against traditional sex stereotypes.

In their study of British young people Furnham and Gunter (1989) looked at a number of sex-role beliefs of adolescents. They found that young people were in favour of a sharing of household responsibilities between the sexes and of women having equality with men in contexts in which, more traditionally, men would be expected to have the upper hand. More than three out of four young people believed that, if a woman goes out to work, then her husband should share the housework. This was extensively endorsed by youth of both sexes, though, perhaps not unexpectedly, more often by females (86 per cent) than by males (70 per cent). Both sexes were agreed to an extent (75 per cent), however, that a woman should be as free as a man to propose marriage.

In the traditional marriage ceremony, the vows made by the woman embody a more extreme commitment than those made by the man, in so far as the woman has to propose to 'love, honour and *obey*' her husband, while the husband only promises to 'love and honour' his wife, without the promise to obey her. A majority of young respondents (58 per cent) in the survey felt that this was an insult to a woman. This belief was prevalent among both sexes, though more so among females (66 per cent) than males (48 per cent).

Beliefs about the relationships of the mother and father in the context of child-rearing were less clear-cut. On balance more young people disagreed that the father should have more authority than the mother in bringing up children (49 per cent against 26 per cent) or that it should be the woman who decides how many children a couple has (41 per cent against 25 per cent). There was pronounced sex difference on the first of these two items, however. Females (58 per cent) were much more likely than males (38 per cent) to reject this proposition.

What do young people believe about women at work? More respondents agreed than disagreed that 'it is wrong for mothers of young children to go out to work' (42 per cent versus 32 per cent), while disagreement outweighed agreement on views such as 'children are essential for a happy marriage' (29 per cent versus 41 per cent) and 'it should be the woman who decides how many children a couple has' (27 per cent versus 42 per cent).

The general picture to emerge was one which reflected endorsement of equal opportunities for women in the work-place and the belief that women were suited to work (as well as have families) and had as much to offer as did men in the occupational sphere.

A large majority (78 per cent) believed that women should have completely equal opportunities with men in getting jobs and being promoted. Females (83 per cent) were more often in agreement with this point of view than were males (70 per cent). There was widespread belief also that women were better off having their own jobs and the freedom that would bring (60 per cent). Once again this sort of belief was much more prevalent among females (67 per cent) than among males (50 per cent).

On the ability of women to do a good job, or at least to be as capable as men, opinions were mixed and differed between the sexes. Over half of the British youth respondents overall (55 per cent) agreed that there are many jobs a man can do better than a woman, though males (67 per cent) believed this much more often than females (46 per cent). Fewer overall (39 per cent) thought that women generally handle positions of responsibility better than men do, especially among males (27 per cent) but much more among females (48 per cent). On the same theme however, there was widespread disagreement that women should not be bosses in important jobs in business and industry (61 per cent) and that women have less to offer than men in the world of business and industry (55 per cent). In each case, though, females were much more likely than males to reject these opinions. The weight of opinions across youth generally indicated that women ought not to allow being married or having a family to restrict their occupational aspirations, though this was not without exception. Most respondents (62 per cent) rejected the view that a woman's place is in the home looking after her family rather than following a career of her own. This opinion was nowhere near as commonplace among male youth (46 per cent) as among female youth (74 per cent), however. There was also widespread belief that a wife should not mind earning more than her husband (61 per cent), again endorsed by more females (69 per cent) than males (51 per cent). There was a less clearly defined viewpoint on the relative merits of women concentrating on becoming good wives and mothers rather than worrying about being equal with men. There was little difference in the extent of agreement or disagreement with this item overall, though males (47 per cent) agreed more often than females (30 per cent) that women should focus on marriage and family matters. Mothers should, it seems, exhibit a degree of responsibility when they have young children. Thus, half the respondents agreed that it is wrong for mothers of very small children to go out to work.

Outside the professional educational spheres certain behaviours are traditionally expected of men and women in social contexts. Do young people specify decent codes of social practice for women? In general, Furnham and Gunter's (1989) British youth sample felt that the female sex should enjoy pretty much the same social freedom as males. Most (72 per cent) felt that girls should be allowed to stay out late just as much as boys. Females (77 per cent) were more likely to say this than males (64 per cent). Most (69 per cent) also felt that women should be able to go everywhere a man goes, including going into pubs alone. Females (76 per cent) held this opinion more often than males (62 per cent). There was a consistent age trend. Older children aged 17+ (77 per cent) were much more likely than the youngest (10–14s) (59 per cent) to feel that a woman should be able to go everywhere a man does.

Most of both sexes agreed, however, that it does sound worse when a woman swears than when a man does (68 per cent). But respondents aged 17+ (90 per cent) were more likely to agree with this than younger 10-16s (63 per cent). Opinions were less consistent when it came to the telling of dirty jokes. Females (52 per cent) were more likely than males (39 per cent) to feel that it is all right for women to tell them just as much as it is for men. Older respondents aged 17+ (27 per cent) less often felt this was appropriate than did younger respondents aged 10–14 years (35 per cent).

Going dutch on dates, especially when girls earn as much as their boyfriends, was very widely favoured (by 59 per cent). Again there were sex and age differences. Males (62 per cent) believed more often than did females (56 per cent) that girls earning as much as their boyfriends should pay for themselves when going out with them. The older respondents 17+ (68 per cent) were more likely to agree with this than younger ones (53 per cent). And, finally, most adolescents (63 per cent) felt that women should be able to have sex before marriage. Females (78 per cent) were more in favour of this than were males (56 per cent), however.

The results from this study are not unlike others concerned with sex role attitudes. Firstly, the results are not dissimilar from those done on British adults (Parry, 1983). Clearly, as Helmreich, Spence and Gibson (1982) have demonstrated, sex-role attitudes and beliefs do change with age and it is quite possible that some, but not all, sex-role attitudes change within an individual over time.

Many studies have shown highly significant sex differences in attitudes to women. Predictably, women are more liberal and egalitarian and less traditional in their sex-role attitudes. There are, no doubt, many reasons for this, including the fact that increasing awareness of sex discrimination has led women to have higher expectations in the social, political and economic realms of life. These sex differences were established in respondents as young as 12 years old, which suggests that these attitudes were formed prior to this age.

However, results suggest that as young people get older they tend to become less traditional and more egalitarian in their sex-role attitudes. Most cross-sectional studies cannot explain how or why sex-role attitudes change with age or, indeed, how they come about in the first place. Nevertheless, various speculations can be made for the finding that some, but not all, sex-role attitudes change over time. Many of the attitudes that show significant age effects concerned jobs and work, which may reflect the fact that older adolescents are increasingly familiar with sex-role equality in the work-place. Presumably, attitudes which refer to swearing, drinking and sexual humour show little difference because these refer to behaviours that are more rule-bound.

Sex and gender

It is interesting to note that in the study of Furnham and Gunter (1989) there were fewer significant social class differences than may be expected by chance alone. The results are at variance with those of Parry (1983), who found quite considerable evidence of class differences, with middle-class women being more liberated and egalitarian than working-class women. It is possible that these differences occur more in adults than adolescents because various changes tend to occur more among the one group than the other. Thus, if middle-class men and women are more likely to meet each other in comparable jobs in early adulthood, it is possible that their sex-role attitudes become modified – particularly those of men.

Before attempting to explain or change sex-role attitudes it is first important to establish what they are, and how they differ among various groups. All studies showed evidence of considerable sex differences, some age differences but few class differences in adolescents' attitudes towards women and sex roles. Only detailed longitudinal work can explain how those attitudes occurred and how they are maintained.

Socialization into sex roles: family influences

Developmental experience within the family tends to prepare the child and adolescent for the sex role he or she will occupy in adult life. Much of the experience of females is orientated towards domestic work and motherhood, much of the experience of males orientated to activities away from the home and to employment in the labour market. In part, this reflects the direct teaching of parents, relatives, schoolteachers and others. In part, it reflects historical traditions, the impact of the mass media, the sexual division of labour in the economy, and the prevailing sex stereotypes. Katz (1983) has suggested there are three overlapping stages in sex-role acquisition: (a) the learning of child sex roles; (b) the preparing for adult roles, sexual, domestic and occupational; and (c) developing and living these adult roles. A person's sex role continues to develop through infancy, childhood, adolescence and adulthood. The influence of different socialization agents, including parents, will vary at different periods in the life-cycle.

The position of parents in fostering the development of sex-appropriate values, attitudes and behaviour has long been recognized. Parents are significant for the young as sex-typed upbringers of children and adolescents, and as exemplars of their sex roles in a particular social milieu. They provide their offspring with on-going, direct experience of sex roles within the family. If a youngster has two parents available rather than one, it provides the opportunity for that youngster to relate closely to a same-sex and an opposite-sex person. It creates a concrete situation from which notions about mothers and fathers, women and men can be generated. A sizeable proportion of the young spend all or a significant part of their pre-adult years with only one parent, usually the mother. The vast majority of females and males are brought up primarily by women.

Studies have consistently shown there are differences in the way fathers and mothers behave towards daughters and sons from birth onwards. This applies to parents who state sex does not influence their treatment of their young. Many parents are, of course, aware of sex differences in their expectations and behaviour towards the young. Some emphasize gender differences and sex-typed behaviour. But parents are often unaware of the full extent of the influence of sex on their reactions towards their offspring.

From birth, females are perceived as physically more vulnerable than males, including, eventually, vulnerability to the risk of an unwanted pregnancy. They tend to be treated with more physical care than males. Relative to young females, young males are encouraged to be independent, physically active, adventurous, mobile and exploratory in their local environment. Parents sex-type youthful interests by means of language, toys, clothes, play, games, sports and other activities. Within the family, the tendency is for females to be assigned tasks traditionally carried out by the mother in the home; for males to be assigned tasks traditionally carried out by the father, often out of doors. Both fathers and mothers tend to encourage emotional control more in their male than female offspring. They encourage achievement and occupational ambition to a greater extent in male than female children.

Although there is some evidence that sex differences in upbringing and education may have diminished in recent decades, the general pattern of differences undoubtedly holds. It appears that fathers tend to play a more active part in child rearing when the mother is employed away from the home. However, the shift in the role of mothers towards paid employment is by no means matched by any shift in the role of fathers towards child care and household duties. As a result of close association with mothers in the home, the young are directly exposed to the housewife-mother role during their pre-adult years. They are not similarly exposed to their father's occupational role at his place of employment. In most families females are expected to undertake more household work than males. Both sexes are thus exposed in their pre-adult years not only to sex-typed household tasks but also to the gross imbalance between the sexes in responsibility for performance of household work. It is not surprising that the young from infancy differentiate household tasks into female or male categories.

Much adult desired sex-role behaviour in boys and adolescent males is conveyed by advice and injunctions – 'boys do this', 'boys don't do that'. They learn the rules associated with the avoidance of femininity.

They make use of older males in their environment and in the media to provide role models of masculine behaviour. Sanctions for cross-gender behaviour are more intense for males than females. They are operated by parents, relatives, peers and teachers from an early age. While reviewing much evidence on sex-role socialization and the family, Sampson concludes:

> Boys must...discover masculine goals for themselves from available understanding of the cultural stereotype, restructuring the negative advice into positive goals and learning by trial and error. There is evidence that boys are not permitted to display as much opposite sex behaviour as girls in childhood because parents fear homosexual tendencies for males more than tomboyish ones for girls. The result is that...boys must actively segregate themselves from earlier aspects of their lives, such as emotional self-expression and childish female play, especially in the presence of their peers...less stereotyped roles for sons and daughters have been observed in families where the mother is employed outside the home.
>
> (Sampson, 1978: 267)

There appears to be a tendency for more inconsistencies and discontinuities in male than in female development from childhood to adulthood.

Within the constraints of material circumstances, parents, or a single parent, are primarily responsible for the composition of the family and domestic situation children live in. Molecular families usually have some contact with relations, and may have grandparents or other close relatives live with them for certain periods of time. In multi-child families older children exercise some influence on younger children, and most children have the experience of living with one or more siblings. When the siblings are of the same sex, it appears that this tends to intensify sex typing in development. When they are of both sexes, it appears brothers make more of an impact on sisters than vice versa with respect to sex-role development. Single or solo parents are frequently subjected to many financial and other pressures which may vary according to the parent's sexual orientation (and why the other parent is absent), and these pressures may also affect the children. In addition, there are other styles of extended-family and group living which provide variations in family influences on the development of children and adolescents. Many of these topics remain relatively underresearched, however.

School influences on gender understanding

We have seen that gender and sex-role development proceed rapidly in the pre-adult years, including infancy and early childhood. This early development is reinforced in pre-school educational and caring establishments. Studies have found that schooling directs girls and boys along what some would call sex-appropriate and others sex-stereotyped paths. Schooling encompasses the important adolescent stage of psychosexual development. Sex-segregated schools are the most obvious expression of educational practices based on the division of the sexes. General segregation of the sexes within a school is another obvious expression. More limited forms of sex segregation are widely practised in schools nominally coeducational, though there is considerable variability among coeducational schools in this regard. The major impact of coeducation on sex and gender is through its influence on the informal social life of teenagers, which interacts with the effects of the commercial youth market.

When the child enters school, the educational system reinforces and institutionalizes expectations of different behaviour, educational choices and employment prospects for females and males, though there are variations associated with fee-charging and state schools, the characteristics of teachers, religion, race and social class (Poole, 1983). Typically there are expectations that males will do better in mathematics, sciences and technical subjects, and females will do better in languages, domestic science and literature. The fact that a majority of women bear children and the fact of enormous inequality between the sexes in the economy are often regarded as providing legitimate grounds for treating the sexes differently in school education, and for having different expectations about the sex roles they should acquire and the lives they should lead. These facts are commonly used to justify the inter-generational reproduction of unequal opportunities between the sexes, which in turn means the reproduction of the subordination of women. Questions about whether there are reasonable grounds for expecting that the young, because of sex, should be treated differently and shaped into two distinct genders following different life patterns in conditions of inequality are often rejected as unrealistic, irrelevant, idealistic, destructive to the family, and so forth. But there is general agreement that schooling is importantly involved in the development of femininity and masculinity.

Sex segregation is extremely widespread in education because of the existence of single-sex schools, particularly in the fee-charging sector of education, and the many forms of sex segregation practised within coeducational schools. Sex differences are highly visible in the organization and administration of schools. The more senior positions in the system are frequently disproportionately filled by males, the subordinate positions disproportionately by females. The male sex is clearly associated with authority and leadership in education. This sexual imbalance is significant for teachers as sex-role models to the young.

The curriculum, that is the actual subjects taught in school, enables pupils to gain knowledge, skills and qualifications. Sex differentiation occurs in pupil exposure to school subjects; for example, mathematics, the arts, science, domestic science, metalwork, woodwork, needlework and typing. Such differentiation also occurs with reference to disciplinary practices, regulations concerning dress and appearance, physical education and sport. Teaching and resource materials, including standard text books, contain much information based on sex stereotypes; and are often completely removed from the circumstances of life for the sexes in today's world. In the school context, Macdonald concludes, 'there is a consistent distorted model of woman which not merely misrepresents her activities in social life but does nothing to correct the social patterns of discrimination' (1980: 41). The persistent pattern of misrepresentations, Macdonald suggests, has three basic elements: (1) women suffer from omission, they do not appear as active participants in history and modern life; (2) when women do appear, they are generally in low status roles, typically without any need to have a job and earn money; and (3) a constant emphasis on women's domesticity amounts to ongoing ideological bombardment. Teaching and resource materials are often far from neutral in terms of race and social class content, creating additional difficulties and unpleasantness for the young in subordinate racial and social locations, especially young females.

School 'rituals' with sex associations, relatively rigid activities that apparently give meaning to sex differences, are for Bernstein (1977) the result of the school passively mediating or amplifying general social purposes. These rituals tend to feature in school assemblies, ceremonies, sports days and fetes, uniforms and dress, sex-typed sporting activities, honours boards and the like. Bernstein suggests that such rituals serve the symbolic functioning of relating the individual pupil to the social order of the school, heightening respect for that order and deepening acceptance of procedures which are used to maintain continuity in that order. However, the ethos of different schools varies. The pupils also vary in their reactions to school society, with some being simply compliant with whatever they encounter, some uninterested in school purposes and some rejecting them. On the basis of their field studies in Australia, Connell *et al* (1982) conclude that school education places limits on the diversity of femininity and masculinity, and promotes hierarchical notions of desirable forms of femininity and masculinity.

In education, parents and their offspring can make choices only within concrete circumstances which inevitably pose constraints; for most people, severe constraints. The social structure in which they live, with its sex, race, economic and other inequalities, is an inescapable part of their life circumstances. A number of analysts have stressed the power of schools to define partial realities (including the reality of social roles in society) for the people who are a part of them, and the influence exerted on schools by those who have power in society (Berger and Luckmann,

1967; Bowles and Gintis, 1976; Taylor, 1982). Berger and Luckmann assert 'Power in society includes the power to determine decisive socialization processes and therefore, the power to *produce* reality' (1967: 137). The contribution of schools to gender and sex-role development and more importantly expectations and belief about sex differences is in the direction of emphasizing different female and male competencies, attitudes, interests, family and occupational expectations. Whether implicit or explicit, intentional or not, schools frequently foster predictable activities and preferences among their pupils along narrow sex-role lines, with a continuous emphasis for the female upon vicarious, dependent living in a male-dominated world. Sex differences and sex roles are perceived by children and adolescents as the objective and intransigent reality of life. They are used by the young and become part of their view of social reality, providing sources of meaning to interpret social life. Eventually young people will come to act on their social world of sex divisions at the same time as they are influenced by it; but not necessarily acting in a conformist or compliant way, hence the possibility of change in sex roles over time.

Other influences

As children and adolescents age they are subject to the influences not only of family and school, but also of their age peers, the mass media, literature of all sorts, pop music, and other institutions and groups. All these influences on development interact in complex, and not necessarily consistent, ways. Young people make their own contribution to self-development after they have learned what sex they are and what sex roles are available. Thus, they are subject to a mix of influences, among which family, school, peers and the mass media are particularly important.

During the school years, the influence of age peers becomes increasingly important. Peers exert a continuing influence by reinforcing the acquisition of sex-appropriate attitudes, behaviour and stereotypes. Where children and teenagers are segregated at school, completely or in some lesser but significant way, such segregation makes it particularly easy for the formation of unisexual cliques and groups. If parents and other adults provide little in the way of sex information for the young, the information gap can be partly filled by whatever information is circulating among peers and other persons slightly older, who then contribute directly to notions of sexuality and inter-sex behaviour.

In his study of peer-group socialization, Dunphy (1978) suggests the pre-adolescent peer group functions to stamp in each individual's gender identity and sex role, while the adolescent peer group is vital in providing role-playing opportunities relating to the transition to full adult expectations and status including sexual behaviour. He comments:

It is as if society separates the sexes at that stage so that the individual will make few mistakes in learning the basic attitudes considered desirable in this society for males and females. These basic attitudes being laid down before the onset of puberty, it is then safe for society to allow these individuals to learn those attitudes and behaviours held suitable for relations *between* the sexes with a minimal risk that association with the opposite sex will lead to identification.

(Dunphy, 1978: 49)

Within the family and society, males are pressed to adopt appropriate sex-typed manners, behaviour and stereotypes earlier and more strongly than females. The sex role is less rigidly prescribed for females than males, and females tend to show a weaker preference than males for same-sex objects and clothes.

The mass media, and especially television, pervade modern life. In general, they transmit stereotyped material about sex, gender and sex roles, together with a good deal of blatant sexism (Barratt, 1986; Durkin, 1985; Furnham and Schofield, 1986; Greenfield, 1984; Itzin, 1986; Macdonald, 1980). Connected with stereotypes are exaggerated or extreme sex-role standards and expectations about the way members of each sex should behave and the places they should occupy in society. Sexism refers to the expectation that individuals, entirely and exclusively because they are female or male, will be different kinds of sex-typed people occupying different social and occupational positions with different, highly unequal opportunities. It often implies discriminatory standards.

Purposive television viewing begins as early as the third year of life, though infants are exposed to television before then. At any age the average child or adolescent will have spent more time watching television than in a school class, because most young people spend more than twenty hours per week watching television throughout the year. Confusion about what is meant to be real on television, and what is entertainment, soap opera material, fantasy or commercial advertising is not sorted out until the second decade of life, and with some people not even then. In one sense all television material is unreal because of the limitations of the medium, with uncensored coverage of live events probably being closest to reality. The amount of time the young spend watching television tends to be positively related to the strength of their sex stereotypes. This finding may reflect what television does to the young or the greater attraction of television for the more strongly sex-stereotyped youngsters or an interactive relation between the two.

Television serves many functions in the lives of the young. Among other things it provides: (a) entertainment; (b) relaxation; (c) humour; (d) information; (e) a prime topic for conversation; (f) a component of peer relationships; (g) electronic friendship including television 'companions';

(h) a mild 'drug' to cope with stress; (i) a time-filling activity. Television use varies among children, adolescents and family groups. The young are not completely vulnerable to television, or mass media, messages. There are some possibilities of testing media messages against first-hand experience of life. However, the young are especially vulnerable to influence when they have little or no first-hand experience of the material in question. With reference to sex and gender, the young have to process distorted, misleading and exploitive material during the period of life when their physical characteristics, sexuality and sex-role knowledge are developing rapidly. There is continuing interaction between the material of television and the other media and the use of such material by the young, with factors such as race, social class and education coming into play.

It is difficult to estimate the extent to which the mass media affect gender and sex-role development because experimental studies using control groups of youngsters unexposed to the mass media are very difficult. The media are a pervasive presence in the lives of children and adolescents. They may well counteract any efforts in the family and at school to combat sex stereotypes and sexism. If the sex stereotypes and sexism transmitted across the media are reasonably consistent, then this may contribute to their apparent reflection of reality.

Adolescent sexuality

Sexuality in children and adolescents has attracted the interests of researchers who have obtained a good deal of information about development in the pre-adult years. For example, in their cross-national study Goldman and Goldman (1982) showed that children are aware of sex and sexuality, are active sexual thinkers in the pre-pubertal period, and that much of their thinking is in terms of traditional sex roles. They demonstrated that by late childhood the young are, in general, concerned with bodily development, menstruation, sexual intercourse, conception, pregnancy, gestation and birth, pre-marital and courting behaviour, but not with parenting skills. Sexual lore and misinformation are part of childhood and adolescence.

Because modern trends of life have reduced the age of puberty for boys and girls, at present the changes of puberty are typically happening between twelve and sixteen years. These changes have developmental significance in their own right. Menarche is a crucial event for girls, though they are likely to feel ambivalent about menstruation. Early puberty tends to be an interpersonal asset for males during adolescence, but not an advantage in later life. In fact, the more stressful adolescence of later-maturing males appears to provide a better preparation for adult life. Bodily changes associated with adolescent progress tend to heighten concern with physical appearance and attractiveness. Attractiveness is a major factor in interpersonal relations, yielding a marked advantage for those with good looks according to prevailing notions. Further, the mass media constantly present fashionable types of beautiful people for adolescents (as well as adults) to compare themselves with. Adolescents often worry about their looks and physical attractiveness, and their capacity to appeal sexually. If there is a failure to meet current standards of acceptable looks, then this may well become an important personal problem for the 'afflicted' (Furnham and Radley, 1989).

Adolescents engage in a range of sexual activities, frequently involving sexual feelings towards self and members of both sexes (Gordon and Gilgun, 1987). The incidence of sexual intercourse among the young, especially females, has increased notably over recent decades. One result of this is that teenage males are less likely to have sexual intercourse with prostitutes or with persons of much lower social status. Having sexual intercourse for the first time is a significant event for most young people, and a milestone on the road to an adult life-style. It tends to be more gratifying for males than females, because many females find first intercourse painful or unpleasant for several possible reasons including male pressure. Teenage females are much more likely than teenage males to have sexual intercourse because of love for the partner. Teenage males are much more likely than females to have sexual intercourse with a partner for whom they feel little. The majority of teenagers are sexually initiated by a partner in a steady relationship, not in a casual encounter. They often expect sex to be a part of a romantic, intimate relationship. Introduction to sexual intercourse is normally gradual, with a progressively intimate order of events from holding hands, kissing and petting, on to activities leading to intercourse. Average age of initiating intercourse is sixteen. During the teen years, committed long-term relationships are the exception rather than the norm. Much more often, teenagers have intense short-term relationships which may cause pain when they end. Many sexually active teenagers are partly motivated by feelings of inadequacy, with sex providing some evidence of personal worth.

There is great diversity in the sexual interests and activities of teenagers, with social class, race, education, religion and other factors coming into play. At one extreme are virgins with little interest in sex, and at the other extreme are promiscuous sexual teenagers with multiple partners of either or both sexes. Sexually transmitted diseases are commonplace among promiscuous teenagers. A minority of ambitious teenagers deliberately or incidentally limit their sexual activities while giving other activities (directed towards future objectives) much higher priority. Such a large minority of adolescents, especially females, have been sexually abused at some time during life that, statistically, sexual abuse of the young is virtually normal. Pregnancy, miscarriage, abortion, childbearing and marriage among teenagers are widely seen as a problem, and are often criticized, denounced and morally condemned (Gilchrist and Schinke, 1987). For most teenagers, pregnancy is upsetting and disturbs any plans for the future. Further, many teenagers who have to cope with such sex problems also have to deal with the problems of racism, sexism and social class discrimination. Adolescents live inside an adult social world suffused with sex and its exploitation, with the mass media constantly extolling sexual activity. This social reality sets their developmental agendas (Juhasz and Sonnenshein-Schneider, 1987).

Among teenagers marriage is a popularly accepted adult way of life. They tend to have a romantic personal perspective on marriage based upon love and companionship, which typically involves setting up a home and usually the addition of children. Yet their first-hand experience of parental and other marriages is often offputting or worse. There is a gap between the reality of their experiences and the romantic images of marriage in circulation among the young. In addition, adolescent females are further disadvantaged by not knowing how a future husband will react to any occupational plans and other aspirations, which makes much of their future contingent upon marriage.

Teenage females appear to be more aware of the disadvantages of marriage and parenthood than males, but typically see no realistic alternative. Though they are more strongly orientated towards marriage than males (who are more strongly orientated to sex and employment), their orientation may well be a negative one. Romanticism about marrying the right partner is a major rationalization of the female situation. Thus, being attractive to boys, dating and courting are major concerns. Expenditure of time, energy and resources on becoming attractive contribute to female dependency. Fantasies about the right partner providing love, companionship, security, physical protection, respectability, a social life and a stable family background for children also feature prominently in teenage thinking. But a smallish minority of teenage females desire marriage to serve the wife and her career as well as that of the husband.

From childhood the prescriptive sexual orientation is heterosexual. With the advent of puberty and adolescence, heterosexual encounters assume more sexual importance. Though most adolescents will move to adulthood with a heterosexual identity, a minority will not. Given that adolescents typically have autosexual, homosexual and heterosexual feelings, it is difficult for homosexuals of both sexes to discover their sexual orientation during the teens. Among females, strong feelings of attachment occur frequently irrespective of sexual orientation. The sexual behaviour of homosexuals during the teen years is likely to be more heterosexual than their feelings, and they are likely to experience less stability in their sexual orientation than heterosexuals. When sexual preference for same-sex members becomes compelling, teenagers experience conflict, fear of the pain of ridicule, feel isolated and cut off from others, possibly including parents. Given a stridently heterosexual world, frequently displaying homophobia and discrimination, teenagers struggling with homosexuality are faced with difficult adjustments, including a reorientation in respect of marriage, and motherhood among females. They often find it difficult to imagine future life as a homosexual. Hiding their homosexuality is one way of coping with their problem. Bisexuals may deal with similar problems by choosing to relate sexually to one sex.

The sexual abuse of children and adolescents is a widespread occurrence. Females are more likely to be victims than males but males are far more likely to be perpetrators of abuse than females. Females appear to be particularly vulnerable to abuse at adolescence. Such abuse takes in indecencies, molestation, enforced sexual activities, rape, incest, sodomy, sexual exploitation for gain including pornography and prostitution. Most prostitutes become involved before adulthood, and sexual abuse frequently precedes such involvement. Once into prostitution, females and males are likely to be victimized by pimps, customers, thieves and drug dealers. A small proportion of teenagers become sex abusers, most having been sexually abused previously. The physically violent male sex abusers are also likely to injure any victim, who may range in age from infancy to old age. Sexually abused children and adolescents suffer a variety of negative reactions to the abuse, and typically have to live with negative consequences of abuse for the rest of their lives. These consequences will impact on self-concepts, quality of interpersonal and sexual relations and behaviour problems.

Conclusion

Social, occupational and economic changes of the recent past make the traditional sex roles, as well as traditional sex stereotypes and beliefs about gender differences outmoded.

Gender and sex-role development still very much accords with traditional and family role expectations, although there is research evidence from several countries suggesting some limited developmental shifts in keeping with current adult roles in society. The shifts appear to be most marked in the family and at school, and seem to be more significant for girls than boys. Hoffman's analysis of change in family roles, socialization and sex differences leads to what is probably an over-optimistic conclusion about the rate at which differences in the socialization experiences of girls and boys are being narrowed: 'Few children, longer life, and working mothers – none of which are new, but all of which are now pervasive, normative, and I think here to stay – add up to new family roles, new socialization patterns and a decrease in the differences between the sexes' (1977: 655–6). This conclusion stems partly from Hoffman's neglect of the mass media and commercial youth market as agents of socialization and as sources of reassurance about the veracity of sex stereotypes and even sexist ideology. The influences emanating from the mass media and commercial interests emphasize sex differences and sex stereotypes. Children and teenagers are affected directly as consumers of media material and products for the young, and indirectly via peer-group pressures partly the result of media and other commercial influences.

Until the latter half of this century, it was widely regarded as obvious that the apparently great psychological differences between the sexes were caused by biology and instincts. Even today many specialists in medicine, psychoanalysis and sociobiology assert there are great psychological differences between the sexes, e.g. in aggression, morality, sexual drive, rationality, intelligence, ambition, emotionality and so forth; and that these can be explained by genetic, hormonal, instinctual and evolutionary mechanisms. Over the years, as empirical research has failed to demonstrate unequivocal major psychological differences between the sexes (while finding massive individual and group differences within the sexes) and has also failed to find major simple biological mechanisms supposedly responsible for allegedly major psychological differences, the scientific view on sex differentiation has changed considerably. In particular, the enormous impact of culture and society on the developing human has become more clearly visible. Studies of abnormal and unusual biological sexual development have demonstrated that environmental pressures can override the biological predisposition of a young human (and may be totally confirmed by medical-surgical intervention). Where there is ambiguity about the sex of a child, the fact that parents and other adults believe the child is either female or male has definitive gender consequences for the young child.

Sex is ascribed to a baby on the basis of biological characteristics. Gender identity is acquired in the early years of childhood and further developed in the following years of childhood and adolescence. From birth, the child encounters the processes of differentiation applied to the two sexes – in the initial sex-typed welcome after birth, naming, dressing, handling, caring, playing, conversation of parents and others. The infant has to learn that there are two sexes, to allocate the self to one or the other, and to use the allocation to facilitate gender and sex-role development. From around the end of the first year it appears that the infant manifests a concept of self. Gender is one of the earliest self-attributes of which the child is aware; the self-concept is gender differentiated. From infancy, gender is an integral part of personal identity. A young child's awareness of its gender similarity to relatives, peers and others of the same sex promotes identification with that sex. Infants, children and adolescents observe, appraise, select, produce and modify the attributes, behaviour and preferences of their own sex.

Gender identity precedes the differentiation of sex roles. However, sex-role development proceeds rapidly during childhood and adolescence. Sex-typed interests and preferences, sex-role behaviour and sex stereotypes have been observed among children in the pre-school and early school years, and are highly visible in later years. Clearly development occurs before the child enters school, with television a constant influence on the young child. For both gender and sex-role development the environmental forces act upon humans, with biological differences characteristic of the sexes, some would argue, to promote human differences in accord with biological forces acting upon the sexes. Any kind of socially divisive outcome in terms of the sex roles and sex stereotypes can all too easily appear natural and at least partly the outcome of biology, because sex is defined by biological characteristics present at birth and of significance throughout life. Yet many of the apparently natural differences between the sexes do not stand up to objective examination, they are the result of illusions and myths.

Actual psychological differences between the sexes tend to be slight differences between central tendencies with a great deal of overlap between the sexes. Physical differences between the sexes are of declining significance in the work of the contemporary world. There are no biological reasons for the constraints and pressures placed on children, adolescents and adults by traditional sex roles, other than those involved in the bearing of children. There is no biological evidence to indicate that activities in society should not be equally open to both sexes. Recognition of this would make it easier to accept that the range of life opportunities open to both sexes would be expanded if we ceased to expect children, adolescents and adults to fill distinctive constraining sex roles with unequal opportunities.

Chapter six

Religion and spiritual matters

Introduction

No child can live for many years in any society without encountering some notions of God and religion. Young people inevitably encounter many of the religious concepts, symbols, beliefs, attitudes and activities that exist in their society as well as churches, synagogues, mosques and other religious meeting places. In addition, the mass media regularly present religious leaders, personalities, events and programmes. Even a child brought up in a family of militant atheists or indifferent agnostics and receiving a secular school education would by no means escape the cultural influence of religion however secular the society they are in. It is not possible for young people to be totally cut off from religious influences and experiences throughout the pre-adult years; that is, to have absolutely no religious socialization.

Children in families where one or more members practise their religion will experience family life influenced (or possibly dominated) by religion. This may have direct bearing upon their upbringing and education, most directly when the family engages in religious practices in the home or chooses a religious school for education or both. Children and adolescents may be socialized or severely indoctrinated into a particular church, denomination or style of religion, or have little or no contact with institutional religion. The moral and value-system development of young people is often powerfully shaped.

Young people also encounter death, beliefs and attitudes relating to death, fictional and actual deaths displayed on television, death in warfare including nuclear warfare, and religious perspectives on death and its alleged sequelae. It appears that young people attempt to integrate their developing concepts and ideas about death with their total world view and their life in this world. Comprehension of birth and growth, health and illness, aging and physical decline, life and death, grief and mourning, the capacity of nations with nuclear weapons to destroy humanity comes gradually with experience and knowledge. The biological reality of death, its final severance of relationships with the living, is difficult for the young to understand and come to terms with. Religious beliefs provide a framework by which to understand death and many other moral issues.

Despite the claims that are frequently made about the declining significance of religion for modern industrial nations, and about ever-increasing secularization, there is consistent evidence from all nations that religion is a prominent feature of young people's lives and is of varying significance to a sizeable section of each population. Common personal indicators of religion include belief in God, identification with a religion, church, denomination, sect or cult, public and private worship, belief in an after-life, praying, intense religious experiences, beliefs and practices relative to sacred things, and treating births, deaths and marriages partly as religious occasions. Public significance is given to religion and religious leaders by their presentation in the mass media. Any ongoing erosion of religion appears to be much more a decline in the power and influence of the churches (that is, in 'churchianity') than in religion as such. In any examination of young people's understanding of society, religious socialization needs to be seriously considered.

Religion is frequently seen as an institutional source of conformity and social control, as a means of legitimating the social structure and promoting obedience to official authorities, as contributing to the maintenance of social order and protection of the status quo. This sceptical functional view of religion appears to have considerable appeal, not least among some of the proponents of the value of religious education (and religious schools) for children. Such appeal is not limited to those who hold a faith. At present, the contention that religion and the churches are one of the most influential forces on the whole socialization process (that powerfully affects young people's understanding of society) produces arguments and disagreement when it is applied to the most industrially advanced capitalist and socialist, though not Islamic societies.

Religion is not identical with creed or other religious institutional affiliation. Participation in the rituals and religious activities of religious associations can be merely habitual, for the sake of convention, to maintain or gain social status, for economic reasons or, in the case of the young, because of parental pressure. One can distinguish between the religious and the religiose. Some specialists in religion have argued that there is a contemporary trend towards private or home religion because of growing religious pluralism, a competitive market situation in churches, denominations and sects, and rapid social change not matched by change in the major denominations (Blaikie, 1978). Some also argue that the family is the basic religious unit. Churches and other religious associations are the generic religious organizations which provide for their members a social base, beliefs, norms and values, procedures for confirmation, and personal support from significant other co-religionists. Many people who have a secular humanistic outlook or have a private religious system of meaning or do not usually participate in any institutional religious practices have contact with associational religion during the rites of passage of different persons – at marriages, baptisms, confirmations or the equivalent, funerals.

Much religious socialization of children takes place in the family, school, church and youth organizations, which make possible considerable diversity of beliefs and attitudes even within the same church or denomination. Religions generate expectations about parental religious duties, and frequently exert pressure on parents to ensure that their children receive formal religious instruction, attend a denominational school and participate in religious associational activities. Children normally adopt the given religion(s) and denomination(s) of their parents, rather than converting to something else or constructing a purely personal religion. Any changes will usually come in adolescence and adulthood. Young people are exposed typically to highly diverse religious beliefs, attitudes and practices within their extended family, neighbourhood and society. There are differences within and between religions, churches and denominations, which are featured in literature, the mass media and sometimes the political arena. Yet all major religions, churches and denominations have their conservatives, radicals and eclectics. Religion can be transmitted across generations with little if anything in the way of associational participation.

There are many definitions of religion. The simpler dictionary definitions contain several elements: belief in God or a supernatural power; worship of God or a supernatural power; a system with a sacred, supernatural or ultimate point of reference; a system of meaning, faith and worship; practical piety; holiness; the manifestation of meaning and spiritual fulfilment in life. Blaikie brings together many common elements that have featured in studies of religion and religious socialization in the following definition:

Religion may be regarded as a system of meaning – beliefs, values, explanations – that form all or part of an individual's world-view; it makes reference to and involves experiences of 'another' reality; it is a social phenomenon created, maintained and modified by people in interaction, but need not be the property of a specifically religious association; groups that share the system of meaning usually engage in particular behaviour practices or rituals that are seen to be religious in terms of the system of meaning; the system of meaning is available through socialization, to each succeeding generation, or through resocialization, to non-believers.

(Blaikie, 1978: 152)

Some specialists in religion would challenge or reject it; for example, if they believe religion is instinctive or inborn in every person.

Much of the empirical research and writing dealing with young people's religious beliefs suffers from certain deficiencies. Firstly, many of the researchers are fully committed to formal religious education for the young in school and some to denominational schooling. This commitment has tended to narrow their research interests, leading them to concentrate on the influences supposedly working for the transmission of religion to the neglect of those working against its transmission. Secondly, many of the researchers are committed believers, usually Christians concerned with Christian education; and they have tended to neglect not only children of other religions but also children in those sections of society which are indifferent to religion, which do not hold to any religious faith and which have very little or no contact with associational religion. Some have limited themselves mainly to issues in religious education. Further, many developmental psychologists (probably agnostic) do not regard religion as having much psychological or practical significance, so it is a rather neglected part of developmental research. This is not to imply that a proportion of the empirical researchers concerned with religion have deliberately biased their research. Rather, in total the research is imbalanced because of the emphasis on Christianity, because certain sections of society have been somewhat disregarded, and some highly visible issues have tended to be neglected; for example, the religious impact of the mass media, denominational school segregation (particularly when it is combined with economic and/or racial segregation) and the negative consequences of religion for individuals, groups and society (Svennevig, Haldane, Spiers and Gunter, 1988). However, a number of empirical studies of religious socialization have been reported in various countries which present varied information from pre-adults in a wide cross-section of society. Further, there is considerable research interest in religious thinking, attitudes and experience in education (Francis, 1987; Greer, 1984a, 1984b), representation of God among the young (Berryman, 1985; Heller, 1986; Potvin, 1977) and psychological theories of religious or faith development (Capps, 1984; Fowler, 1983; Heywood, 1986; Rizzuto, 1974).

Young people's religious beliefs

Surveys done in many countries have shown that there are systematic differences between the religious beliefs and practices of young people and adults. Younger people tend to believe less than do older people. The surveys by Gallup in Great Britain revealed that 57 per cent of 16–19s believed in God compared with 75 per cent of over 65s. Among the younger ones, 33 per cent believed in a life after death compared with 45 per cent of elderly people. Young people seem less likely to hold a whole range of religious beliefs than elderly people. There are some interesting exceptions though. The under-20s are more likely than older people to believe in astrological predictions (Heald and Wybrow, 1986).

Surveys of religious belief have indicated a decline in religious commitment in recent years. Haldane (1978), for instance, reported that 58 per cent of a national sample claimed to be 'very' or 'fairly' religious in 1968 compared with 49 per cent of a London-only sample in 1978. In 1968, 50 per cent said they were certain there is a God; in 1978 42 per cent agreed with this. The 1978 survey revealed that marginally more women than men fell into the group to whom religion is an important element in their lives. There was a marked increase in religious belief with age and a considerable difference between social classes, with the working classes much higher than the middle classes. Although the samples in these two surveys are not precisely comparable, the same questions and statements were used and they do serve to provide some general indication of trends in religious belief. There have been a number of studies of adolescents' religious beliefs and attitudes in different countries, including America, Great Britain and Sweden.

In their relatively recent nationwide youth survey Furnham and Gunter (1989) found most of the respondents (61 per cent) claimed to have a religion, whilst just over one in four (28 per cent) said they did not. These figures were reversed when the young people aged 12–18 years were asked whether they belonged to or attended a local religious organization or a church. Twenty-eight per cent said that they did, while 61 per cent said that they did not.

One measure, albeit crude, of having some connection with religion is attendance at church. Church attendance for special occasions may be more for social events than for religious ones. Among the youth sample only a minority (12 per cent) had been to a religious service to mark a special occasion such as a wedding, funeral or festival during the previous year. Around one in three (35 per cent) said they had not been at all, while more than half (54 per cent) did not know for sure whether they had or not. This poses an interesting question as to whether young people are able to distinguish a religious from a civil ceremony. The youngest respondents, aged 10–14 (19 per cent), were more likely than the older ones (9 per cent) to have attended church. Among those who indicated that they had attended some special religious service, the largest proportion (43 per cent) had done so just once or twice in the past year. The 10–14-year-olds (19 per cent) were more likely than 15+year-olds (7 per cent) to have been five times or more. It seems likely, therefore, that among a minority of young people there is considerable uncertainty about church attendance. Among those who claimed they had attended religious services in the last year, for many this was a funeral (44 per cent). For around one in four (25 per cent) it was either a wedding or a funeral.

Attendance at occasional religious services for festivals, weddings or funerals may signify little about religious belief. Routine church attendance, however, is probably more likely to occur among those who have a religious affiliation or conviction. Outside special occasions, only a small minority (12 per cent) of these British young people had been to a regular or normal religious service in the last year. Most (60 per cent) said they had not, and 29 per cent did not know. Males (15 per cent) attended services more often than females (9 per cent) and 10–14-year-olds (19 per cent) more often than 15–16-year-olds (12 per cent) or 17+-year-olds (5 per cent).

Of those who volunteered that they had been to a regular religious service, one in three (33 per cent) had attended at least once a week. Somewhat more (39 per cent) had attended less often, while nearly one in three (30 per cent) were uncertain. The 10–14-year-olds (48 per cent) were more likely than 15–16-year-olds (35 per cent) or more especially the 17+-year-olds (18 per cent) to attend once a week or more. Regardless of whether or not individuals go to church or some other place of worship regularly, how important do young people think it is to do so? And how important is religion in the lives of young people? On the first question, one in three (34 per cent) felt that it is important actually to go to a place of worship regularly. These were outnumbered by young people (45 per cent) who did not endorse this sentiment. More than six out of ten youth respondents (62 per cent) said that religion was important to them, entirely outnumbering those who said that it was not important to them (39 per cent). When asked to identify the more important things about religion, teaching a good life was the aim most often endorsed (by 45 per cent), followed by believing in God (29 per cent), and then going to a place of worship (23 per cent). Another behaviour associated with religious affiliation and belief is prayer. Only a minority of youth respondents (14 per cent) said that they prayed regularly. More than two and a half times as many (37 per cent) said that they never prayed, even in times of crisis. The youngest, 10-14-year-olds (20 per cent), claimed to pray more often than the oldest, 17+-year-olds (7 per cent), with the 15–16-year-olds (15 per cent) falling between the two. Among those who said that they did pray, many (43 per cent) did so several times a day, 17 per cent once a day, and 8 per cent only during times of stress or crisis. Among those who prayed, females (48 per cent) were more likely to pray several times a day than were males (37 per cent).

Furnham and Gunter (1989) were also concerned about belief in God as opposed to some other 'supernatural being'. While the belief that life's events are influenced by the stars may be widespread, this does not preclude the belief that life is predetermined in some way by some higher force – whether this is God or some other supernatural being. Around one in four of the British youth sample (26 per cent) said they believed in the existence of a higher force which has some influence over events in their lives. Somewhat more (36 per cent) dismissed this belief, while 39 per cent were uncertain. The youngest respondents, 10–14-year-olds (40 per cent), less were far more likely to believe in a higher force than either 15–16-year-olds (26 per cent) or 17+-year-olds (15 per cent).

On the question of the existence of God, fewer than one in five (17 per cent) said that they thought about it from time to time, 24 per cent said they did not, while more than half (55 per cent) were unsure about this. Regardless of whether they gave the matter any thought, equal proportions of young people (28 per cent) either believed or did not believe in God. Many (45 per cent) did not know, however, which might be taken to be an agnostic position. Finally Furnham and Gunter were concerned about what young people thought about the after-life.

A little over one in four (25 per cent) of young people said they had thought about whether there is a life after death. Half as many again (18 per cent) did not believe they ever had, even at moments of crisis. Most (70 per cent), less however, claimed that they did not know. The youngest respondents, aged 10–14 year (19 per cent), were more likely to say they had ever thought about an after-life. Despite the apparent lack of enthusiasm for thinking about the idea, one in three (33 per cent) admitted to a belief in life after death, outnumbering those (24 per cent) who did not believe. Forty-four per cent did not know. Once again the youngest group were more likely (43 per cent) than the older one (29 per cent) to say they believed in life after death. A similar proportion (32 per cent) also believed in heaven and hell, though rather more (30 per cent) on this occasion held doubts. Males (34 per cent) were more likely to have doubts about heaven and hell than were females (25 per cent).

In their study of 8165 adolescents and their parents in America, Forliti and Benson (1986) found between 46 and 56 per cent of American adolescents found their church or synagogue extremely or very important to them. Between 38 and 44 per cent (depending on age) agreed their church or synagogue helps them (very much/quite a bit) answer important questions about life, while between 50 and 60 per cent agreed that being part of a church or synagogue was something they wanted very much indeed. They found evidence for three important patterns: Girls have somewhat more positive attitudes towards the church than do boys; for both boys and girls, attitudes to the church become somewhat less favourable with age; and the decline in favourable attitudes is more pronounced among boys. Adolescents appeared to hold fairly orthodox beliefs about God, Jesus Christ and the Bible. The study showed that younger adolescents (11–14-year-olds) tend to experience religion more as liberating than restricting. Also the more central they see their religion to be, the more likely adolescents will have positive attitudes to the church; have high self-esteem; engage in helpful, considerate behaviour towards others and refrain from drug and alcohol use. However, those who experience religion as restricting (stressing control, discipline, limits) tend to be sexist, racist and high on anti-social behaviour. Forliti and Benson note:

> Boys are more likely to adopt a restricting religion orientation than girls are. Perhaps boys receive more 'God will punish you if you do that' messages than girls. It is conceivable that a restricting orientation is felt as oppressive by boys, and this in turn might be a factor which helps explain why boys attach less importance than girls to both church and religion.
>
> (Forliti and Benson, 1986: 224)

Other studies on fairly large population groups have been interested in the correlates of religious attitudes and beliefs. For instance, Mark (1982) in a study of nearly 2000 British 11–16-year-olds found age, sex and school related to religious beliefs. Young people become less affirmative in their attitudes to religion and less sensitive and compassionate in their attitudes to other people as they grow older. Essentially there appears to be a linear decline with age of what might be called an institutionalized understanding of Christianity.

Infancy and childhood understanding of religion

Many parents follow the custom of infant baptism, or a similar form of initiation ceremony, usually followed by a celebration. Often they have a vague or unusual understanding of the ceremony's religious meaning or commitments and pledge that they are making. Conventionally it is regarded as significant for the religious life of the parents and their community rather than as a means of beginning to train the very young. The later consequences, if any, of infant baptism for religious development have yet to be determined.

In families where some members engage in religious activities, the very young are likely to become increasingly aware of them without comprehending their meaning, even if they are taught and/or imitate some of the words and actions involved in religious practices. Parental influences are probably the major factor in religious socialization in the pre-school years. It has often been claimed that religious development is profoundly affected by infant and early childhood experiences. To date this has not been demonstrated empirically.

Early in the century, Freud attempted to analyse the infantile origins of the concept of God. In *Leonardo da Vinci and a Memory of his Childhood* (1910) he observed: 'Psychoanalysis has made us aware of the intimate connection between the father complex and the belief in God and has taught us that the personal God is psychologically nothing other than a magnified father.' In *Totem and Taboo* (1913) he stated: 'God is in every sense modelled after the father' and 'God at bottom is nothing but an exalted father'. Freud's biographer, Ernest Jones, generalized this psychoanalytic position by claiming that religious life represents a dramatization on a cosmic plane of the emotions, fears and longings which arise in the child's relations to her or his parents. More recently, Rizzuto (1974) has argued that (a) there is an extraordinary congruence between a person's experienced image of God and the internalized aspects of that person's parents, and (b) the elements used unconsciously to form the image of God originate in early relations with parents, the product becoming more or less integrated with the conceptions of God provided by the child's environment.

These psychoanalytic notions have been subjected to empirical testing by a number of researchers, who have worked with samples of people falling within various age ranges including childhood. It is clear that the image of God held by young and old may have paternal, maternal and self features, or some mixture of these, or indeed none of these features. On the basis of the empirical evidence, it is not possible to accept unequivocally that the images of God in the population are modelled on father or parent figures rather than any other major referents. Further, children have varied experiences with parents. Some children are deprived, beaten, hated, sexually abused, cruelly treated or deserted by parents. When children in a school class are told, for example, 'God is a father up in the sky', they may relate the information to exceedingly different experiences of fathers.

The infant's important discovery that objects and persons are permanent or conserved in a changing world where they appear and disappear, Elkind (1970) suggests, comes eventually to interact with the discovery that they and others must ultimately die. The conflict between the desire for permanence and the inevitability of death, which often impacts fully at adolescence, is solved by religion with the concept of God. By accepting an immortal God, a young person can accept the religious answer to the problem of conserving life involving beliefs about an after-life, eternal life or resurrection or salvation or reincarnation. Elkind concludes that, for the young person who will accept it, 'religion offers an immediate solution to the seemingly universal human problem posed by the conservation of life and reality of death' (1970: 38). It also provides, in worship, a means whereby the young person can relate themselves to the deity.

Religious concepts, beliefs and practices are not of course based upon direct sensory experience of the divine, but are formed on the basis of experience, cognitive abilities, needs, imagination and cultural influences. The analogies, metaphors, high-level propositions and abstractions which abound in religion raise enormous, often unsurmountable, intellectual difficulties for children of all ages. Their conceptualization of God (or disbelief in God) develops over time. Parents, siblings, teachers, schooling, peers, television programmes, clergy, books, art, all contribute to this development.

Elkind (1964) distinguishes between the 'acquired' and the 'spontaneous' religion of children. They acquire many religious terms, ideas, beliefs and practices directly from others, through instruction, observation and imitation. They can memorize religious material and practices without understanding them. This can easily mislead adult observers, who assume the memorized verbal and behavioural performances of children indicate religious understanding. Children's spontaneous religion consists of those notions, ideas and beliefs that they construct in their attempts to come to terms with religion and religious practices, much of which is beyond their comprehension. For example, a 6- or 7-year-old may believe 'You become Jewish by eating Kosher foods' or 'You become Catholic by going to a Catholic school' or may wonder 'How did God become God?, or 'Does God have a first name?'

Theological efforts to comprehend the nature of God range from rather detailed formulations to complete aversion to any specification. Elkind (1970) argues that once the growing child accepts the concept of God, allowing that such acceptance is multi-determined and difficult to predict in the individual case, the issue of God's representation is an inevitable outcome which is part of the search for forms of representation in general. Religion provides representations of the deity in Scripture.

In attempting to understand the psychological features of the concept of God among lay people, including children and adolescents, various researchers have undertaken studies aimed at developmental as well as other issues. For example, Harms (1944) asked several thousand American children to draw their idea of God or the highest being they thought to exist, and to comment upon their drawings. Harms concluded that there are three stages in the development of religious beliefs:

1. 3–6 years   The fairy tale stage. God is in the same category as giants and dragons, only bigger and greater.

2. 7–12 years   The realistic stage. God is seen as a real person, say as a father. The influence of institutional religion is visible in the acceptance of many orthodox ideas.

3. 12+ years   The individualistic stage. Here there are a variety of interpretations: conventional, mystical and personally imaginative.

There have in fact been a number of attempts to construct stage-wise theories about religious thinking or indeed relating it to Piagetian or other developmental theories (Lawrence, 1965). Moore (1988) has argued that adolescent spiritual development can be described in terms of three stages which have consequent strategies attached to them. The three stages are as follows:

Purgative   and characterized by developing self-esteem, synthetic conventional religious beliefs and an affiliative faith;

Illuminative   which includes a searching faith with warm images of God and strategies of asceticism, meditation, bible sharing, etc;

Unitive   which is more integrative and involves the surrender of total control over one's life and a dissolution of prejudice.

Fowler (1983) has specified a six-stage theory of development of religious concepts which describes how an individual's scheme of faith progresses from simple, narrowly defined concepts of faith to highly complex, multi-faceted concepts.

Stage 1: intuitive-projective faith

The lowest level of development is based on an intuitive and imitative knowledge of faith. Beliefs are focused primarily on an omniscient but magical view of God. Natural phenomena such as lightning, thunder, and northern lights are seen by the child as rewards or punishments for their own behaviour; for example, 'God made the sun shine for my birthday', or 'Why did God make me sick on the day I was to go to the dance? The child's conception is usually highly egocentric. But adults are not immune to stage 1 feelings. When driving to an appointment and in danger of being late, and every traffic light is green, adults are likely to think something like 'I must have done something right', implying that some magical power has caused the lights to be green as a favour to us.

Stage 2: mythic-literal faith

The next stage, most common to childhood and pre-adolescence, is a faith dominated by a literal acceptance of the dogma of religion and a strict adherence to the concreteness of its symbols. That is, the young person regards the symbol as important not because it represents something but because it has concrete reality. Not uncommonly, this concrete reality may also acquire stage 1 magical characteristics, as in a good-luck charm. Rules and guidelines are inviolable and absolute. Once again, in this simple construction adherence to the rules leads to rewards by God, disobedience to punishment.

Stage 3: synthetic-conventional faith

In this study, faith provides a social structure within which to handle the complexities of daily living. Religious rules are interpreted rigidly, and members of the faith community are all expected to adhere to the rules. The strict interpretation is often extended to imply, sometimes implicitly and sometimes explicitly, that the rules are the only true ones.

Stage 4: individuating-reflexive faith

During late adolescence young people find themselves in a struggle between loyalty to the community and a quest for individuality, between concrete objectivity and abstract subjectivity, between feeling obligated to serve others and desiring to fulfil themselves. Those struggles may and do generalize to the adolescents' relationship to religion. Stage 4 requires a personalizing of religion and a recognition of personal responsibility to a particular faith.

Stage 5: paradoxical-consolidative faith

During this stage of religious development, individuals recognize and appreciate integrity and validity of positions other than their own. Recognizing the value of other faiths, and exploring their extra dimensions, often expands the individual's personal faith development.

Stage 6: universalizing faith

The rare person who achieves this level is able to live in harmony with all people. The feeling of oneness does not interfere with the person's sense of individuality, because the oneness with humanity is transcendent.

Subsequent studies of a similar kind indicated that the emphasis of different religions and denominations can be found in representations of God by the young. It appears the general trend is for a masculine God to predominate in socialization, with the concept of a feminine God producing anxiety for a proportion of boys. The mass media – especially television – can influence God imagery by presenting spectacular, miracle-working, omnipotent and fantastic versions of God (and religious superheroes of all epochs) which compete with representations offered by others. Heller (1986) concludes, on the basis of his small-scale detailed study of American children aged 4 to 12 years, that their religion is a spontaneous phenomenon of the heart in which God is inter-connected with their own and other people's lives.

In constructing images of God, children elaborate, combine and interpret many pieces of information, selectively drawing upon their previous experiences and the materials for religious thinking in their environment. Children may use religious ideas, symbols, themes and practices in their play. Elkind (1970) argues that religion functions as an aid to the adaptation of the growing child and adolescent to problems of development. Working with a sample of English youth, Goldman (1964) showed that children are introduced to religious material before they are capable of understanding its religious meaning; and the misconceptions that result may actually interfere with the growth of religious understanding. The research of Goldman, and others in various countries who have followed him, has demonstrated that the development of religious understanding is significantly determined by the development of cognitive structures (Slee, 1986). Children often think of God in anthropomorphic terms. The childhood tendency to think of God anthropomorphically continues for many people throughout life. Conversely, a section of the adult population believe themselves to have been affected by childhood religious experiences that have been of value throughout adult life.

Many children inevitably encounter instrumental, utilitarian views of God and religion in the family, community, school and mass media. Religion may be presented as being a matter of conventional morality, respectability and personal conduct; at the extreme, presenting the most socially desirable life-style and belief system. In different locations God and religion are used to legitimate national, social class, racial and religious segregation in schools (including religious schools) and social life. God and religious education may also be harnessed to career development, financial ambitions and social status, particularly in the middle and upper classes. God may be presented as a supernatural source of gifts and rewards. Claims that religion reconciles all people, breaking down barriers of nationality, class, race and religion, have very little, if any, validity within the sphere of religious socialization. Views of God and religion acquired in the pre-adult years are often part of a world view which is markedly influenced by factors such as nationality, race, social class, political and military interests.

Adolescent beliefs and understandings

The biological changes prominent in early adolescence are accompanied by important changes in cognitive functioning. The young person becomes able to think much more logically and consistently about abstract concepts, including religious concepts; to examine thoughts and feelings as if they were external objects; and also to imagine radically different or ideal alternatives. There emerges what Elkind (1970) calls the 'search for comprehension' which recurringly uncovers new problems and puzzles for understanding in the passage of time. He concludes from pertinent research that for adolescents who accept God and religion the solution to this search is provided by theology or a 'body of myth, legend and history which provides a means for comprehending God in his various aspects' (1970: 41). He also suggests that young people who seek comprehension on their own are likely to become bewildered and disheartened.

The cognitive development which takes place in late childhood and early adolescence is well illustrated by Elkind's (1964) study of the religious (denominational) identity of American Catholic, Jewish and Protestant children aged 5 to 14. He found that young children have a global, vague impression of their family religious denomination, that religious identity is no more than a name. Children of around 7 to 9 have a concrete conception of their religious identity rooted in the behaviour of people; for example, 'you go to a Catholic church' (or synagogue or Protestant church). From age 10 to 12 upwards young people acquire an abstract conception of religious identity involving faith, beliefs and conviction, that is, an inner subjective reality. Older children and young adolescents reflect upon their own thinking about religious identity as well as observing characteristic ways of behaving associated with different denominations. Elkind concludes that 'until adolescence the child *knows much more than he can understand about his religious identity*'; and that 'it is no accident that religious conversion occurs most frequently in adolescence' (1964: 40) when the conceptions of religion and denomination become much more matters of inner conviction.

Adolescence is associated with religious 'conversions', though the term has several meanings in this context. It can refer to a heightened commitment to a family denomination; to a complete change in commitment from one denomination or religion to another; to a gradual, rapid, dramatic or crisis conversion. Sudden conversions in adolescence often involve prior intense feelings of anxiety, guilt, sin, deprivation and frustration, possibly criticism of conventional or superficial religiosity, which convert to contrasting feelings of faith, virtue, satisfaction and peace. If a society generates much anxiety, deprivation and frustration among adolescents, it naturally produces favourable circumstances for conversions. Adolescent converts are usually ready to change and have the opportunity to change, often with personal relationships aiding the change. Religious crusaders and evangelicals use techniques with prospective adolescent converts which separate them from former associates, emphasize the benefits of the new faith, reward conforming behaviour, provide models to guide behaviour, a supporting environment and a new world view and way of life that often includes generous financial support for the chosen church or sect.

Potvin and Lee (1982) present a developmental approach to adolescent religion drawing upon published research and their own study of a national sample of Americans aged 13 to 18. Their main thesis has three elements: (a) up to early adolescence religion is largely a product of parental and institutional religion, that is of relations of authority; (b) in mid-adolescence peers begin to influence belief and practice directly, and the adolescent begins to co-construct with peers a meaning system which supports or doubts or rejects the earlier religion; and (c) in late adolescence a new religious stability emerges which may be compatible with the past or may abandon the past or may create something new. Potvin and Lee (1982) stressed the salience of relationships among adolescent peers, that is, relations of mutuality, which allow 'objective discussion' free of adult constraints. This approach possibly over-emphasizes the impact of the peer group during the religious flux of adolescence at the expense of some other non-parental interpersonal influences. If present in the family, older siblings or other close relatives can be influential during adolescence. Close relations with schoolteachers or youth workers or clergy are also possible influences. The presentation of adolescent themes and problems in the mass media may impact on adolescent ideas and expectations within their interpersonal relationships. Finally, any peer-group influences may have a transient rather than a lasting impact.

Religious leaders are concerned that the young new generation will come to accept the faith, doctrines and institutions which they value. They usually assert that parents have the right and responsibility to educate their children, but with emphasis upon the inter-generational transmission of religion often involving school segregation. Research findings support the conventional view that the family is significant in religious socialization. They indicate that mothers tend to have a greater influence on development than do fathers. Within-family transmission tends to be strongest in families where the parents have definite religious beliefs, agree on them, carry out religious education in the home, have no more than minor disagreements with their offspring and avoid adolescent rejection of their religion. Himmelfarb (1979) suggests that the most substantial impact of parents is indirect, through channelling their offspring into circumstances where they are influenced by other socialization agents. However, in general researchers have found weak relationships overall in the level of within-family religious similarity across generations, with denominational orientation showing a slightly stronger relationship than many features of religion. To some extent this may reflect the shared position of parents and offspring in the social structure. Researchers have not much explored the religious impact of the young on parents for it is possible that any within-family relationships stem partly from the influence of the young on their parents. In a complex society with many influential socialization agents, in most cases adolescents simply may not resemble parents in terms of religion.

A large number of studies in various countries have found females to be more religious than males in late childhood and adolescence. Girls are more likely than boys to believe in God, to feel close to God, to attend church and church-based youth groups, to believe religious doctrines, to pray, read the Bible, have positive attitudes to religion, to be anti-militaristic, more pessimistic (realistic) about nuclear weapons and the possibility of nuclear war, and to feel they have had spiritual experiences (Furnham and Gunter, 1989; Forliti and Benson, 1986). The greater religiosity of girls can be attributed to socialization rather than inherent personality traits or biology. The traditional religious gender differences are deeply rooted in culture. Females and males learn the appropriate roles and behaviours for their sex.

Although the research evidence is not altogether consistent, it appears that there is a tendency for Catholic teenagers somewhat more frequently than other teenagers (save for Protestant fundamentalists) to believe in Christian doctrines, to have positive attitudes to religion and to attend church. In addition, there appears to be a tendency to greater anti-communism and hostility to the USSR among young Catholics. Catholic educational and family influences are significant here. Research into denominational school education, Catholic, Jewish and Protestant, suggests denominational influence is strongest on youth from the most religious homes. Working with data from American Jews and Catholics, Himmelfarb (1979) suggests that religious schooling does not have a significant independent impact on adult religiosity until close to 3000 hours of religious studies are undergone. This finding is probably relevant to the vast literature on the religious ineffectiveness of schools.

The emphasis in Catholic education on segregated schools, on isolation from the outside culture in order to pass on the Catholic faith, has been criticized within and outside the Catholic community as inimical to the Christian cause. However, there appears to exist a widespread assumption among Catholics and other fundamentalists that a negative relationship exists between participation in non-religious or outgroup institutions/organizations/activities and orthodoxy of belief. It is argued that outgroup associations introduce the young to disturbing alternatives as well as different and sometimes opposing world-views.

One conclusion to emerge from studies of the religious beliefs of the young and religious education is that religious beliefs and practice decline with increasing age from around 8 to 10 years through to the late teens. Females display this decline somewhat less than males. Positive attitudes to religion, prevalent among 6- and 7-year-olds, display a similar decline with age. Young, regular churchgoers do not contribute to this trend. Regular church attendance, religious belief and positive attitudes to religion are interrelated among the young. By the time teenagers leave school, institutional religion has largely been put aside or rejected by them, though it is not always clear which of a number of potential factors is the major cause of this. It has been argued that this religious decline is part of a general adolescent discontent with authority, orthodox values and school itself; and possibly also something of a reaction against parents in pursuit of independence. Francis (1987) dealt specifically with this issue in a study based upon a sample of 800 English boys and girls aged 7 to 15. His results indicate there is a genuine decline in positive attitudes to religion and religious education, and that the decline is not an artefact of general adolescent discontent. In discussing the decline he made much of the unpopularity of religious studies in school and of religious education among older children and adolescents.

The socialization and counter-socialization of religion

Studies of religious socialization typically suggest that during pre-adult years the young become, to some extent, conventionally religious (Black, 1978; Blaikie, 1978; Elkind, 1970; Faulkner, 1980; Francis, 1979, 1987; Greer, 1984a, 1984b; Potvin and Lee, 1982). The significance of parents and family, teachers and schooling, peers and friendship, and the churches as socialization agents is acknowledged, though the mass media are largely ignored. There is general acceptance of a decline in positive attitudes to religion from late childhood onwards, a widespread youthful dislike of religion as a school subject and a partial failure of religious education, even in religious schools.

The young who are indifferent, unsure, critical and antagonistic in their religious orientation do not feature in such treatments. Even the concerns, problems and criticisms of the religious young are usually not seriously considered, with Heller's (1986) developmental study of God being a notable exception. It is clear that, by the teen years, among the religious there are enormous differences in the perceived importance of religion, its salience to finding meaning in life and death, its role in personal decision making, its application to everyday life and to public affairs.

Some of the religious concerns, problems and criticism of the religious young are presented in detail by Heller (1986). He studied the development of conceptions of God and religion in depth among forty American Baptist, Catholic, Hindu and Jewish youngsters aged 4 to 12 years. Among the issues he presents, the following are relatively important:

1. General anxiety among the religious young in the face of Godly power.

2. Resentment with the constraints of formal religion (in home, school and church); that is, with the constraints of religious concepts, practices, propriety and control, and with religion functioning in a parental role.

3. Resentment at the interference by formal religion with the religious experience of the young. This includes the tendency of parents, teachers and clergy to act as go-betweens for the youngster and God, as though they had direct contact with God; often leading to the use of religion to sanctify obedience.

4. A formal religious tendency to block non-institutional, unconventional and original ideas and views among the young.

5. Disenchantment with formal religious routines and the promotion of obsessive routines, including routine worship.

6. Inordinate adult concern with the expectations of adults rather than with those of the young.

7. Unhappiness with religion among the young is usually acceptable in the home and school.

8. Science and technology are influential on the young and may be viewed as a human-made competitor to formal religion.

Heller (1986) uses the term 'excessive socialization' to cover the implications of these and other issues for the young. He points out that they struggle against excessive socialization, and strive for personal exploration and discovery. He also reports that 'scientific and technological imagery work their way into deity representations and frequently inhibit personal discovery' (1986:138). Some of the young, Heller found, search for a certain spiritual and expressive freedom, and may break through to have moments of great faith in a God beyond apparent socialization influences.

Religious education is directed towards producing participation in the corporate life of a religion or denomination together with adherence to official beliefs and doctrines; that is, education in religion to produce conformity to certain orthodoxies. It is not directed predominantly towards the religious experiences and spiritual awareness of children and adolescents. Yet many have a variety of religious experiences, including 'moments of great faith' to use Heller's (1986) phrase. At the same time, many youngsters do not have religious experiences. Clearly adolescent awareness of religious concepts, beliefs and practices is not dependent upon religious experiences or commitment.

In general, there is little adult concern with the religion of youth as such, rather than as it relates to adult concerns, and there is adult suspicion of unusual experiences among the young. In practice, this means that the quality of religious experience of a proportion of the pre-adult population is of an altogether different quality to that of their parents and teachers. Further, there is very little adult concern with the possible negative individual consequences of religion for the young; for example, from the encouragement of anxiety, shame, guilt, obsessive practices, fears, unreal aspirations, stereotypes, and hostility both to religious and non-religious out-groups. In some circumstances stereotypes, prejudice and hostility are positively promoted, often in association with national, racial and/or political issues.

Relatively little attention has been given by researchers to the socializing impact of the mass media, including television. The treatment of religion as news by the media differs little from their treatment of other subject matters. The media specialize in excitement, action, success, conflict, violence, deviance, scandal and personality. This means they specialize in religious leaders and evangelists, papal announcements, televangelists and their misdeeds, libertarian theology, financial misdemeanours of the churches and clergy, defrocked priests, lesbian nuns, red vicars, important clerical appointments and elections, faith healing, the abortion controversy, anti-communism, miracles and such like. The religion of children and adolescents is rarely newsworthy.

The treatment of religion as entertainment by the media is largely a mixture of Madison Avenue advertising and Hollywood versions of God and religion. The media present countless versions of God and gods; Biblical stories; Christian and non-Christian characters, superheroes and miracle workers; ancient and modern, conventional and exotic, religious ceremonies and rituals. This entertainment is certainly consumed by children and adolescents. The treatment of religion as religion by the media (as, for example, in religious telecasts and broadcasts) tends, in presentation, towards the conventional, seasonal, inoffensive, clean and wholesome, bland and family-orientated. When associated with Christian evangelism there may be a strident request for money especially in the USA. Religious presentations apparently attract little interest among the young. At the level of informed speculation, it is difficult to conclude that the mass media have a generally positive religious influence on pre-adult socialization, and easy to conclude that they have negative and anti-religious influences. Heller reported that 'the popular media stereotypes do impede the child's own spiritual explorations' (1986: 139). The religious material in the media provides some alternatives to that in the home, school and community, with a palpable emphasis upon the newsworthy and entertaining.

The religious and world views of adolescents who criticize, reject or are antagonistic to religion differ considerably from those of adolescents who profess to some extent to be religious. Predictably, anti-religious adolescents show marked tendencies to disbelieve in God and religious doctrines, to have negative attitudes towards religion, and to disapprove of religious education in school. In addition, without being consistently radical, they do tend to be much more politically radical than religious adolescents and somewhat less supportive of capitalism as a system. At the extreme are those adolescents who believe religious leaders and clergy to be consciously fraudulent for their own vested interests, and possibly for those of the powerful and rich. Religious adolescents tend to be politically conservative though they may be radical about certain issues. Religious beliefs among the young can be linked with support for governmental and non-governmental terrorism as, for example, in South Africa, Israel, Northern Ireland and parts of the USA (Coles, 1986). Religious adolescents are more likely than others to believe that nuclear war is prophesied in the Bible. They apparently reflect much more than others upon the meaning of life, illness and death. The anti-religious seem to place more weight than the religious on the role of luck, chance and fate in life. The origins and development of scepticism, agnosticism and atheism in the pre-adult years have not attracted the attention of researchers.

The limited evidence available suggests adolescents who are unsure about religion tend to be unsure about the whole range of religious issues. They also tend to be unsure about politics and political issues. Their unsureness about religion is possibly part of a general pattern of relative unsureness in their world views. Adolescents who are indifferent to religion apparently tend to be indifferent or apathetic towards religious and political issues. They seem to be the group least engaged or involved by religion. It is however difficult to disentangle cynicism, disinterest and scepticism in the young.

Parents, teachers and others caught up in the religious socialization of children and adolescents undoubtedly generate contradictions and unintended consequences as agents of socialization. There are obvious possible contradictions between what these adults say and what they actually do, contradictions readily perceived by the young. The contradictions between what they say in the home, school and church, and the organization and operation of these institutions are more subtle. For example, do Catholic teenagers in a denominational school experience the segregated school and school life as a fulfilment of the Christian ideals they are taught, especially if racial, social class or other factors impinge on the school? Could they experience this education as a partial rejection of those ideals in the adult pursuit of worldly aims? The degree of acceptance, indifference or rejection of religion as a youngster grows is outside the attempts of adults to control it, and always open to influence from the mass media. The reaction of a sizeable proportion of the teenage population against school and the widespread dislike of religion in school are other influences.

When agents of socialization criticize and attack the religion of others, might they be providing the young with reasons to doubt their own religion? When they criticize and attack secular world-views and out-groups, including humanists, atheists and Marxists, might they be visibly contradicting religious values of tolerance, co-operation and peaceful coexistence? When they reject out-group religion and secular world-views in attempting to perpetuate what they value, might they be undermining at least some of what they value, and possibly encouraging a habit of rejection of religious world-views? On the basis of his study of religious socialization, Faulkner concludes 'there exist simultaneously, within the organized religions of the West, psychologically conflicting moral forces for good and evil – teaching brotherhood with the right hand and bigotry with the left, facilitating mental health in some and mental conflict, anxiety, and psychosis in others. I realize this seems an extreme interpretation: but the research bears it out' (1980: 210). It is clearly easy to introduce stereotypes, bigotry and hostility into religious upbringing and education, and sometimes this is done deliberately. It is probably easier to turn religious socialization into counter-religious socialization than is commonly realized. This may well be involved in the marked tendency of older children and adolescents to dispense with or reject religion.

Conclusion

Young people acquire a conventional understanding of God, and spiritual matters in their early teens. Abstract religious concepts are very difficult to grasp before this time which may account for the instability of religious beliefs over time. Many researchers have pointed out that religion plays a major part for some young people in the general identity-formation process. Religion helps by giving answers to questions about right and wrong, acceptable and unacceptable.

Religion serves at least four broad functions for young people (Meadow and Kahoe, 1984). It serves to meet *egocentric* needs of individuals. That is, religion functions to meet needs of feelings of security and belonging. Religion also serves a *growth* function by fostering a sense of self-worth in the individual which is tied to self-connection to the religion. Religion serves a *social* function by establishing and passing on a code of conduct and ethics. Religion serves a *cognitive* function by offering reasons and answers to the 'why' questions of existence which plague us all. All religions and cults are built around one or more of these functions. In particular, cults and repressive religions often provide a regimented, simplistic code of conduct and a sense of belonging within a closed community. The individual member feels wanted and needed and is provided clear rules which reduce personal anxieties resulting from having to make one's own decisions.

Young people's value systems and moral development are intimately bound up with religious thinking. Adolescents' attempts to clarify and internalize their own value systems frequently affect their assessment of religious beliefs. Their reactions to religion may range from mild discomfort and uncertainty to radical redefinition of their religious selves. It is not uncommon for young people, particularly during their later adolescent years, to reject institutional religion, temporarily or permanently, in favour of a more personalized belief system. Adolescence may also, of course, be a time of intense religious experiences which serve to confirm religious beliefs.

The end of adolescence does not bring with it a permanently resolved set of value structures. Adults working with young people may serve an important role by helping adolescents realize that adults are also dealing with refinement and clarification of their own values and beliefs.

Chapter seven

Race, colour and prejudice

Introduction

Given the importance attached to race and skin colour in so many
countries around the world, it is not surprising that children begin to
develop race and colour awareness at a very early age. The physical cues
on which young children's initial racial classifications are based are easily
discernible, rather like the cues for sex involved in the gender categorization of children and adults (see Chapter 5). Ideas, beliefs, feelings,
attitudes and behaviour relating to race and skin colour are communicated
to the young throughout the pre-adult years by parents, siblings, teachers,
peers, the mass media, churches and other cultural agents. In many
countries, including Australia, Britain, Canada, France, Germany, Japan,
New Zealand, South Africa and the USA, racial differentiation is widely
considered to be of great importance yet it appears less important in many
South American countries.

It was once common to describe national populations as races. An
eighteenth-century example is Daniel Defoe's description of the English
as a 'mongrel half-bred race'. This use of the term is now rare. Today
geographical groups of people of common ancestry with distinguishable
physical characteristics, and the compulsory or voluntary migrants from
such groupings, are referred to as races. Scientists delineate a race as a
reproductive population which shares a common gene pool. The implication of this is that there exists an infinite number of possible races within
our species which can be regarded as a vast human race. The popular or
everyday use of the term often reflects the non-scientific belief that races
exist as biological entities because certain human surface characteristics,
such as skin colour, hair texture and shape of nose, vary in highly visible
ways. In fact, these surface characteristics are relatively unimportant in
themselves, and are continuously variable rather than divisible into a few
broader categories. The term 'racism' refers to the ideology that race is a
primary inherited determinant of human characteristics, abilities and

performance, almost always implying a racial hierarchy of superiority and inferiority, and often implying hostility to peoples of different race. Racial prejudice is not essentially different from religious, national, linguistic or other prejudices. Prejudice and discrimination have developed (and been fostered) between people who are physically indistinguishable, as in Northern Ireland and Japan, but their promotion is made easier where there exist visible physical differences between groups, however biologically unimportant. Racial prejudice is of course accompanied by the negative stereotyping of out-groups of people. Racial stereotyping involves the attribution of supposed and actual characteristics of a whole racial category to its individual members, however appropriate or not. As with sex stereotyping, it has the effect of greatly exaggerating human uniformity within categories and differences between them.

Groupings of people by virtue of national background, religion, language and culture, or by membership of a largely endogamous community, or by racially mixed parentage, are often described as 'ethnic groups'. Examples are people of Mexican, Puerto Rican or Cuban background in the USA; or Italian, Greek or Lebanese background in Australia; or of Turkish, Italian or Jugoslav background in Federal Germany. The vague and eclectic term 'ethnic groups' is sometimes used to refer to racial groups, and the words ethnic and race overlap in meaning; for example, when applied to Afro-Americans and Jews in the USA, Pacific Islanders and Aborigines in Australia, Indians and Pakistanis in Britain, Arabs and Jews in France, or Maoris and Pacific Islanders in New Zealand. The word ethnic is usually applied to socially designated groups that occupy a subordinate position in society, which means it is often applied to recent immigrant groups (Rosenthal, 1987). Such ethnic groups may also be referred to as minority groups. The term immigrant can imply racially different in the EEC, Northern Europe and the USA, even when applied to white immigrants from Southern Europe or Latin-American countries.

Understanding of skin colour

Humans inevitably differ in skin colour. Many people believe skin-colour differences are of major importance in human behaviour, and that people who are differently coloured must be fundamentally different. The notion of race is bound up with skin colour and its associations, combinations and symbolism. The colour names 'black' and 'white' are the most frequently encountered colour terms in language. In most cultures the colour white is associated with positive attributes and the colour black with negative ones; in fact, black has many highly pejorative associations and connotations.

When young children are acquiring their language, they will learn colour names including black, white, brown, red, yellow. The custom of designating racial (and ethnic) groups by colour names encourages children to label racial groups by skin colour. Obviously the colour designations are often inaccurate as with red Indians, yellow Chinese and white Australians. Given that children experience colours as different, the colour labelling of racial groups carries for them the implication that different groups are different kinds of people, and attaches some of the non-racial associations, connotations and symbolism of colour names to groups of people. This is particularly important for the labels black and white, because black is culturally associated with the undesirable, dirt, darkness, bad, evil and the Devil, whereas white is associated with the desirable, purity, virtue, goodness, light and God. The slogan 'black is beautiful' is aimed at detaching the negative cultural symbolism of black from the skin colour of Afro-Americans (and other dark-skinned people), and at establishing black as a complementary and equal term to white in the racial context. The slogan is also an attempted counter to racist slogans asserting black is primitive, backward, dirty, inferior, ugly and, within the Christian tradition, to beliefs that black (skin) represents sin, evil, the black arts and the Devil; that 'black is the badge of Hell' as Shakespeare expressed it. All children are born and grow up in a world in which particular perceptual cues have social significance for categorizing and conferring status upon individuals. Racial and sex cues are highly significant for understanding social organization and behaviour from the earliest years onwards, and are important in socialization from infancy through the pre-adult years.

Babies are able to make discriminations on the basis of colour within the first few months of life. Within their first year, they must be able to observe light-to-dark differences in skin colour, and distinguish people on the basis of colour cues. A sizeable proportion of 3-year-olds and most 4-year-olds are able to react to skin colour cues, are aware of race, and also exhibit evaluative responses to different colours indicating race preference. For instance, in western societies young white children prefer white and, until relatively recently, a sizeable proportion of young non-white children displayed a pro-white bias (Alhibai, 1987; Katz, 1983; Milner, 1983).

Cross-cultural research evidence shows that children, from as young as 3 years, react differently to the colours black and white (Milner, 1983; Williams and Morland, 1976). White tends to be positively and black negatively evaluated, with children exhibiting this evaluative tendency to varying degrees. Racial background appears to have a slightly modifying influence on the way children react to these and other colours.

Williams and Morland (1976) suggest the white over black bias is initially attributable to a preference for the light of day to the dark of night, the feelings of discomfort and fear aroused by darkness, the fear reduction associated with lightness and the reinforcement of cultural symbolism which treats white positively and black negatively. This means that certain feelings about black and white terms, colours and race are carried forward from infancy to adolescence and adulthood. They also suggest this bias develops in children of all races for the same reasons, though racial experiences modify slightly the effects of the general determinants in certain circumstances. The preference for lightness over darkness is developmentally prior to preference for light over dark skin. They reject the proposal that children have a natural inclination to evaluate colours by reference to their own skin colour. However, they feel the American research findings indicate a recent trend for older black children, teenagers and adults to evaluate the colour black more positively, and attribute this trend to influences from within the Afro-American subculture. In the less severe racial situation of New Zealand, Vaughan (1978, 1987) has reported a comparable trend among the indigenous Maoris.

Williams and Morland believe there are some causal links between the white over black colour bias and racial bias among children:

> We observe the parallel between the lightness of white vs the darkness of black and lighter-pinkish-tan skin of Euro-American vs the darker, brown skin of the Afro-American. The opportunity which this provides for primary stimulus generalization seems quite evident (i.e. *the generalization of a response to a given stimulus to other stimuli*). We also note the current practice of designating racial groups by colour names ... a clear invitation to generalize colour bias to racial groups. Under these conditions, it seems most unlikely that the preschool child who views white as good and black as bad could avoid generalizing some of his colour bias to persons who differ both in skin colour and in the colour labels by which they are designated.
>
> (Williams and Morland, 1976: 243)

They present American, French and Italian research findings which indicate: (a) children who have a strong pro-white colour bias also display a strong white racial bias; (b) modification of children's colour bias is accompanied by a change in racial bias; and (c) young children who display negligible knowledge of racial classification respond more positively to light-skinned than dark-skinned persons. They interpret these findings as supporting their belief about causal links between colour bias and racial bias by assuming that the white over black colour bias takes developmental precedence over racial bias or at least that they develop concurrently.

Williams and Morland (1976) propose that the white 'racial bias' exhibited by young people is not racial in its origins, but a consequence of all children's early experiences with light and darkness which result in their acquiring a tendency to evaluate light things more positively than dark. Among black children, positive associations to dark-skinned people should emerge to counter early light preferences. The very early racial bias, or pro-light/pro-white skin colour bias, becomes racial in its implications as children learn about race in a society pervaded by racism. Katz (1983) makes the point that to the extent young blacks have negative and unpleasant experiences with white racism, they should progressively devalue the colour white and the racial group. Williams and Morland assert that the links between colour bias and racial bias create the general evaluative context in which the young learn about race, while admitting that their racial concepts and attitudes are much more complex than a light over dark and white over black bias.

The emphasis of Williams and Morland (1976) on the white over black bias as contributing to the childhood development of skin-colour preference, and as providing an evaluative context in which racial bias may be developed, coincides closely with Milner's (1983) conclusions about the relationship of colour values to racial preference. He places more emphasis upon the direct and indirect tuition of the young about race. He points out that racial values appear more strongly established than colour values among 3-year-olds, and speculates that values about white and black people may influence the acquisition of colour values in childhood and later. He concludes:

> We should regard this area of theory and research concerning colour values *not* as a viable account of the genesis of prejudice, but rather as describing some contributory factors: colour values provide an evaluative framework, chiefly operating through language and pictorial imagery, which reinforces race prejudice and gives it greater credence. In addition it assists the learning of race prejudice ... by simplifying for young children the division of the world into categories of opposites, whether they be colours or evaluation.
>
> (Milner, 1983: 105)

It must be emphasized that the young, from early childhood onwards, not only categorize people into racial groups but also evaluate the groups. They tend to think in terms of contrasts or opposites, that is, comparing their own group with other groups. Eventually they will learn that race is a fixed characteristic that does not change with age. The constancy aspect of race seems to be acquired around 7 to 9 years, and their racial beliefs reflect the society in which they live.

Racial attitudes and preferences

Children begin to develop racial awareness in the pre-school years: they have the capacity to discriminate differences between major racial groups, to label racial groups, and also to categorize self and others in evaluative racial terms. Research in a number of countries has demonstrated that children develop racial awareness from 3 to 6 years, with non-white children being more precocious in development (Milner, 1983). By 6 years few children cannot perceive and label racial differences accurately. This age-related development among children reflects general cultural influences which assert that race categories are of great significance in social life. The child is born into a social structure with racial characteristics in which relations between their in-group and other relevant groups already exist. Children in nearly all societies frequently encounter people of different races and racial labelling. Even if children have personal contact with only one racial group, they will view race, colour, prejudice and race-related conflict through the mass media. For most children, race awareness is well established by the time they enter primary or elementary school.

At the pre-school level, children attribute more positive traits to light-skinned as opposed to dark-skinned figures and persons, but whites do this to a greater extent than non-whites. Whites also prefer persons whom they evaluate positively, which means they show a pronounced tendency to prefer light-skinned persons. With regard to skin colour preference for self, children tend to prefer light to dark, but this applies to a greater extent for white than non-white children. Of course, preference for any one skin colour or race over others does not necessarily imply rejection of, or hostility to, other races; simply a preference. However, a definite minority of young white children do reject dark skin colour and dark people.

In white-dominated multi-racial societies, young children of all racial backgrounds tend to prefer figures and persons in the white category, and to see themselves as similar to their preference (Davey and Mullin, 1980; Milner, 1983; Vaughan, 1987; Williams and Morland, 1976). This implies that children, sensitive to the nature of existing race relationships, tend to prefer the racial category with the most favourable position in the social structure. However, the pro-white bias is less strong among non-white than white children, though it exists among a majority of black children. The evidence suggests this bias is least strong among the darkest-skin-coloured children.

During the school years, white children continue to be pro-white in their racial evaluations, attitudes and preferences. Racial attitudes consist of enduring beliefs and stereotypes concerning racial/ethnic groups and their members, which are evaluative in content and which have an emotional overtone. They develop considerably during the school years and become resistant to change, largely because of their evaluative and affective components. This racial/ethnocentric bias of white young people seems to be most intense around 6 or 7 years, when it takes a simple polarized form. For many children it appears to decrease somewhat in later childhood as a result of learning that all racial groups can display good and bad attributes, and because of the impact of conventional notions about racial tolerance. However, by age 12 children have assimilated many of the racial attitudes circulating in their society. Adolescence is the time when many young people seek to define themselves and relate themselves to others on the basis of race or ethnicity (Rosenthal, 1987). The family, peers and friendships, school and teachers are salient personal influences and potential sources of conflict, especially with reference to interracial relationships. During the school period, then, white youth's views, feeling and attitudes undergo development together with some integration and consolidation, so that there is greater consistency between them. Wilson (1963) suggests that attitudes towards more salient racial objects may develop earlier than do attitudes to less salient objects; that is, there are differential development rates for attitudes to various racial objects.

Milner (1983) makes the point that, while the messages about race which the young of different races receive are the same, the implications are radically different. The developmental pattern is more complex for non-white children and adolescents (Davey and Mullin, 1980; Milner, 1983; O'Donnell, 1985; Rosenfield and Stephan, 1981; Vaughan, 1987; Williams and Morland, 1976). After entry to primary school, as they get older non-white young people become progressively better at race classification, show an increasing preference for their own race and more frequently categorize themselves as non-white until the extent of their own-race categorization is comparable to that of white youth. Yet these trends are not completely mirrored in attitudes towards the races, in which something of a pro-white bias remains, particularly in the evaluative features of attitudes. The evaluative climate which surrounds non-white youth is subjectively significant to these young people. At the same time the external world dictates to the young that perceptible racial cues place them and others in relevant racial categories, however they evaluate the categories and whatever their feelings about them may be.

The reactions of non-white youth to non-white groups other than their own are similar to those of white youth to black groups. Ethnic and racist attitudes and preferences are common among non-white as well as white children and adolescents. They are often exhibited in school and in other public places. At sporting events racism may be expressed by racial name-calling and taunting of the players or competitors or of other spectators. In all racial groups, at the extreme there are a minority of viciously racist adolescents.

The apparent disjunctions during pre-adult development among non-white youngsters, which involve delayed own-race identification, appear to spring from them perceiving the inequalities of life between races and the relatively favourable position of the dominant white race. It may be that they are simply orientated positively to the 'haves' in the upper reaches of the social structure who are overwhelmingly white. White young people tend to be less (rather than more) aware of race issues and their significance than non-white youth. The latter perceive the world as more threatening and hostile than their white counterparts.

Mixed-race children have received very little attention from researchers. Vaughan (1987) points out that whether or not it is possible for a youngster to develop a truly interracial identity in a multiracial society is an unresolved question. He reports the suggestion that the mixed-race young may attain an interracial identity only when society formally recognizes the interracial group involved as, for example, the 'coloured' minority within the South African apartheid system. Since the 1920s it has also been repeatedly suggested that mixed-race people are marginally positioned between conflicting racial cultures which intensifies their self-consciousness. From the experience of his cross-cultural studies, based on young citizens of various countries around the world, Coles (1986) remarks that 'coloured' South African young people are not only confused and troubled about their situation, as a weak minority caught between the dominant whites and oppressed blacks, but also find it exceedingly difficult to put aside the worries of race in their everyday thinking. Predictably, Coles found negative and hostile racial attitudes among the young of the 'coloured' and other racial groups in South Africa. This hostility also occurs between the young of the two white 'sects' (Afrikaner and English), though they share the Afrikaner apartheid outlook and accompanying hostile attitudes to non-whites.

On the basis of a small-scale study of mixed-race children aged 6 to 9 in Britain, Wilson reports they 'see the racial world in an unusually self-conscious, detailed and questioning way in order to make sense of their own ambiguous position' (1981: 40). She found that these children understand the main racial distinction in society to be white or non-white, but that they have to deal with a more complex and confused racial situation. Wilson states that the complexities of their racial assessments are impressive. Some mixed-race children use fine gradations of skin colour – white through yellow, beige, tan, brown to black. Others contrast 'pure' racial categories with 'mixed' racial categories. Others focus on cultural background – English, Indian, African, etc. And some children combine all these assessments. Whatever their approach to racial assessment, mixed-race children place themselves very much in the middle.

More research studies dealing with racial development in the pre-adult years have been carried out in the USA than in any other country. The American research emphasis has been upon black Afro-Americans and white Euro-Americans, but with some studies based upon Asian-, Indian-, Jewish- and Hispanic-Americans. The pattern of research results in the USA has been similar for all non-Euro-American racial groups, with the largest attenuation of the pattern apparently being of regional origin – in Hawaii where race relations are somewhat less tense. Similar patterns of results have emerged from studies in many other countries, with some attenuation of the pattern in Hong Kong, where the Chinese and British live in parallel and are both represented in the upper reaches of society. The pattern of white own-race bias combined with hostility to other races appears to be heavily pronounced in South Africa as one might have predicted.

Reviewing evidence on the development of ethnocentrism, Tajfel concludes 'Thus there is a good deal of evidence ... that members of groups which have found themselves for centuries at the bottom of the social pyramid sometimes display the phenomenon of "self-hate" or self-depreciation....The self-depreciation, relating to social comparisons with the outside world, leads to a variety of conflicts' (1982: 12). There is accumulating multinational evidence of a swing, since the early 1970s, away from out-group preference and towards own-race preference among the young of racial/ethnic minorities. This change in the pre-adult years has been interpreted as one indication that the ideology of white supremacy is being effectively contested (Milner, 1983; Tajfel, 1982; Vaughan, 1987). It has been partly attributed to societal changes that have promoted a growth in group pride and self-respect among non-white minorities. Milner observes that 'it has been increasingly possible (not to say appropriate) for blacks to externalize blame for their predicament onto whites, rather than internalize it' (1983: 162). But, it must be stressed, research over the past fifty years has consistently shown that a proportion of the young in all non-white racial groups do not prefer the white race, and this proportion appears to have been growing significantly in the recent past.

Furnham and Gunter (1989) have noted that, although research has not been able to answer questions like 'Do children who exhibit early awareness develop different attitudes than those who manifest it later?' or 'What is the relationship between earlier expressed preferences and later racism?', it is clear which are some of the major factors that lead to racism. These include:

direct instruction – most prejudice appears to be taught (by parents, schools, the media) rather than caught (from other sources); reinforcement components – racial attitudes can be punished and rewarded by all sorts of factors which may in turn create or eliminate them;

parental personality – parental personalities often affect their child-rearing techniques and there is evidence that authoritarian parents tend to encourage beliefs and attitudes that are racist;

cognitive factors – people who tend to overcategorize assume that all people from the same category (i.e. racial group) behave in the same way and exhibit the same traits. This cognitive style tends to lead people to be relatively impervious to new information that contradicts their beliefs;

perceptual factors – many children believe that visible differences imply real differences and that the more strange these 'different' people appear the more negative will be people's reaction to them.

Katz (1976) has suggested that the development of racial attitudes is different from that of other attitudes for two major reasons: often information about race comes from people of the same group and there are few models from the out-group to dispel misconceptions; the evaluative (good/bad) component may be more intrinsically involved in early learning with regard to race. Katz also sets out eight steps in the development sequence of racial attitude acquisition:

1. early observation of racial cues;

2. formulation of rudimentary racial concepts;

3. conceptual differentiation between people from different racial groups;

4. recognition that racial characteristics are irrevocable and not subject to change;

5. consolidation of concepts of racial groups;

6. perceptual behaviour between 'us' and 'them';

7. cognitive elaboration;

8. formulation of racial concepts.

What of current day racial attitudes? In another study of stereotypes with 281 white English teenagers, Bagley and Verma (1973) noted the positive, neutral and negative stereotypes of different groups. The Irish were thought to be clean and civilized, but also aggressive, lazy and untrustworthy. Indians were perceived as civilized, peaceful and trustworthy but Pakistanis were thought of as untrustworthy and dirty. Overall, the children seemed to have more positive and less negative stereotypes about West Indians than about Indians who, in turn. were seen more favourably than the Irish and Pakistanis. The negative stereotypes most associated with West Indians were that they were dirty, smelly, aggressive and unkind; while Indians were thought to be dirty and smelly; the Irish stupid, complaining, troublemakers, aggressive and drunken; and the Pakistanis dirty and smelly. They conclude:

> Clearly, there is a depressing amount of hostility in the attitudes of white students to their West Indian and Asian class mates. Asian students too have hostile views of other ethnic groups. Only West Indian students have anything approaching an attitudinal set which could be categorized as 'tolerant'. Interestingly, commitment by West Indians to black power ideology is unconnected with hostile perception towards whites.
>
> (Bagley and Verma, 1973: 258)

In their recent study of over 2000 British young people Furnham and Gunter (1989) asked their subjects how they would describe themselves – as prejudiced against other races or not prejudiced? Asked if they thought of themselves as prejudiced, a disarmingly large number admitted to being either very (10 per cent) or a little (38 per cent) prejudiced, while 42 per cent said that they were not at all prejudiced and 10 per cent did not know. More males (57 per cent) than females (41 per cent) admitted to some degree of prejudice and more older (53 per cent) than younger (42 per cent) respondents admitted likewise. It could be argued either that these respondents are being particularly honest, as fewer adults admit prejudice, or that a certain amount of bravado is associated with racial prejudice and that this tended to over-inflate scores.

Identical questions were asked about the racial prejudice experienced by Asians (Indians and Pakistanis) and Blacks (Africans and West Indians) and almost identical responses occurred. In all, 42 per cent thought the above groups suffered a lot of prejudice in Britain nowadays, 32 per cent a little prejudice and between 8 and 11 per cent hardly any. Between 15 and 18 per cent did not know and there were no sex or class differences. In all, therefore, nearly three-quarters of our sample believed that racial minorities experienced some racial prejudice. Interestingly, more older (83 per cent) than younger (63 per cent) children thought that prejudice against these racially identifiable minority groups occurred. On the issue of racial equality 60 per cent agreed that coloured people were equal to them, though more females than males agreed (65 per cent vs. 55 per cent) and more older than younger adolescent respondents (66 per cent vs. 51 per cent). Roughly the same number (18 per cent) as 'did not know' thought 'coloured' peoples inferior (17 per cent) and a small minority (2–8 per cent) thought them superior. There were no sex, age and class differences.

The young people were asked whether they thought Asian and Black Britons suffered job discrimination and again the results were so similar that it could be argued that respondents saw no difference in job discrimination against these two groups. About a third (30–40 per cent) thought racial job discrimination happened a lot and 45 per cent that it sometimes occurred and 10–12 per cent said it rarely happened, thus indicating that, overall, three-quarters thought that it is a non-rare occurrence. On this issue there were no sex, age or class differences.

As regards attitudes to racial discrimination legislation, about half (48 per cent) were in favour and just under a third (30 per cent) 'did not know' but a fifth (22 per cent) opposed it. Females more than males (52 per cent vs. 45 per cent) and older more than younger children (57 per cent vs. 39 per cent) were in favour of this sort of legislation. Naturally there was a higher incidence of 'don't know' among the younger children.

Finally, Furnham and Gunter (1989) attempted to measure the social distance concept which relates to contact with other races. There were completely consistent sex and, to a lesser extent, age differences on the five questions that we asked. Although nearly half (47 per cent) said they would mind a little or a lot if a relative married a person of Asian origin, only a third (36 per cent) said they would mind (a little or a lot) if a close relative married a person of black or Irish origin.

Two out of three (64 per cent) adolescents said they would not try to avoid having neighbours from the West Indies, India or Pakistan. On the issue of whether local authorities or private landlords should refuse accommodation to West Indians, Indians or Pakistanis, just over half (54 per cent) believed that accommodation should be let to these groups and about one in four said they did not know (26 per cent). One in five (21 per cent) believed that these three groups should not be given accommodation.

In every instance, females reported less prejudice than males, and the older respondents seemed less prejudiced than younger respondents who nearly always had a much bigger 'don't know' score. While roughly two-thirds of the sample either expressed no desire to avoid contact with other groups or did not express an opinion, between a fifth and a third of the respondents clearly would prefer to avoid any sort of contacts with members from other groups.

Furnham and Gunter conclude:

> For some, these results should bring hope. There was evidence of racial prejudice and discrimination, indeed over a third admitted that they were a 'little prejudiced', but the vast majority who expressed opinions believed in equality between 'races', the use of anti-discriminatory legislation, close integration between groups. The majority did not oppose the view that explicit racial attitudes be banned. There was some evidence that stereotypes were confirmed – the Irish as drunken and bellicose, the West Indians as musical – but fewer than half the

sample endorsed these stereotypes. Moreover, some stereotypes were disconfirmed – that Asians are hard working, for instance.

Three consistent findings occurred. Females nearly always express less negative racial prejudice than males. That is, they were more in favour of equality, endorsed fewer negative statements, and agreed with more positive statements than the males. This is consistent with previous findings on sex differences though it is not always clear why it arises.

There were also a fairly large number of age differences which were usually linear, though there were a number of inconsistencies. Older respondents tended to be more 'liberal' in their responses. For instance, they believed that more discrimination occurred, were more against the silencing of publicly expressed racist views but tended to reject stereotypes and negative statements and accept positive statements more often than did young children. A number of reasons could be put forward for these findings – such as the fact that older adolescents are more aware of racial issues in society; more sympathetic to the plight of others and less egocentric; or quite simply more aware of the socially desirable responses that could be given. Each of the above, or indeed other explanations, could be put forward for these findings.

(Furnham and Gunter, 1989: 126–7)

Socialization

Though the young in different racial or ethnic groups are subjected to much the same socializing forces within society, they are by no means in an equivalent position. As a result of being a member of a particular group, the young person is subjected to forces which differentiate her or him from members of other racial groups and, in the case of some groups, from members of the dominant racial group. Of crucial importance, the young person will be categorized and treated as belonging to a racial group by other people, including members of that group. Such categorization may carry expectations about how the young person should behave and how others should behave towards her or him. It will inevitably lead to experience of racial stereotypes, some derogatory and racist. Thus, if a youngster is categorized as Aboriginal, Chinese, Irish, Jewish, Maori or whatever, he or she will become the recipient of the stereotypes that are attributed to their own group.

The young undoubtedly receive some direct instruction about race, race differences and race relations from parents, older relatives, school teachers, church persons and others. The instruction influence can be directed predominantly towards acceptance and tolerance or prejudice and discrimination or some mixture of these elements, possibly a contradictory mixture. Related to the direct instruction of parents and other adults are the examples they provide by their speech and behaviour, which may not be in accord. Such examples convey to the young how significant elders in their lives think and speak about race and how they behave in a variety of situations. The young identify with some of these people, and may use them as models for imitation. On occasions a child may purposefully imitate the relevant patterns of behaviour of significant others. The same applies to their racial views, beliefs and attitudes. Various developmental theorists have argued that imitation of models, in either real-life or fantasy situations, is particularly important in the acquisition of aggressive behaviour, verbal and physical. In any multiracial society, for a definite proportion of parents the choice of their residential location, and that of their children, is determined in part by forms of racial avoidance and congregation. Conflicting standards can be communicated to the young. For example, in the USA the main churches prescribe racial equality and interracial tolerance, yet American churches and synagogues are largely segregated by race. It appears that being a member of the dominant group in a multiracial society facilitates the achievement of racial identity.

Many analysts have claimed that parents (or guardians) are the primary agents most responsible for children's racial concepts, beliefs, preferences, attitudes and related behaviour (Katz, 1983; Milner, 1983). Many have also claimed that parents are most responsible for passing on prejudice from one generation to the next. Milner (1983) argues that parents are in positions of great power, particularly in the early years of socialization when they order the child's racial world and encourage particularly ideas and behaviour. He writes:

> society teaches children not only ways of doing things but also ways of seeing – that is, its *values*. Parents are central to this process; they are the interpreters and instructors. They encapsulate and inculcate society's message, by accident and design. Children come to hold many of these values as their own; among them are values concerning other groups in the society – social classes, religious denominations and racial groups are the most obvious of these. Not all parents share the majority's attitudes and values so that their children may develop dissenting views.
>
> (Milner, 1983: 67)

However, to date research has not substantiated the view that parents are the primary socializers, that parents exert a discernible major within-family influence on their young and adolescent offspring.

Any parental influences inevitably interact with (and possibly have to contend with) racial, community, school and general cultural influences, including those emanating from the mass media. A family preoccupation with race or particular racial groups may promote an early concern with race in the children, and a belief that race and skin colour are of great importance. It has also been argued, with supporting evidence, that authoritarian parents who use harsh and rigid techniques of upbringing generate racial prejudice in their offspring (Sanford, 1973; Williams and Morland, 1976). This is because the young person identifies with uncompromising parents who are racist in outlook, and complies with parental racism for expediency or displaces the aggression created by this frustrating family situation on to racial out-groups. Racial, ethnic and immigrant groups can always be treated as scapegoats or as an excuse for society's ills. On the opposite side of the rejection–acceptance continuum are those parents who show no concern about race and who are indifferent to racial issues. At the end of the continuum are parents who actively accept other racial groups and attempt to promote interracial tolerance.

Racial categories are widely accepted by the members of society as ways of describing persons of all ages. Such categories also indicate the norms of interracial communication and behaviour; that is, the social roles of racial groups. In multiracial societies, race is likely to be one of the significant aspects of social reality. A racial role carries, up to a point, prescriptions for behaviour which vary to some extent with age, sex and social class. Role learning by children and adolescents is an important part of their race socialization; it is influenced by direct and indirect instruction, and by peer relationships. Enormous social pressures are applied to the young to produce conformity to race standards prevailing in their social milieu. In acquiring a racial role, the young person learns behavioural norms and expectations similar to those of other persons who occupy the same racial role. During the early years, as the role is acquired, the child becomes aware of enacting a role and of the way in which it relates her or him to others occupying similar or different roles. The child also attains a racial perspective on the social world and on the self in this world, from a particular role position. The results can be extremely unpleasant. For example, in South Africa the black child or adolescent is encouraged by black socializing agents to acquire knowledge, skills, qualifications and achievement-orientated characteristics appropriate to a modern technological economy, while the apartheid system forbids their use in competition with whites and insists upon racial division, racially based inequality, and politico-economic subjection of non-whites.

From the perspective of race socialization, the mass media communicate (a) an enormous amount of race-related material about persons, celebrities, events, pseudo events, fiction and what is passed off as fact, (b) news dealing with race, racial groups, immigration and race relations, and (c) expectations about social life for different racial groups. Young people would not encounter the vast bulk of these types of material if they were not manufactured and conveyed by the media, particularly television. Inevitably the young have a limited range of experiences in which they actually participate. The media create a second-hand reality (or version of reality) about race, racial roles and race relations, as they do about sex, sex roles and relations between the sexes. Much of the second-hand reality is blatantly unreal (Wober and Gunter, 1988).

Overwhelmingly, in western countries, the media are owned or controlled by whites, staffed by whites and aimed at a largely white audience. To a considerable extent the media determine the public agenda concerning race and race relations. They may not be able readily to change public attitudes towards important issues, but they influence what people of all ages can attend to, become interested in and talk about. The media confer importance on chosen people, events and issues by putting them before the public eye. They turn obscure nonentities into public figures by covering their ideas and actions. All this is conveyed to children from their pre-school years onwards. The young in minority groups and in the lower socio-economic strata (which greatly overlap) are typically the most vulnerable to having their views of social reality shaped by television. Further, television is an important source of information for the young throughout the social structure (Wober, 1980).

Direct interracial contact

Children and adolescents strive to understand racial and ethnic differences and similarities. They acquire racial concepts, attitudes, preferences and roles. They come to categorize people and events, become aware of regularities in race relations and eventually order their multiracial world. The young of all racial groups are sensitive to the evaluative differentiation of races and the climate of race relations. Direct interpersonal contact between children of different races provides them with concrete, first-hand experience of members of other racial groups. Notwithstanding customary patterns of interracial behaviour and adult influences, contact makes possible companionship and friendship which cuts across racial and ethnic categories. It allows practical experience and personal factors to come into play, and possibly disturb conventional race stereotypes, roles and behaviour. Such contact can occur in the home, the neighbourhood, at school, in sporting or recreational activities, or youth organizations.

Differences in the socio-economic characteristics of racial groups ensure that children and adolescents in the middling and higher strata of the dominant white group will have relatively little direct contact with the young of non-white racial groups. This is largely because of the considerable extent of de facto residential stratification (and associated racial

segregation), and the related school stratification (and partial segregation), in different countries; and the apartheid system of racial separation
in South Africa. So direct interracial contact is not experienced in a
uniform way by children through any nation's social structure. And at the
top of the social structure, white children of the rich may encounter
non-white children of domestic servants in a particular form of direct
contact (Coles, 1977, 1986).

A number of investigators in various countries have examined interracial contact among children and adolescents, most frequently in the
school context (Coles, 1977, 1986; Davey and Mullin, 1982; Figueroa and
Swart, 1986; Milner, 1983; Rosenfield and Stephan, 1981; Taft, 1978;
Williams and Morland, 1976). Unfortunately the interplay of socio-economic and racial factors has often been ignored by investigators and
confounding variables have made explanations difficult. But general
agreement has emerged that it is not the *amount* of contact which is
significant, but rather the *kind* of contact or the qualitative aspects of the
interracial situation. The notion that increasing interracial contact, say in
school, would necessarily reduce racism and prejudice is naive and false.
So is the notion that simply increasing interracial contact between children
and adolescents of equal family status would tend to lessen their racism
and prejudice. In practice, white and minority group young people often
do not meet on an equal-status basis in school. Interracial contact therefore
provides opportunities for stereotypes and prejudice to be reinforced,
interracial competition to be emphasized, hostility and overt aggression
to be expressed and personal status to be enhanced within the own-race
group by interracial conflict.

The results to emerge from these investigations of interracial contact
point to an age-related trend of own-race choice for companions and
friends in day-to-day situations. In the pre-school years there is least
frequent choice on the basis of race, though young white children appear
to be less accepting of other races than young black children. A majority
of children, at this stage, accept children of other races as companions and
playmates.

Race becomes an increasingly significant factor in companionship and
friendship during the school years. There is a rapid decline in cross-race
acceptance, until there exists a marked cleavage along racial lines in later
childhood and the teen years. Davey and Mullin (1982) observed that the
generality of own-group friendship in the various racial/ethnic groups
suggests that friendship is influenced more by category membership than
by personal characteristics.

The research findings reflect the racial climate of society, and imply
that direct interracial contact is not, in itself, likely to modify significantly
the impact of that climate on school life. They suggest there is a crude
consistency between racial attitudes and interracial behaviour for children

and adolescents in school. They do not necessarily imply widespread active rejection by the young of young people in other racial/ethnic groups, though much active rejection takes place. There is considerable variation among the young in their interracial behaviour. A sizeable proportion of the young do accept the young of other racial/ethnic groups and a small minority do form interracial friendships. Young persons who generally reject others, or who have mainly negative relations with others, will not be favourably disposed to persons of different race. The young with low self-esteem tend to be prejudiced; increasing their self-esteem together with increasing their interracial contact tends to reduce their prejudice. Voluntary co-operation in multiracial groups of the young composed of equal-status individuals of similar outlook, with institutional or normative support for the contact, yielding positive outcomes, tends to promote favourable intergroup relations. The notion that a teenage youth culture exists which cuts across divisions of race (and social class) is erroneous.

Tajfel (1982) proposed a formulation of intergroup relations during periods of social change which stresses minority group rather than individual coping strategies (Davey, 1983; Milner, 1983; Tajfel, 1982). The formulation is applicable to children, teenagers and adults. When individual attempts by minority group members to integrate with the dominant majority are perceived to be hopeless, then group strategies provide an alternative to individual frustration. Tajfel does not specify in detail how the transition from individual to group strategies comes about; though factors such as racism, discrimination, deprivation, the provocation of racists and racial attacks, together with recognition of the immutability of race, must be involved.

Tajfel (1982) argued that every racial group has a need to create and maintain a positive social identity in comparison with other racial groups. Group members do, in general, have a more positive image than others of their own racial groups; that is, they display own-group favouritism. Interracial disparities can be modified through positive social differentiation of own from other racial groups, including the dominant white group in western countries. Such differentiation may take a number of forms: for example, accentuating linguistic distinctiveness and vitality; changing the value assigned to own-group attributes (such as skin colour, hair style, clothes, language, music, religion) in a positive direction; changing the bases of social comparisons between racial groups in a favourable direction; positively evaluating own-group products; competing directly with other racial groups for resources. A common means of elevating one's own racial group is to depress the positions of other groups, which encourages conflict among minorities. Rastafarianism is an example of such social differentiation. It is highly conspicuous and offers a social identity, but it is safe because it is innocuous and does not confront the powers-that-be or really disturb conservatives. Forms of positive social differentiation are communicated to the young and become a feature of their race socialization. When intergroup relations are unstable, and racial minorities are seen to be changing faster than the dominant group, the interracial status quo is threatened. Racial minorities become aware that their social location is not fixed or legitimate, that something better is possible for them; while for the dominant group what was taken for granted in the past cannot be taken for granted in the future. This situation will be reflected in the ideas and behaviour of children and adolescents. Positive social differentiation may well generate some conflict, hostility and antagonism which, among other things, will influence direct interracial contacts between the young. The 'bad news' aspects of this differentiation will be publicized by the mass media, rapidly disseminated nationally and, for sensational 'bad news', internationally. Minority group demands for civil rights and better opportunities will be seen as a racial threat by some members of the dominant racial group. It has been suggested that this is a most important factor in contemporary racism and prejudice.

Racial prejudice

Racial prejudice predisposes individuals, and social groups, to perceive, think, feel, believe, judge and act in a favourable or unfavourable way towards racial groups. Unfavourable feelings can vary from mild distaste to dislike, antipathy to hatred. Predispositions to behave unfavourably range from avoidance to discrimination, social rejection, ostracism and even outright violence. When the term prejudice is applied to racial or ethnic groups, it is nearly always with reference to the unfavourable aspects of prejudice.

At an early age, children acquire awareness of race, and this is accompanied or shortly followed by evaluative feelings towards people of different skin colour and race. By the time children enter school, their racial awareness is not affectively neutral, and they have racial preferences, with some children rejecting others of different race. There is a substantial foundation of racial terms, concepts, evaluations and preferences available for children to develop further their outlook and behaviour. Child and adolescent development takes place in a society where racism and prejudice are commonplace and deeply rooted in the culture of the dominant race. The racial character of the society impinges inevitably on every person's socialization, whatever her or his individual characteristics and family background. In western countries, the ethnocentric bias of white children is widespread and strong by the early school years; in school, white ethnocentric frames of reference are the norm.

While school pupils do not fully comprehend racial terms, ideas and stereotypes, they can nevertheless use them in a reasonably appropriate manner, with some or all of the emotional force intended. They can use them to hurt other-race young people (Figueroa and Swart, 1986). During the school years, from rudimentary beginnings the young elaborate racial ideas and stereotypes with the addition of more information and misinformation about race, including that obtained by direct contact with persons of other races. These elaborations contribute to the emergence and development of racial attitudes, including highly prejudiced ones. Wilson suggests that there exists a negatively accelerating growth curve for racial prejudice in childhood and adolescence – 'the level of prejudice increases with age, but at a progressively declining rate until it levels off and stabilizes at the adult level' (1963:248). With age the young become increasingly aware of the racial norms of behaviour in their own social milieu, and increasingly conform to them. In children's preferences for companions and friends, the age-related trend in own-race favouritism is in line with the other features of development. By the end of childhood, most children display marked ethnocentrism. This is maintained through high school.

Where racism and prejudice have become commonplace in society, it seems inevitable that many children and adolescents will absorb them, and adapt them to current concerns. The young are vulnerable to influential sources of racism and prejudice in their environment, including the mass media, literature and comics.

In addition to meeting race in the family, neighbourhood, school, religion and wider world, children encounter race in television, motion pictures, radio, newspapers, school textbooks, books and comics (Milner, 1983; Open University, 1977). Young people partly develop their views of racial reality from such material. In western countries the non-white races are usually under-represented in these sources of information. When non-white people are presented, it is frequently in a stereotyped and derogatory way: sometimes as the white man's burden or problem; sometimes as undesirable, evil or savage because of race; sometimes as targets of intense prejudice.

Television, the most important medium of contemporary entertainment, drama, news and current affairs, is undoubtedly a major purveyor of racial stereotypes, racism and prejudice (Greenberg and Reeves, 1976; Milner, 1983; Collins and Korac, 1982). The non-white races and their members are greatly under-represented on television; and when they are portrayed, it is typically in an unflattering, unfavourable or overtly prejudiced manner. Television does not convey the racial diversity of (a) particular countries such as Australia, Britain, France, New Zealand, South Africa, the USA and USSR, or (b) the whole world. Racial diversity is most likely to be evident in external public events such as the Olympic

Games or Commonwealth Games. Television news and current affairs programmes continually stress contentious race and immigration issues. They are manufactured on the assumption that racial minorities and immigrants are the problem, not the racism and prejudice rooted in the dominant culture. In fact, all the news media use race in the same way, influenced by the media norms that 'bad news is good news' and 'racial conflict and violence is good news' (Milner, 1983; Open University, 1977). Commercial television advertising is particularly racist in content (as well as ageist, sexist and social class biased). Its incredible fantasy world is peopled mainly by affluent, skinny, white stereotypes who are voracious consumers of everything, without their bodies ever showing the consequence of their greedy behaviour.

The mass media, books and comics reflect the culture of the dominant race. The racial ideas, beliefs, images, fantasies, stereotypes and events they purvey so blatantly reflect the racial concerns of that culture, including its racism and prejudice. As a result, the young of all races encounter daily a second-hand representation of the social world, which is racially biased and misleading, with visible components of racism and prejudice. But it is reasonably congruent with the racial biases, racism and prejudice encountered at first-hand in everyday life and, apparently, an independent source of confirmation of racist versions of reality. This promotes the socialization of racial stereotypes, biases, racism and prejudice. The socialization effects seem to occur cumulatively, from infancy onwards, through repeated exposure to racial ideas, images, stereotypes and piece-meal bits of information that favour particular views of a multiracial world. Children and adolescents holding racist views can choose material, including television programmes, that supports their views and apparently confirms them.

When the young have established some racial stereotypes and biases, these tend to affect their cognitive processes. Then, they are inclined to notice and remember events that are consistent with, rather than those that contradict, their racial view. When they encounter behaviour that is clearly contradictory to their racial expectations, they can discount it by attributing it to factors unrelated to their expectations, for example to luck or to an exception or to cheating. The young are inclined to attribute the behaviour of other-race persons to factors consistent with their racial expectations and biases, regardless of whether the behaviour is really consistent with them. When the young see acts performed by own-race and other-race persons, they interpret the acts differently and in accord with their expectations. Racially prejudiced children and adolescents are prone to see the behaviour of other races in an unfavourable light, and to interpret such behaviour in a derogatory way. It follows that racial bias, racism and racial prejudice among the young will not change easily if evidence and events which contradict them are largely ignored. Further, if the immediate social environment (including peer groups) strongly supports racism and prejudice, and threatens interracial companionship, the probability of the young being independent enough to make positive interracial contacts is extremely low.

Conclusion

In this chapter the emphasis has been upon youth's understanding of a multiracial world, which involves coming to terms with the racial/ethnic features of social reality. Developmental analyses which stress that the children and adolescents of racial minorities suffer from problems of culturally imposed inferiority, low self-esteem and racial misidentity are inadequate. They are (a) excessively narrow in focus, (b) unduly confined to individual coping strategies without due consideration of group strategies, (c) questionable in equating a pro-white racial preference with low personal self-esteem and an unsatisfactory racial identity (that is, with negative self-conceptions), and (d) neglectful of the much worse conditions of life of racial minorities. Here, the perceived attractions and advantages of the social location of the dominant race to all children and adolescents have been stressed to a greater extent than in other comparable analyses. This applies particularly to perceptions of its upper social strata and its representatives portrayed in the mass media. It is suggested that changes in race relations within the last quarter-century have had some positive psychological consequences for the pre-adult racial minorities in the western world. Finally, many of the young of the dominant white race develop false notions of superiority and an erroneous outlook on their world, which can only impair them and be damaging in the long run.

Chapter eight

Law and justice

Introduction

In any modern society law is a crucial institution and a primary means of regulating human affairs. Further, the laws and statutes of a country can and do become associated with rules, customs, conventions and social practices that are strictly not matters of law. Laws are often seen as mechanisms for: achieving justice; a moral social order; a consensus about right values, rules and social practices; binding legal obligations; respect for the legal order; social cohesion; and such like. Alternatively, laws are often seen as mechanisms for achieving: rationalized power; an organized coercive apparatus; 'law and order'; the obedience of the masses; coercion by violence; ruling-class domination; and so forth. In practice, national legal systems exhibit characteristics of both of these two broad perspectives on law. These perspectives reflect many of the arguments about what the law is and what it should be. Clearly law can be coercive, immoral and unjust; it can be used to maintain inequalities between the sexes, races, social classes and other social groups. But law can provide the means for people (and organizations) to act to defend themselves against powerful interests, the immoral and unjust. In addition, there can exist a great difference between law in publications and the routine practices of people applying and enforcing the law, especially when they are dealing with social inferiors, minorities, nonconformists and deviants. The difference is particularly relevant to certain teenage sections of society.

In the 1970s the term 'legal socialization' came into popular usage. It refers to the development of legal ideas, concepts, attitudes, reasoning and behaviour, including a sense of legal obligation. It is often related to ideas about justice, morality and politics. Legal socialization has been viewed as part of young people's socialization into compliance systems (family, school, sporting codes, church, local and national government). It has been suggested that the socialization of the young into the legal system is of great importance because the law serves to regulate and control much human conduct, and is used as an instrument for achieving governmental ends. Respect for private property is often stressed in this context.

Researchers concerned with legal socialization have been almost unconcerned with anti-social, delinquent and criminal behaviour among the young, including interracial violence. They have been primarily concerned with the understanding of general and hypothetical aspects of law in young people, rather than with their actual conduct. This means little is known about law as a regulator of youthful social conduct. However, it is known that a great deal of law-breaking occurs amongst older children and teenagers. Many teenagers are unwilling to comply with law that interferes with their activities or that they disagree with. But with age the young do become progressively sensitive to issues involving unfairness, injustice and human rights.

An early, much-quoted paper by Adelson and his associates illustrates the concerns of many researchers in this field. They studied issues such as the growth of the idea of law, law's mutability and the effects of law among a sample of 120 young people aged 11 to 18 in the USA (Adelson, Green and O'Neil, 1969). Their research data were obtained by means of an interview which probed in some detail the reactions of these young people to problems faced by 1000 migrant people building a new community on a Pacific Island.

Adelson, Green and O'Neil (1969) reported that during the second decade of life the young are increasingly able to think in terms of legal principles, to see the positive aims of the law and to treat the law in a relativistic, functional way as an instrument for achieving community ends. Their younger subjects were found to have concrete, authoritarian, moralistic ideas of law and government, emphasizing their restrictive and punitive functions and also the strict enforcement of law. In the early teens a more abstract idea of the law was observed to develop, involving some appreciation of the community benefits of law and of possible improper legal interference with individual liberties. Older teenagers were found to deal with the law in an even more general and abstract way, taking in the needs of the community, governmental practice and individuals, but they were wary of the interference with individual liberties. Notions of amendment and repeal, rather than strict enforcement, as ways to deal with unpopular, ineffective and unworkable law were much more common among their older teenagers. Adelson, Green and O'Neil (1969) stressed the rapid growth, in the years from 13 to 15, of abstract thinking about law and governmental realism. Using the research strategy, Adelson subsequently found a similar pattern of development among comparable samples of British and German youth. Cross-national differences were observed to be far less significant than age-related changes. Young Germans were the more authoritarian of the three national samples, the

British most concerned with social welfare and the Americans most concerned with individual and minority rights.

Developmental perspectives and stage-wise models

Three major developmental perspectives on law and justice can be seen, the first two being derived from theories of moral and political development, the third being a role-theoretical model of socialization with an emphasis on following rules. The theory of legal development proposed by Tapp and her colleagues (Tapp and Levine, 1977) derives largely from the moral development theory of American psychologist Lawrence Kohlberg. In this theory there is a central interest in the processes and products of reasoning about legal norms in both 'legal' and 'rule' systems, as well as the assumption of a sense of consciousness of rules and laws. The theory proposed by Judith Torney derives primarily from the political socialization theory of Hess and Torney (1967). Four models of the socialization process applied to the development of political attitudes are applied to legal development. Hogan and Mills (1976) have advanced a role-theoretical view of socialization which assumes that compliance with legal authority is over-determined; certain pre-legal attitudes are important determinants of compliance with law (especially rule attunement); and social learning consists largely of learning about different kinds of social relationships.

Moral theory of legal development

Tapp's interest in legal development was stimulated by her involvement in a study of authority, rules and aggression among older children in Denmark, Greece, Italy, India, Japan and the USA. A subsidiary theme of this study was children's socialization into various compliance systems including family and school. Many questions about law, justice, compliance, punishment and authority were put to the 5000 children involved in the six-country study. These results indicated the importance of rule and legal systems in development. They encouraged Tapp to conduct further studies of legal development in the USA on samples of subjects ranging in age from kindergarten to college level (Tapp and Levine, 1977). These studies led her (and her colleagues) to conclude that there are commonalities across cultures in legal development including legal reasoning. Tapp also became concerned with rules and laws as mechanisms for promoting a just and moral social order.

Kohlberg's moral development theory was applied by Tapp to legal development with particular reference to laws, rules, legal reasoning, legal compliance and justice. In Kohlberg's theory there are three general levels of morality: preconventional, conventional and postconventional. Each level has two stages. The levels and stages have the following core features that organize moral beliefs, values and judgements.

Preconventional level – a deferential, sanction-orientated outlook associated with judgements of good and bad, avoidance of punishment, a morality of power and authority favouring the strong, with power maintaining social order.

(1)   Physical power stage – typified by absolute deference to power and authority, compliance with rules, avoidance of bad conduct; resulting in an obedience and punishment orientation.

(2)   Instrumental relativism stage – in which is displayed a hedonistic outlook where there is a pragmatic desire to satisfy personal needs and interests but with some elements of fairness, equity and reciprocity in relationships; resulting in a concrete individualistic orientation.

Conventional level – an outlook supporting established rules, norms, conventions, arrangements and social order, and opposing nonconformists, stirrers, troublemakers and dissidents.

(3)   Interpersonal concordance stage – typified by an emphasis on pleasing others and gaining approval, which promotes helpfulness and generosity to valued others; resulting in a social-relational orientation in which interpersonal moral reciprocity is prominent.

(4)   Law and order stage – in which the emphasis is upon obedience to rules, norms, regulations and conventions, good citizenship, maintaining social order (avoiding disorder and chaos), with justice being a matter of rules and laws binding an individual to their society; resulting in a member-of-society orientation in which the functioning of the social system is placed ahead of individual interests.

Postconventional level – an autonomous principles outlook in which morality is detached from rules, conventions and laws, and which guides behaviour via principles that are moral and just.

(5)   Social contract stage – typified by concern with rational principles, for making as well as maintaining rules, regulations, laws and social arrangements, embodying a social contract outlook on the relation between individual and society with an emphasis on individual rights; resulting in a prior-to-society perspective where basic rights, values and justice are considered prior to rules and social arrangements.

(6)   Universal ethic stage – in which there is commitment to universal, non-relative, moral principles above other considerations including

the law; resulting in a rational moral orientation that places individual rights and justice before the claims of authority.

The preconventional stages predominate among children; the conventional stages predominate among teenagers and adults, with the highest incidence of Stage 3 morality being among younger teenagers; the postconventional stages are reached only by a small proportion of people. It is accepted that people go through the stages, from one to four or higher, during their moral development because each stage depends upon experience of prior stages. It should be noted that this theory assumes not only that the direction of moral development is towards internalized individual moral controls but also that the higher stages of morality move beyond dependence on culture and society to dependence on a selfless, rational, morally autonomous individual. In the theory, behaviour is treated very much as the externalization of thought. Clearly there is a strong possibility that, in many circumstances, moral stage may relate to thinking about behaviour rather than determine behaviour.

Tapp and her colleagues interpreted the research data obtained from their American and cross-national studies in terms of the Kohlberg moral development theory (Tapp and Levine, 1977). That is, a legal levels account of development was produced involving progression from the preconventional to the conventional to the postconventional. The conventional, law and order, system-maintenance level was found to be modal in different countries and in most social groups including teenagers. This led to the conclusion that the predominance of conventional legality among teenagers and adults indicates that the socio-legal environment can limit an individual's natural capacity for legal development. It was asserted that 'acquiring knowledge about law (whether one endorses the law or not) is essential because it expands the ability to understand problems, define expectations, relate to events, press claims, and structure choices' (Tapp and Levine, 1977: 174). Stimulation of legal reasoning skills in school and community settings, it was argued, would counteract environmental limitations.

At the preconventional level, children (and some adolescents) have a rule-obeying perspective which guides their legal thinking. Rules and laws are seen as preventing bad and harmful conduct, including violence and crime. They function as commands serving no positive social good. Punishment avoidance and deference to power are the reasons for compliance with them. Rules and laws are external to the child and interpreted in personal terms. There is no awareness of a general legal system or of differentiation between the legal and moral. Rules and laws are accepted as fixed and immutable things derived from authority. There is no understanding that social life entails shared standards of behaviour involving law, justice and morality.

At the conventional level a rule- and law-maintaining orientation prevails which flows from membership of society. The main concern is law and order. Conventional adolescents (and adults) respect rules and laws for providing behavioural prescriptions, sustaining morality, ensuring good conduct and maintaining social order. Most conventional individuals make no distinction between underlying principles of justice and laws maintaining 'good' behaviour and social order. Compliance with rules and laws is regarded as fair to all because it prevents violence, crime, disorder and chaos. It is accepted that laws can be changed if they are not for the good of society and, in extreme circumstances, a person may be justified in breaking the law. Law and order are accepted requisites for the existence of society and social welfare.

The small minority who reach postconventional level have a flexible legal perspective orientated to principles of morality and justice. Rules and laws are regarded as norms mutually agreed upon by people to maximize individual and social welfare. Laws function preferably to achieve the rational purposes behind their enactment. They should be obeyed for rational, moral and utilitarian considerations, or for reasons of justice. Laws should be changed if they are unprincipled, purposeless, unjust or immoral. If law violates moral principles, individual rights or principles of justice, it should be challenged or broken. The limits of compliance should be determined by principles of morality and justice, not convention.

Tapp is critical of traditional upbringing and education which aims for simple compliance with existing rules and laws, pushing the young towards a law and order orientation. She is concerned with developing legal reasoning skills and a sense of legal obligation and justice; with developing critical competence rather than conventional compliance. To stimulate legal development Tapp recommends a number of socialization strategies that can be used in school and community. Among these are, firstly, the transmission of legal knowledge to the young, including knowledge about legal conflicts and alternatives. Secondly, encouraging youthful participation in decision making where rules, regulations or laws are significant; for example, in school, church organizations, clubs and societies. Thirdly, encouraging adults in contact with the young, including the police, to be examples of moral, fair and just behaviour. Fourthly, exposing the young, with reference to law, justice and morality, to diversity and conflict in ideas, values, practices and roles, to promote cognitive development. Tapp stresses the potential importance of the school, as a functioning system, in legal socialization. Her aim is clearly to stimulate more young people to move to a postconventional orientation.

Legal development

Socialization into the American legal system was examined by Torney (1977). Four psychological models of the socialization process were outlined. These models had been utilized earlier by Torney and her colleague Hess in an American study of political socialization focused on attitude development and change (Hess and Torney, 1967). The data gathered in this study from about 12,000 white children in school grades two through eight (aged 5–6 to 13–14) were analysed with reference to the legal system, law and legality. Subsequently, Torney moved on to developmental issues surrounding injustice and human rights (Torney-Purta, 1983).

Torney believes that four models of the socialization process are useful for understanding socialization to the legal system. This implies that at least four distinct types of influence impact on children and adolescents. The models are:

Accumulation model – holds that the young steadily acquire information and knowledge about law and the legal system from scattered experience. This includes knowledge, accurate and inaccurate, about government, legislation, lawbreaking, the police and courts. Parents, teachers and the media are amongst the sources of information and knowledge. It is assumed the often unrelated bits of knowledge are not tailored to the individual needs of the young, who receive the material in a relatively passive way, hence this socialization process is very limited.

Identification model – focuses on youthful imitation of elders towards various aspects of the law and the legal system. The young can imitate beliefs, attitudes, values and behaviour of salient elders. This may result in both obedience and disobedience to rules and laws. This model accounts for the copying element of socialization.

Role transfer model – involves the young transferring or generalizing towards authority figures in society the attitudes and behaviours developed towards authority figures within the family. Such transference tends to be emotionally loaded and vulnerable to distortion because of actual differences between family and societal authority figures. The result is usually early idealization of the authority figures in society.

Cognitive developmental model – treats ideas, concepts, thinking about law and justice as developmental change in the organization of knowledge and in making judgements. The model explains the development of ability to deal with more complex, abstract aspects of law and justice, and to take perspectives other than one's own on issues. With the passing years the specific cognitive limitations of early life are progressively overcome.

Using these models in this way implies that legal socialization is one facet of socialization broadly defined. Torney's own work closely relates legal to political socialization; and in this she is similar to Adelson. Torney's approach emphasizes the cognitive features of legal development at the expense of the behavioural; and in doing this she is similar to Adelson and Tapp.

The results from the large-scale school survey (Hess and Torney, 1967; Torney, 1977) showed that the legal system has an impact on the young through its personal representatives and authorities. But with advancing age the personalization of law (and government) decreases. Early attitudes towards the system's representatives, notably the police, may be the origin of many attitudes towards the legal system. The police are seen as powerful by young people of all ages. Primary or elementary school children generally believe laws are fair. They tend to accept that might is right, admire power and take its possession to imply goodness. Torney found that girls react more positively towards the police than boys at all ages, though this sex difference becomes more pronounced with age because the police-positive attitudes of boys decline more substantially as they get older. Torney interpreted this (and other) sex differences primarily by means of differing role transfer influences and, to some extent, by differing accumulation and identification influences. Other empirical studies in the USA and elsewhere have shown that the young in certain social groups are far less positive to the police than Torney's sample, and that they can become highly negative or hostile in the teen years, especially when relevant adult evaluations of the police are negative or hostile (for example, Department of Education and Science, 1983).

Torney concluded that many of youth's ideas about the functions of law have transferred from ideas about school rules. Younger children see the preventive functions of rules and laws; pre-adolescents and early teenagers also perceive them serving positive social functions. Rules and laws are believed by the young to control behaviour and sustain order to make a real difference to social life. Torney suggests that by age 12 or 13 the functions of law and the police are understood relatively well. The young believe rules and laws should be fair, with ideas of fairness changing somewhat with age and cognitive ability. However, with the passing years there occurs a marked decline in the belief that laws are fair, particularly among boys. Associated with this decline is growing recognition that legal injustice can occur. Other studies suggest that disadvantaged social class and racial groups become widely suspicious of the prejudices of the legal system during adolescence (Stern and Searing, 1976). Further, boisterous and unruly behaviour, under-age alcohol offences, conventional but illegal drug taking, social life in the streets, peer group rivalries and confrontations, hooliganism at sporting events, interracial conflict and other activities can result in unpleasant or criminal teenage involvement with the police. In addition, property offences bring many older children and teenagers into criminal contact with the police and courts.

Prior to adolescence the young regard law and government primarily as coercive powers, using the police to keep people from behaving badly or criminally. With adolescence, this perspective changes to a less authoritarian and coercive outlook which features rising awareness of positive functions of law and justice, of freedoms and rights, and more realistic perceptions of law, government and other authorities. Torney states that socialization shows 'pronounced changes leading to less syncretic, more differentiated perspectives toward legal functions and authority figures, greater abstraction, and less idealistic views of the operation of the legal system' (1977:143). She suggests that pre-adult socialization outcomes are significant for adult ideas about, and attitudes towards, the legal system.

The review of studies dealing with injustice and human rights by Torney-Purta (1983), which refers to the work of Adelson, Kohlberg and Tapp among others, indicates that several factors are important in the development of such views among the young. For example, the sense of injustice is acquired in the early school years, becomes strong and is then stimulated by issues of injustice at all ages. Towards the end of primary school most children regard basic violations of human rights, such as slavery, unfair trial and enforced residence in a locality, as wrong even if they should be lawful. Older children and adolescents are prepared to see law and social policy as closely associated with justice issues. By adolescence, a majority of the young feel that the social order has some responsibility to promote justice. There seems to be a general tendency for older children and adolescents to judge civil and political rights as more important than economic and social rights. There is a marked tendency for teenagers frequently to support tolerance, rights and freedoms in the abstract (like adults), but far less frequently in concrete situations for specific political, racial and religious persons who are disagreed with. Torney-Purta (1983) argues that often exposing the young to legal, governmental and other conflicts, and to the clash of opposing interest-group viewpoints in school and community, would be beneficial to development. She insists the young need to develop understanding of remedies for injustice as well as of injustice itself.

A role-theoretical view

This view was initially derived from Hogan's research into moral character and moral conduct. It is predominantly concerned with the developmental processes and social experiences that produce an internalized orientation to law (Hogan and Mills, 1976). Internalization implies the assimilation of law to a person's character, which is not necessarily a rational process. Internalization is contrasted by Hogan with compliance or rule-obedience and with identification or rule-following to preserve social relationships. Internalization generates a 'higher' level of felt legal obligation than compliance or identification. It is argued, from this viewpoint, that children and teenagers acquire those legal, moral and political concepts, ideas, etc., described by Adelson, Kohlberg, Tapp and others, primarily because they reflect important elements of culture, not primarily because processes of cognitive development and social learning take place. In this view, law is taken to be interrelated with justice, morality and politics at the individual, group and societal levels (Emler and Hogan, 1981). Moreover, individual and group differences in legal, moral and political matters are often associated with conservative–radical differences in outlook.

Three assumptions underlie the role-theoretical view. Firstly, compliance with law and authority in general is over-determined for reasons of belief, duty, deference a need for order and predictability in life, and necessary obedience to power. Secondly, early attitudes, including those connected with attunement to rules and social sensitivity to others, are important determinants of compliance with rules and law. Thirdly, social learning consists largely of learning about social relationships in family, school and community, and this will influence the attitudes to law and justice of children, adolescents and adults. For the young, these social relationships entail experience of varied relationships with parents (or caregivers), relatives, peers and teachers, and the formal relationships of competitive games and sports. The experience of injustice in relationships may be a potent influence in social learning.

Beginning with an unsocialized state in infancy, certain consistent changes occur with age in the orientations of children and teenagers to rules, values, principles of their culture, law and justice. For the rules and laws to be accepted as obligatory in adulthood, internalized compliance passes through three levels in reaction to changing life circumstances. These levels are characterized by the following transformations:

(1) Attunement to the existence and operation of rules, and accommodation to adult authority. Initially, internalization occurs through accommodation to parents. Subsequently, the child discovers that social situations are governed by rules, and the situational demands are to determine what they are and effectively adjust to them.

(2) Sensitivity to social expectations, and accommodation to peers in school and community where certain rules and standards are maintained. This accommodation involves fairness, co-operation, participation in

games and sports, and participation in role relationships (especially in school). At this level the young develop an internalized orientation to adult rules, values and norms which are implicit in the law. This transformation is a reaction to concern for relevant others and to emerging sensitivity to social expectations.

(3) Autonomous observance of rules and laws without dependence on public opinion; that is, upholding the legal and moral principles of culture or society irrespective of their popularity. This is usually accomplished by accommodation to the rules, values and principles of admirable reference persons and groups, and to the best traditions of one's culture or society. Over time the young find out that there exist many answers to moral and related questions; and this diversity reduces the monolithic impact of adult opinion upon them. Some individuals organize their experience, beliefs and attitudes into an ideology, perhaps beginning in the later teens.

Hogan and Mills comment 'At the first level of legal socialization one must learn to live with authority, at the second level one must learn to live with other people, but at the third level, one must learn to live with oneself' (1986: 270). In doing this, from childhood onwards an individual's politico-economic orientation and social alignments influence reactions to many issues. The conservative–radical ideological continuum comes into play, impacts on reactions to rules, law and justice, and underpins divisions among young people and adults. The age factor is not considered in any detail in the role-theoretical view.

School as a bureaucratic organization and as an educational influence plays a major part in transmitting the principles that underlie role relationships to children and adolescents. The developmental trend is from personalizing role relationships to understanding the role-specific nature of such relationships in adolescence. Emler and Hogan argue 'Experience in school profoundly shapes attitudes to authority and bureaucratic relationships' (1981: 312). They associate success in school directly with the development of positive attitudes to authority, and failure with negative attitudes. Success in school indicates the ability to adapt to a bureaucratic system and authority, while failure indicates poor attunement to the demands of the system and authority. Related to this polarity is the fact that a disproportionate number of young criminals come from the ranks of those who failed in school.

Hogan and Mills (1976) suggest that there are three conditions a law should meet in order to be highly effective, conditions represented in the three levels of socialization. Firstly, the lawmakers must be generally regarded as legitimate, credible, concerned with the welfare of people and in authority. Secondly, the law must be seen as promoting the interests of all people in a fair and even manner, not favouring or abusing particular subgroups of people. Thirdly, the law must be in accord with the traditions and values of the people to whom it applies. These conditions lead them to the conclusion that the possibility of using law as an instrument of social reform in the USA (and other countries?) is bleak. This is because politicians do not have the trust of a majority of the people, government (with its public institutions) is widely believed to favour preferred subgroups of people and the economic system is generally seen to be unfair. The dominance of what Hogan and Mills (1976:275) call 'the crass market place mentality of laissez faire economics' where 'little is sacred beyond the profit motive' means there is not a significant set of traditions and values with which a law can be aligned to aid the achievement of social reform. Reform is further constrained by the stress on individualism and societal ambivalence about modes of compliance with law and morality.

Attitudes to law enforcement and crime

Adolescence may be a critical period in the development of attitudes concerning law, crime and the judicial system. On the one hand, important changes in logical reasoning abilities and the capacity for philosophical reflection enable adolescents to adopt ideological systems of beliefs and attitudes (Adelson and O'Neil, 1966) and social attitudes in general are in a formative stage (Niemi, 1973). On the other hand, adolescents are likely to encounter the criminal justice system, either directly or indirectly, through peers, police, courts or other experiences. Such encounters are likely because of the prevalence of delinquent activity among youth, conflicts between youth culture and the laws governing the use of drugs, and the assumption of legal responsibility and potential liability when the adolescent begins to drive.

Youth attitudes towards crime- and law-related matters, however, are not always simply formed. Recent research has indicated that such attitudes tend to be multidimensional. Nelson, Eisenberg and Carroll (1982) investigated the structure of high school students' attitudes relating to crime, law and justice. They wanted to find out if these attitudes formed into clusters which could be clearly defined and differentiated. They gave a group of high school students a battery of items derived from a selection of other scales (e.g. liberalism, just world, authoritarianism and social responsibility). Respondents were required to endorse each item along a four-point agree–disagree scale. Responses were factor analysed to reveal six interpretable factors labelled: retributive responses to criminals; self-attribution of social-legal responsibility; belief in effective versus ineffective law enforcement; law abidance; government by authority versus government by law; and adverse, exploitative orientation to the law.

Furnham and Gunter (1989) have data on a large group of British youth's attitude to the law. They found that whereas 53 per cent of adults (Jowell and Airey, 1984) said that they would obey the law without exception, only 36 per cent of adolescents agreed that they would. Similarly, while 46 per cent of adults said they would occasionally break the law to follow their conscience, nearly two-thirds (64 per cent) of the adolescents claimed they would on occasion break the law. They were then asked, are there any circumstances in which you might break a law to which you were very strongly opposed? Whereas less than a third of adults (30 per cent) thought there might be circumstances where they would break the law, over half (51 per cent) of the adolescents could think of examples. Predictably perhaps, nearly one in three of the adolescents (29 per cent) claimed that they did not know the answer to the question.

They were also asked whether they were in favour of or against the death penalty in various cases. Overall, the adolescent sample were in favour of the death penalty for murder – nearly three-quarters (73 per cent) were in favour of executing terrorist murderers, two-thirds (66 per cent) in favour of the death penalty for general murderers and slightly fewer (62 per cent) in favour of executing those who murdered policemen.

As one may expect, the adolescents in general appeared to be more willing to break the law than adults. Paradoxically, however, they are very conservative in their reactions to murderers.

They were also asked about crime prevention. Most adolescents (61 per cent) held the opinion that stricter policing was the best way to prevent crime. Females (67 per cent) believed this more than males (57 per cent). There was a feeling also that ordinary people could play an important part (63 per cent) in the prevention of crime and maintenance of law and order. Finally, carelessness on the part of individuals in looking after personal belongings was thought to be in no small way to blame for criminal theft (55 per cent). Males (58 per cent) were marginally more likely than females (50 per cent) to believe this. Among young people there is clearly some feeling that the efficiency of law enforcement and personal crime prevention measures contribute to some extent to current levels of crime. But, in a broader social or psychological sense, are criminals a special breed who originate from a certain kind of background?

Furnham and Gunter (1989) asked the adolescent sample whether they agreed or disagreed with each of these statements. First, 'crime is more often the fault of our society than of the criminal'. Second, 'most criminals will never be able to live right no matter how much we do for them'. Third, 'crime is caused by people without morals or standards'.

Although not held by an overwhelming majority, the weight of opinion among young people interviewed in this survey was that crime is caused by people without morals or standards. Agreement with this (37 per cent) was more common than disagreement (28 per cent). Even more prevalent (44 per cent) was the belief that criminals cannot be 'made good', with 29 per cent disagreeing. But the criminal is not himself or herself to blame. In the view of nearly half (48 per cent) the respondents, crime is more often the fault of society than of the criminal. Only 24 per cent disagreed with this statement. There were no sex, age or class differences for any of these opinions.

On the whole, young people felt that the world is a place where criminal elements are not always dealt with effectively. At the same time, however, there were some disparate opinions and differences of opinion among respondents.

Among the opinions held most commonly were that even the guilty have their rights (72 per cent), crime doesn't pay (66 per cent) and discouragement with the law when a smart lawyer gets a criminal free (60 per cent). Males (83 per cent) were keener to see a guilty man getting his rights than were females (69 per cent), while females (75 per cent) were more often of the view that crime doesn't pay than were males (61 per cent).

There was not total belief in the system of justice. Certainly, more (46 per cent) believed that it is rare for the innocent to go to jail than did not (27 per cent), and fewer (28 per cent) agreed that it is impossible for a person in this country to receive a fair trial than those who disagreed (41 per cent). But most young people (58 per cent) felt that the courts do not treat everyone fairly and, equally, more agreed (41 per cent) than disagreed (25 per cent) that it is common for the guilty to go free; also more disagreed (40 per cent) than agreed (35 per cent) that law-breakers are almost always caught and punished. Finally, there were mixed opinions about how useful it is to co-operate with the police since criminals usually aren't effectively punished anyway.

The lack of faith in the justice system to deal effectively with criminals and to allocate punishments to fit the severity of crimes was widely evident. It further emerged that young people in Furnham and Gunter's (1989) survey are largely in favour of strict punishments for serious crimes. Most (66 per cent) endorsed capital punishment for murderers; 18 per cent were against this. Most (62 per cent) were also in favour of severe punishment (e.g. public whipping for rapists and child molesters), while just 16 per cent were opposed. Finally, a majority (61 per cent) supported strict enforcement of all existing laws. Females were more in favour than were males both of capital punishment for murderers (70 per cent versus 65 per cent) and of strict law enforcement generally (65 per cent versus 57 per cent).

The British youth sample were not simply in favour of strict law enforcement, most (69 per cent) also felt that there should be tougher laws against crime in this country. Nine per cent were against tougher laws. According to nearly two out of three (63 per cent), everybody should take part in the development and enforcement of laws for the good of local communities and the country as a whole, while 11 per cent were not keen on this. A weight of opinion (46 per cent) indicated that these young people felt that laws were not enough; 36 per cent were unsure and 18 per cent disagreed. According to 46 per cent, the country also needed strong, courageous and trustworthy leaders in whom people could put their faith, while 21 per cent disagreed and 33 per cent were undecided.

Furnham and Gunter concluded:

> Our sample of young people did not seem to have total faith in the criminal justice system, which was seen to have both merits and faults. This was manifested in a number of conflicting beliefs about standards of justice in this country. For instance, most felt that crime doesn't pay, while at the same time there was widespread disillusionment that smart lawyers can and do get criminals off the hook. Most respondents felt that it is rare for the innocent to go to jail and that fair trials in this country are the rule. But there was a common belief that not everyone is treated fairly in the courts. Many respondents held the opinion that the guilty often go free, but law-breakers are usually caught and punished in the end.
>
> (Furnham and Gunter, 1989: 57)

Conclusion

This chapter has examined the development of young people's understanding of law and justice. What strikes one about the material is emphasis upon cognitions, attitudes and rule-following, often focused upon the general, abstract or hypothetical, and the enormous value placed on autonomous, individual legal and moral reasoning about 'higher' and 'universal' principles. There is very little concern with actual behaviour, legal and illegal; the specific impact of situational factors on such behaviour; levels of obedience to the law among the young; youthful sharing of responsibility for legal and moral actions (or their opposites) with others; reactions against existing law, for example over drugs; legal obligations as reflected in conduct; and with the power of government, institutions, companies, authorities or 'them' to coerce and their use of their power of coercion. The direct influence of very many studies of moral development, often primarily about higher levels of abstract thinking, on studies of legal development is partly responsible for this general outcome. The studies in both fields tend to be at a great distance from the legalities and moralities of everyday life.

People of all ages do not judge and react to others in a uniform way irrespective of their background characteristics. They take account of age, sex, race, social class, voice, possible religious and other characteristics. When children or teenagers judge or react to the actions of others as right or wrong, fair or unfair, just or unjust, their general beliefs about the kinds of people involved will affect these judgements and reactions. They will tend to be favourably disposed towards people who belong to their in-groups and groups which they like or trust, and to be unfavourably disposed to out-groups and groups they dislike or mistrust. Children, teenagers and adults display a marked tendency to be ethnocentric in outlook, and far from tolerant of the whole spectrum of social, racial, political and religious groups present in society. Sections of society do not believe in providing the protection of the law to everyone, in particular deviants, outsiders and nonconformists; or in using the law to create social justice for everyone. Such beliefs can readily be supported by recourse to commonplace just world beliefs that people get what they deserve and deserve what they get. Little is known about the influence of ethnocentrism on legal (and moral) development, including issues of inter-group relations and behaviour.

The arguments of Emler and Hogan (1981), that, firstly, the conservative–radical dimension is important in law and morality and, secondly, legal and moral reasoning cannot be seen as self-enclosed and as obeying cognitive dynamics inherent in development, are convincing. They quote research evidence showing that student conservatives functioning at Kohlberg's conventional Stage 4 can imagine the responses to issues of radicals functioning at postconventional Stage 5. They suggest that, as the views of individuals change over time, there is cognitive movement from the postconventional Stage 5 to the conventional Stage 4 as well as vice versa. The notion that radicals are morally and legally more advanced than conservatives because they are more advanced cognitively is clearly partial because it ignores the significance of political responses to legal and moral issues. Emler and Hogan believe that Kohlberg's developmental distinction between his Stages 4 and 5 'largely reflects a difference in the ideological content of attitudes toward law and justice' (1981: 309). This means that Kohlberg's developmental stages represent preferences for different legal, moral and political positions rather than a cognitive-developmental movement towards a universal ethic stage of morality and justice. It implies that researchers need to be careful about ideological confusions in the study of legal and moral development, and to avoid confounding issues with ideological preferences.

One of the issues which has attracted much attention from developmental researchers has been individual rights and freedoms, especially in the early teen years which are watershed years for thinking about law and government. Associated with this is the matter of the limits of law in the face of these claims. This attention reflects a stress on individualism, often at the expense of the community. The stress on individualism has not been matched by a stress on public rights and freedoms, collective concerns and civic responsibility. Yet ordinary citizens who do not have the financial means to reside in affluent, relatively crime-free locales are likely to be much concerned with safety and security, violence and crime, vandalism and hooliganism, alcohol and drug abuse, effective policing, the uniform and regular administration of the law and such like. Law and order, caring neighbourly relationships, and system fairness to the common people are much more relevant to daily life, and to the upbringing and education of the young, than high levels of abstract thinking about law and morality. The difference between these two types of stress reflects the intellectualistic biases of researchers in the field; their tendency to overvalue abstract thinking; their lack of consideration of the death and destruction caused by powerful people acting from the highest principles; their idealization of morality and justice rooted in autonomous thought; their relative lack of concern with conduct and with deviations from the norms of conventional, non-criminal life.

These biases raise the issue of whether different levels of legal and moral reasoning are really differences in cognitive-linguistic style. There is no evidence that the levels are consistently related to legal and moral behaviour. There are immoral and criminal people who function cognitively at the higher rather than the lower moral levels; people who can talk well without behaving well by conventional standards.

These conclusions indicate some of the complexities associated with legal development. They suggest researchers should be more concerned with individual and group differences in legal development. They also need to become concerned with the role of the mass media in this development. The media are a major source of information and misinformation about law, justice, violence, crime, punishment, the courts and police work. They are certainly not preoccupied with legal constraints and morality as internalized self-control. Their daily exploitation of crime and violence can hardly contribute in a positive way to legal development. But what they contribute to this development is not known. At present we must look forward to a more realistic and reasonably complete account of legal development emerging from future research.

Chapter nine

Social class and stratification

Introduction

Amongst the most noticeable features of society is the existence of human inequalities associated with social differences and the stratification of society. The structures and institutions of society ensure continuing social inequalities and stratification, the sometimes highly unequal status quo, from generation to generation. A number of social mechanisms for generating acceptance or support of inequalities and stratification are routinely presented in analyses of social structure. These include: the demands of the system of political economy; the influence of property and money interests on government and throughout society; coercion by the powerful, the conservative influence of the mass media; people's fear of major change and losing their established way of life, their hopes for a better future (including possible upward mobility), their feelings of powerlessness; the inability of many to imagine an alternative type of society; and the perceived basic or natural legitimacy of inequalities and stratification.

Despite their differences and disagreements, social analysts regard legitimation of social class as important in the maintenance of inequalities and stratification because it promotes their acceptance or support. Legitimation refers to the extremely widespread view that some inequalities in the distribution of resources such as riches, income, power and status, together with accompanying social differences, are justified and desirable. Clearly the specific arguments used to support this view vary among individuals and groups from one time and place to another, as do beliefs about the desirability of different types and patterns of inequality. Research evidence from around the world indicates consistently that a negligible proportion of any nation's populace holds to an egalitarian view though, of course, dissatisfaction with prevailing inequalities and social differences is not uncommon.

During the period of pre-adult development, the inequalities and stratification of the larger society become incorporated in the development of the individual. This applies to the most disadvantaged, poverty-stricken children and adolescents as well as to the offspring of multi-millionaires (Coles, 1977; Coles, 1986). Young people develop beliefs, ideas and concepts (representations) of inequalities, social differences and stratification; that is, of their current social reality. Eventually they become aware that alternative representations are held by different individuals and groups. The development of such a representation is particularly susceptible to influences within the family, community and society. Further, the availability of information and experience to young people is to some extent related to age, race and social class, and is by no means totally dependent on level of cognitive development.

Many adults, including a proportion of parents, teachers, professionals, media personnel and politicians, are concerned primarily with exploiting particular inequalities and social differences, with compelling the young to fit into the kind of society they want maintained. In practice, this means compelling the young to accommodate to complex hierarchically structured social class differences. For some older teenagers, this may well entail immediate disadvantages in terms of income, taxation, vulnerability to unemployment, relatively poor conditions of employment when in work, prejudice against females and minorities, and the intergenerational transfer of public debt and environmental degradation to rising generations. Obviously it is easy for adults to rationalize any actions by the arguments that their own interests are in the best interests of the young or that they do not owe future generations anything. In the upper middle and upper social classes, where advantages are often provided for the young, this sort of rationalization always carries great force because of its association with relative developmental 'advantage', and it is also comprehended by some people in other strata of society.

Many beliefs, ideas and concepts relating to inequalities and stratification appear during childhood and adolescence. They have economic, occupational, political, psychological, racial and social features. They may be based upon rudimentary 'knowledge' of social divisions and limited cognitive ability, especially among younger children. They may be based upon a great deal of information and fairly sophisticated reasoning, particularly among those in their teens. In the pre-adult years, experience is limited by lack of direct exposure to the labour market and adult world of employment. But teenagers enter the adult world familiar with stratification and inequalities. With advancing age, the young become increasingly aware of the unequal, stratified social order and their own place within it. With age, they become increasingly like adults in their construction of social reality.

For instance, Emler and Dickinson (1985) asked middle- and working-class Scottish children (aged 7 to 12 years) to estimate incomes of people in different occupations and make judgements about the fairness of that income. Most children thought differences in income justified but middle-class children made overall higher estimates and perceived a greater spread. Also, compared to the working-class children, middle-class young people possessed a more extensive rationale for inequality and were more committed to it. Middle-class young people also seemed more sensitive to other consequences of income differences. The authors concluded:

> Knowledge specifically concerned with socio-economic stratification is unequally distributed in society and its distribution is related to the socio-economic structure. This knowledge takes the form of 'social representations'; it consists of shared, socially generated and sustained systems of ideas, beliefs and values. Children assimilate most readily those social representations that are most dominant, widespread and important within their community. The current findings, we believe, reflect the fact that social representations of economic inequalities are more detailed, extensive and salient in the middle class. Hence children who are members of that class assimilate these representations more rapidly and thoroughly. The same representations are more 'external' to the working-class milieu and so children in this class have acquired more simplified and tenuously held versions. We take the much more differentiated income estimates, the greater resistance to equality of income, the greater emphasis on income as the differentiating factor in housing, and the greater variety of justification for inequality charac-teristic of the middle-class group to be reflections of this difference. This interpretation does not exclude developments in the structural complexity of children's social knowledge, social representations pos-sess a complexity which limits their accessibility to children. But social representations are also defined by content. Cognitive-developmental principles can tell us something about the sequence in which children acquire knowledge but not everything about the particular knowledge they will acquire. This also depends on its currency and availability in their various social milieux.
>
> (Emler and Dickinson, 1985: 197)

The development of knowledge of stratification and social inequalities has been studied predominantly as an individual achievement, as a part of cognitive development in general. Experiences that challenge ways of thinking about such phenomena or create conflicts in thinking about them are seen by cognitive-development researchers as promoting the develop-ment of a more accurate representation of social reality. There has been relatively little concern among researchers with institutional and other external influences on young people, particularly with attempts to in-fluence directly or to indoctrinate young people. Yet such influences flow from government, political parties, the economic order including commercial advertising, the mass media, schools, churches, parents and relatives. In particular, these socializing agencies are all concerned with legitimating certain kinds of inequalities and hierarchy and with opposing others. Children and adolescents inevitably experience pressure from adults, the media and peers to perceive and evaluate social inequalities, divisions and hierarchies in particular ways. Obviously different sections of society react in different ways to stratification and inequalities. Their members communicate various representations to the young; and they may well emphasize what is regarded as significant information, beliefs and values. They do not communicate value-free, neutral information. Young people who simply accept the conventional representations of society in their own social milieu may not test them against objective reality or may not experience cognitive challenges and conflicts. Stratification and inequalities may be so much a part of their life that such young people absorb them into their version of social reality without any individual cognitive conflict, especially when they are conforming to the norms in their own social milieu. Awareness of other representations of social reality may also fail to be cognitively challenging.

Developmental trends and stage-wise theories

Ideas, images and conceptions of the social structure are assimilated by young people before they leave school and well before they reach adult status (Connell, 1977; Leahy, 1983; Stacey, 1978). This includes awareness of social mobility. In fact, the awareness of socio-economic differences and social class emerges in early life.

Perceptions or recognition of everyday social differences on the basis of cues such as clothes and physical appearance, type of motor car owned, type of housing or accommodation, residential area, type of employment and behavioural style can occur as early as 5 or 6 years. It is commonplace by later childhood. Knowledge of life-style and behavioural correlates of social differences is displayed in later childhood and adolescence. Teenagers become concerned with the ownership of consumer items, the financing of their activities or pastimes and with aspirations to ownership of major items, which they see as significant for their own status and life-style. In this they are often influenced by the prevailing fashions and symbols of the commercial youth culture. With increasing age the young become more like adults in their representations of stratification and social differences, and thus more mature in a conventional way.

Since concepts such as class, status and inequality are complex, it might seem unsurprising if children found them vague, meaningless or confusing, and adolescents had great difficulty with them. But by the time they are 10 years old, children in general are aware conventionally of social differences, status symbols and inequalities (Emler and Dickinson, 1985). Adolescents are familiar with these phenomena, and usually talk about them with ease. The social thinking of children and adolescents may outrun their linguistic abilities; class, status and inegalitarian thinking can occur without the linguistic capacity to express them. This has been brought out in observational and experimental studies of the young which rely to a limited extent on their linguistic abilities. However, most studies of stratification and social inequalities have been based on the use of interviews and questionnaires.

Working in Australia, Connell (1977) described three main stages through which ideas about the class structure pass during the school years. These are:

I   The stage of dramatic contrast (around 5–8 years).

II The stage of concrete realism (around 8–12 years).

III The stage of true class schemes (around 12–16 years).

At each stage, ideas about the class structure depend partly on intellectual capacity, which includes thinking about money, poverty and riches. Communications from the adult world, including television, provide materials for the ideas and thinking of young people. These will include materials dealing with money, finance, banks, crime, education, jobs and careers, social hierarchy, social mobility and inequalities.

In the first stage, Connell found children have no overall conception of the class structure. However, they perceive socio-economic differences which they interpret using a mixture of detail and vagueness. The major feature of their thinking is the use of dramatic contrast – between poor and rich, tiny house and large house, money/gold and complete lack of it, rags and riches, poverty and wealth. The most striking aspect of this is the contrast between poverty and wealth. The prominence of this distinction comes from children's literature, songs, rhymes and films which employ dramatic contrast for impact. At the second stage, Connell found that children construct a rough class scheme by placing an intermediate group between contrasting extremes. They learn much about the concrete details, particularly financial, of the class structure. Their ideas about money, incomes and jobs become more realistic, reflecting the society in which they live. They develop the conception of an occupational hierarchy, though it is only loosely connected with their perception of social class. By the end of this stage children are aware of the competitive standing of many jobs in terms of income and status. At the third stage, class schemas which embrace the whole society make their appearance and reflect the main types of class schema existing among adults. Most of the teenager schemas fall into three categories: (a) classless or one-class schemas which typically express satisfaction with the status quo; (b) dichotomous schemas which commonly involve some hostility to the upper class; and (c) gradation schemas usually without effect. Ideas and notions about education, employment, income, a job hierarchy, residence segregation and privilege are integrated into a true class schema. Teenagers are at ease with the language of class and social differences. They readily see competitive advantages and snobbery in education, employment and other spheres of life. But, in general, they do not develop a firm consciousness of class position or class membership and they do not judge themselves from a class frame of reference. They display a marked tendency to locate themselves in a 'middle-class' position to deny being rich or poor rather than to commit themselves. Given the opportunity, many teenagers shun expression of class membership. Connell concludes that the young are 'subjectively classless in a class society, informed and ignorant at the same time' (1977:151). He believes that money is an important agency of socialization because it symbolizes social relations, in a property-based economic order, that appear as given and independent of the people involved. However, the inevitable participation of the young in the class system is, for Connell, the really powerful educational experience.

Working in the USA, Leahy (1983) proposed a cognitive-developmental model of social class conceptions. The focus of his research was on the rich–poor contrast. His model has three levels of class conceptions. These are:

I   Peripheral-dependent conceptions (around 6–11 years).

II   Psychological or central conceptions (around 11–14 years).

III   Sociocentric conceptions (around 14–17 years).

At the first level, children make distinctions on the basis of the external qualities of the poor and rich such as clothes, possessions, residence and activities. Explanations of stratified group differences refer to the peripheral or observable aspects of poverty and riches. At the second level, stratified groups (classes) are distinguished on the basis of the psychological qualities of their members; for example, intelligence, ability, manners, motivation and effort. Explanations of group differences are now in terms of psychological characteristics. At the third level, teenagers distinguish classes on the basis of differences in life chances and class consciousness. There is growing recognition of competing class interests, and a minority of teenagers recognize the existence of class conflict. Sociocentric conceptions reflect some understanding of relationships within the class structure, though peripheral and central conceptions continue to be used in the teens (and later). Leahy reported an increasing tendency with age for the young to engage in social comparisons and to refer to comparisons in evaluating themselves.

In Leahy's (1983) model the development of understanding of class and inequalities becomes progressively less concrete and less tied to external appearances; it progressively moves to use of differences in personal attributes and then to use of politico-economic factors. This means that with increasing age the young are able to explain inequalities in more diverse ways. The model implies, apparently, that the many teenagers (and adults) who explain inequalities by means of differences in personal attributes are limited in their level of cognitive development. However, the norms and values in some sections of society would promote individualistic explanations and resist politico-economic explanations. In such circumstances social pressure is exerted on the young to conform to particular stances of the elders they are tied to and gain experience from. This is not to suggest that, usually, parents and teachers formally instruct the young about the class system; rather in home, school and community adults communicate informally what they know, accept and reject about the class system. Such circumstances would still allow potentially much scope for young people to utilize their own experiences and intellectual resources.

Some of the foregoing issues are discussed by Jahoda (1984) in his analysis of the development of thinking about socio-economic systems. Since the late 1950s Jahoda has carried out a number of studies of socio-economic development using a variety of research techniques and working with different populations. Jahoda (1984) suggests that there are two main elements involved in this development: (a) general information about the socio-economic world; and (b) knowledge of the norms and rules regulating relationships within the socio-economic world. He interprets the available evidence as indicating that young people receive relatively little explicit teaching about the socio-economic world, and, in so far as they receive teaching, it tends to be limited to conventional information about this world. The result is that young people pick up much additional information informally both at first- and second-hand, and also face the difficult task of getting to know the norms and rules of the system. In this development Jahoda stresses money and money-related matters such as price, selling, banking, interest and profit.

Though Jahoda (1984) does not discount the significance of socially transmitted information, including that from the media, he emphasizes the role of the activities and social interactions of the young in their development. He also refers to the availability of information to the young being partly dependent upon social background. His own research provided evidence that some youngsters can exist comfortably with socio-economic inconsistencies and contradictions, possibly seeking refuge in fantasy. Intellectual problems and conflicts among the young do not necessarily stimulate attempts to resolve them.

Social differences

Children become aware of social differences and inequalities at quite an early age, during the beginning school years. They can perceive and react to differences in appearance, possessions, residence, cars, recreation and jobs. They fairly quickly learn that there is a link between having a job and getting money, probably because of adult comments on the subject. At first, this link appears to be a general idea that the child may apply to an activity regarded as a job, though not all jobs are seen as such. As young people move through primary and secondary school they develop more realistic, conventional ideas about jobs and income, and become able to compare jobs. With advancing age, young people progressively integrate ideas about jobs, incomes, possessions and life-style. In association with this, the young learn that some sorts of people do not interact on equal terms with others. In the development of such ideas, there do not seem to be marked differences between youngsters of different social and racial backgrounds.

Studies in several countries have shown that during the school years there is a substantial increase in the similarity of pre-adult and adult ratings of the status of occupations. Young people begin to assimilate adult values of occupational status in primary school. They also begin to assimilate adult values about inequalities of employment, status, income and possessions. Before they enter secondary school, young people have a crude conception of an occupational hierarchy, though it is only loosely connected with class concepts. They become aware that 'good jobs' have real advantages over other jobs, that they are more desirable. Without having adult experience of the labour market, teenagers see the world of jobs in near-adult terms of competitive access to a hierarchy of occupations. For teenagers, full-time employment is an important symbol of the adult world to which they aspire; and it is a source of money, lack of which is a major teenage concern. The consistent research finding that with age the young become more like adults in socio-occupational thinking is predictable; and suggests that age is, among other things, an index of experience with stratification and inequalities.

While investigating perceptions of stratification in the USA among their sample of 1917 youngsters aged 8–17 years, Simmons and Rosenberg (1971) studied the growth of class consciousness with reference to barriers to equal opportunity. They found that about four out of five young people in school believe that economic, racial and social barriers to equality exist. However, a great majority of youngsters are optimistic about their own prospects while believing others will be handicapped by the stratification system. They found that it is the more disadvantaged youngsters with the poorest prospects who are least aware of the characteristics of the stratification system. It is the well-placed young people who develop the sharpest perceptions of occupational status, social class, poverty and riches, and barriers to equal opportunity. This finding was replicated by Stern and Searing (1976) among samples of American and English adolescents. Simmons and Rosenberg also found, among manual working-class youth, that it is the more personally ambitious rather than the radical who tend to be most class conscious. They concluded that the somewhat unrealistic expectations of working-class adolescents and their lack of comprehension of their deprivation produce a low level of class consciousness and much false consciousness (associated with elevating their family status) which in turn operates to counteract pressures towards working-class action.

Simmons and Rosenberg (1971) interpret their findings in terms of the functionalist theory of stratification. According to this theory, stratification differentials and rewards are necessary to motivate people to train for jobs indispensable to society, and then carry them out. Simmons and Rosenberg suggest the youthful desire for upward mobility depends on a knowledge of the stratification system and optimism about mobility opportunities. Of course, the desire for upward mobility could promote concern with the stratification system.

In Britain, several investigators have reported that awareness of 'social class' and a sense of class membership increase with age (Stacey, 1978; Stern and Searing, 1976). By the end of secondary school almost all teenagers are aware of social classes, and they have acquired some ideas about class relationships. The small minority of teenagers who attend fee-charging boarding schools tend to be more intensely aware of class and are more approving of existing class divisions in Britain than the majority in state schools. Among the latter, a majority do not regard class as important, though they tend to think about society in a hierarchical way. Working-class youth trail behind youth in the higher strata in developing ideas about class. It appears that teenagers in state schools who are sensitive to social barriers are more aware of class and class relationships. On the basis of their cross-national study, Stern and Searing (1976) concluded that upward mobility aspirations intensify alertness to stratification phenomena. As compared with adults, teenagers tend to claim higher social status for themselves than community evaluation would warrant. In fact, adults in Britain (and other western countries) tend to perceive themselves somewhat higher in the social structure than they are actually located.

Inequality in educational provisions and educational attainments is related to patterns of stratification, and is not shaped by the abilities of young people. The school system reflects the stratification system. In functionalist theory, schools are held to provide both basic socialization to fit the young into society and differential socialization to fit them into the stratification system, hence contributing to the efficient functioning of society. In Marxist theory, schools are held to serve the needs of the economically dominant by contributing to the reproduction of a stratified labour force, hence serving the interests of the ruling class. In practice, many people believe that schools should teach the young 'their place in society'. Within schools, social differences and inequalities are accepted as natural and often as desirable (particularly in the more advantaged schools). Goals and ambitions are communicated to youth on the assumption of an unchanging class system. State schooling does not routinely encourage the young to evaluate the class structure and its impact on their lives and future prospects. Schools throughout the education hierarchy contain rebels who reject the means and ends of school. Rebels are most numerous in working-class schools, where they may well create a counter culture associated with the commercial youth market. Some research analysts have argued that family origin is a far more important social influence on the young than schooling, and that schooling itself counts for very little.

Research studies have consistently shown that the vocational expectations of teenagers are associated with their position in the social structure. By the mid-teens they have a reasonable appreciation of the practical implications of their positions within the school system. Their expectations are generally 'realistic' and 'mature' from a labour market perspective. The school system implicitly locates the reason for lack of educational success in the individual. Connell (1977) stresses the idea of (lack of) brains or intelligence as an ego-protecting interpretation of reality by the young who are not among the successful. Connell suggests the educational system can be conceived as a strongly segmented system with different socio-occupational groups linked to different segments of it. The private property system and distribution of income are involved with these links; that is, the educational system in its basic features and mode of operation is a product of class processes.

During the teen years, young people become more aware of conflicting positions on social, economic and political issues. They see private business and trade unions as representing competing interests and as being associated with political parties. They come to connect occupational status with parties and voting behaviour. But some awareness of an association between stratification and party politics does not necessarily produce understanding of a relationship between class interests and party politics, especially in the manual working class; and it does not produce political polarization among the young from a class situation, again especially among the manual working class. It appears that class consciousness and class politics are most developed among the young in the upper social strata.

Uses of stratification information

Teenagers typically value family, domesticity, easy social relationships, personal recognition, natural behaviour and their leisure activities. They tend to dislike etiquette, formality, affectation, postures associated with rank and being socially out of place or discomforted by invidious distinctions. Most of their leisure time is spent in the home. Many experience conflicts between achievement-orientated values of home and/or school and the hedonistic, consumer-orientated youth market. Only a small proportion of teenagers reject adult status, values and society. Most do not want 'responsibility' in an adult sense, but the young are attracted to what are seen as adult 'freedoms' and financial independence. The majority of teenagers desire enjoyment, fun, excitement, and they are not committed to hard work. They moderate their vocational and social aspirations to fit in with circumstances and ongoing concerns, including money. Unemployment is a significant issue for many of the young. Becoming aware and knowledgeable about their world, the young understand that society is stratified and that the stratification system applies to them and their family as well as to others (see Chapters 2 and 4).

Teenage perceptions of stratification and inequalities interact with ideas about jobs, incomes, possessions, consumer patterns and life-styles. Teenagers locate their peers in society by stratification criteria such as voice, dress, family home, possessions and leisure activities. A sizeable proportion prefer the company of socially homogeneous groups; of others like self. One way for the young to deal with the discomfort that may arise from socially heterogeneous situations or unfamiliar encounters is to avoid unnecessary contact across stratification lines. Stern and Searing suggest that teenage Americans have to learn that the country's norm of 'public egalitarianism has definite limits in a hierarchical society' (1976:193).

A significant feature of adolescence is the growth of concern with self-identity, taking in self-image, confidence in relationships, independence, personal aspirations and freedom of choice within their own spheres of activities (Department of Education and Science, 1983). This growth brings out the matter of self-definition in relation to family, peers and the social world. Stratification information facilitates self-definition and interpretation of personal circumstances, though not necessarily in a positive way. Directly or indirectly such information helps the young to adapt to, or plan, their future. In some cases the young are not able to estimate reasonably well what their adult place in society will be. They may not be able to estimate how the stratification system will impact on their life at some future time. Young people realize that at some point adulthood will inevitably be reached. In relation to adults, with advancing age the young have to learn to overcome any feelings of immaturity and inferiority, and to begin to consider themselves as on the same adult footing as others. This may well entail some consideration (and evaluation) of their place, and possibly their future place, in society. This in turn is likely to stimulate social comparisons involving inequalities. Awareness of stratification and inequalities implies awareness of superiority and inferiority which can be expressed in interpersonal encounters. However, for most teenagers social class is not a salient criterion for defining the self. Sex, age, nationality, race, religion, school attendance or its alternative are typically more salient criteria.

Teenagers, like adults, show a strong tendency to hold the view that there is a need for a greatly unequal distribution of incomes and goods, and to be positively evaluative of people with riches. A belief in the proposition that material rewards should be contingent on work and effort is widespread amongst them. A proportion of the young use this belief to explain riches by hard work and great effort. In practice, teenagers tend grossly to underestimate the level of high incomes and the personal fortunes of the rich. Most are not engaged by arguments for a radical change of the class system. Such radicalism as occurs tends to be abstract rather than concrete in content; that is, based on concepts such as equality and democracy and on rejection of bourgeois values. Among teenagers, there is more concern with improving one's standards of living without disturbing the system a great deal. Connell (1977) stresses that the concerns of teenagers are mainly personal; that they have developed a commitment to private goals and fulfilments rather than community and national ones.

The situation of the very rich young in the highest social strata is completely different. Family assets and money create a particular functional relationship with the social world for the young as well as their parents. This, among other things, results in much money-based control over life and its experiences together with money-based opportunities for chosen experiences. From the perspective of the common people, among rich young people there is a certain level of functional incompetence because there is a limited need to function in an ordinary competent way. Servants, tradespersons, professional specialists and therapists are always on tap. Parents may prevent their young from doing ordinary things which to them are socially unacceptable, while they encourage the right behaviour, stylishness, manners, grace and charm. The riches and status of the family overshadow any achievements of the young, while there are very high demands for adult success. In the upper-class great 'success' is the norm not the exception. The normality of ordinary or average success is totally unacceptable. The offspring of the very rich gain awareness of their family's upper-class position and an associated class outlook including appropriate politico-economic beliefs and values. They may well regard themselves as deserving what they have and the privileges which go with it, including special consideration from social subordinates. Some researchers have referred to them acquiring a sense of entitlement. The disadvantage for teenage rebels, if they do not have the capacity eventually to change their way of life, is that they may become prisoners or victims of their class and its riches.

Conclusion

Taking the whole social structure, a small minority of teenagers have a firm consciousness of their own class position or strong feelings of class allegiance; that is, not only consciousness of stratification but also a sense of class interests and opposition or hostility towards other classes. Though there exist associations between family socio-economic status and politico-economic beliefs, the young (outside the upper class) do not usually interpret their own interests from a class position. There is a tendency among teenagers to elevate the status of their family, usually by claiming to be middle class (though their family has no significant income-earning assets and is totally dependent on paid employment or welfare income). Often the claim to be middle class is a claim to be placed in the middling strata of the socio-occupational structure, to be neither rich nor poor, rather than a claim to be middle class with reference to income-earning assets, occupation and life-style. Teenagers who regard themselves as working class tend to be politically to the left and hold left-leaning views about the economic system, business, welfare, trade unions, treatment of workers by employers and the government's role in the economy.

There are pockets of heightened class awareness and of class consciousness that seem to have some basis in the stratification system and economic events. At least three such pockets exist: (a) the youth of the upper middle and upper classes (who typically go to expensive private schools); (b) teenagers who anticipate meeting social barriers in life, particularly those with upward mobility aspirations; and (c) those in families which experience financial upheaval including bankruptcy or prolonged unemployment. However, a most striking feature of pre-adult development within the stratification system is that the young, outside the highest social strata, develop an awareness of the system and its inequalities without developing a firm consciousness of class membership. Amongst teenagers, there are definite socio-economic differences in outlook on political and economic issues, including in beliefs about democracy where there is least support for democratic norms in the higher social strata. But there is great diversity of outlook among teenagers in the working class and great homogeneity of outlook among the young in the upper class. Differences and divisions within the working class clearly help to prevent the organization of united working-class opposition to the existing social order. Whereas greater homogeneity in the upper reaches of society contributes to the formation of a united upper-class defence of the social order.

Chapter ten

Conclusion

Introduction

This book has been concerned with young people's understanding of society. Compared to psychological research on children's and adults' understanding of the physical world, their understanding of the social world has been relatively neglected. Hence one finds in many schools teaching about chemistry, mathematics and physics being given more attention and certainly more prestige than other traditional disciplines like history or the unhappily named social studies that deals with how societies operate.

This is not to suggest that an understanding of the physical world is unimportant or irrelevant. Rather it is to suggest that young people would benefit from explicit, comprehensive instruction in many of the topics covered in this text. The reasons for this are manifold:

Many studies have shown the lamentable state of young people's knowledge on clearly important issues like economics, law and politics. Some appear to be, and often remain, in ignorance of some of the fundamental processes governing western, capitalist societies.

Many young people have full-time jobs, vote and may even be called upon to do jury service. The consequences of their ignorance may have serious effects on themselves or their society if they misunderstand, misuse or abuse rules, institutions or processes designed to protect their rights.

Ignorance may engender apathy and it could well be that young people may not appreciate the importance of, or indeed necessity for, institutions which have arisen to protect their rights.

The cost of ignorance in terms of health, marriage break-up, lack of management skills, under-employment, etc., might be considerably higher than the relatively low costs of education.

Civic education or explicit education about various aspects of society is fraught with difficulty. For some it has overtones of propagandist indoctrination associated with right-wing regimes. For others it is simply too 'soft', too trivial compared to acquiring an understanding of mathematics, physics or even geography. The major problem associated with formal education in economics, religion, the law and marriage is that social facts are difficult to disentangle from social values. In other words, some people argue that knowledge about the social world cannot be imparted in an acceptable manner, and educationalists should not impose, transmit or advocate their personal socio-political value system to young people because that is not their job. Another major problem is the clash among different sections of society; for example Protestant and Catholic in Northern Ireland, Islamic and Jewish in other countries, atheist and fundamentalist.

This argument about educating young people in how society works begs the question however as to how and when young people gain knowledge. As has been pointed out in each chapter, young people gain knowledge about society not only through formal schooling, but through personal experience in the family, with their friends and through the media. Furthermore they are clearly able to assimilate and accommodate different types of information at different stages of their cognitive development.

Any debate as to the wisdom, necessity or benefits of education aimed at educating young people about society should first consider:

the optimal time (in terms of average developmental phases) for the imparting of facts, figures and available values;

other sources of information that young people have which may contradict, supplement or complement any formal education;

the optimal way in which to explain, describe and evaluate information about society;

the value-laden nature and implications of providing particular information in a certain way.

Interestingly, it appears that our view of young people is probably conditioned by the economic conditions we find ourselves in. Thus, Enright *et al* (1987) found that in times of economic depression theories of adolescence emerge that portray teenagers as immature, psychologically unstable and in need of prolonged education, while in wartime the psychological competence of youth is emphasized. Clearly debate concerning educating people about the workings of society is partly of the function of socio-economic conditions prevailing at the time.

The structure of social attitudes to society

In each chapter we have examined young people's attitudes to various topics like marriage, religion, law and class. Their actual attitudes are of particular interest because they reflect, to some extent, their knowledge and they also potentially influence their behaviour. But two related questions are of particular interest regarding young people's attitudes: firstly, what are the basic dimensions underlying their attitudes to a particular issue, say marriage? And, secondly, what is the relationship between their attitudes to different but related topics, say politics and economics?

Certainly there is fairly extensive work among adults that may go some way to answering both of these questions. A great deal of work has been done on the structure of social attitudes which has been concerned either with the underlying dimensions of the attitudes to a particular issue or with the basic structure of all social attitudes. As an example of the former one might consider the work of Ekehammar and Sidanius (1982), who found evidence of five stable dimensions underlying Swedish young people's political attitudes, or Furnham's (1982a) work on the underlying perceptions of the causes of unemployment. Nearly every researcher interested in young people's attitudes to a specific topic has, through statistical techniques like cluster- or factor-analysis or multi-dimensional scaling, attempted to find underlying basic dimensions. However, these dimensions tend to be specific to both the particular attitudinal question-naire used and the topic examined. Hence it is very difficult to compare dimensional solutions.

Others have attempted to look at the basic structure of all social attitudes. Thus, Eysenck (1951) has proposed two basic dimensions underlying social attitudes: radical–conservative; tough–tender minded. This yields four quadrants and, according to Eysenck, all social attitudes can be economically and validly classified by this system. Although there has been extensive replicative work on this 'system', it is true that not all agree with this two-dimensional classification, believing it either too simple (i.e. there are other basic dimensions as well) or in fact wrong (the dimensions as specified by Eysenck are in fact not orthogonal).

Most of the work on the structure of social attitudes has, however, been done on adults and it is not certain whether the same analyses done on young people would yield comparable results. It may be that similar patterns do emerge but that they are less reliable because of the fact that young people's attitudes are more capricious and less fixed. On the other hand, a rather different structure might emerge for young people which changes over time into a rather different adult pattern.

More important perhaps than a robust and general dimensional struc-ture is a theory underlying or explaining that structure. One-off studies on the structure of social attitudes can be the worst kind of dustbowl empiri-cism unless the study is theoretically driven or programmatic. Most of all it is important to explain the aetiology and development of 'attitudinal types' as well as explaining the consequences of those attitudes, their stability over time or the various psychological functions that they reflect and fulfil.

The second major question concerns the extent to which attitudes predict or relate to social behaviour. Most people interested in social attitudes are interested in predicting and changing behaviour but for many there is the naive assumption that attitudes predict behaviour. That is, if we can measure a person's attitude to contraception, a political party's creed, or religion, then we can accurately infer their behaviour with respect to contraceptives, their voting habits or their praying, church going, etc. The answer, as many people have found, is that overall attitudes are a fairly poor predictor of subsequent behaviour and there are many obvious reasons for this. Consider firstly the *level of specificity* at which researchers usually measure attitudes and behaviour. Frequently, attitudes are measured at a very general abstract level and behaviour at a highly specific level. The more the two are in alignment, the better the one predicts the other. Secondly, there is the problem of *single versus multiple act* measurement. If people are interested in attitudes to men or to women, it is better to look at a series of possible behaviours associated with these. Attitudes are much better predictors when a whole series of behaviours (multiple acts) are taken into account. 'One-shot' measures of behaviour do not give much information about the relationships between attitudes and behaviour. Thirdly, *situational* factors may strongly influence attitudes as well as behaviours. Where situational pressures are strong, such as at the scene of an accident or in a religious building, people of widely different attitudes may act in a similar way. Fourthly, it is possible that a given behaviour might relate to a whole *range of attitudes*. For instance, consider predicting how likely people are to help in accidents, specifically how likely to help a black child knocked over by a motor cyclist. A person might be unfavourably disposed to black people, very positive about children and very strongly against motor cyclists. It is difficult to know which of these attitudes would best predict behaviour.

Other factors, too, mediate between attitudes and behaviour. However, these factors are known and appear to have a systematic relationship. Thus, rather than despair it may be possible to show a strong relationship depending on how one measures both attitudes and behaviour. For instance, Ajzen and Fishbein have concluded from their extensive research that 'A person's attitude has a consistently strong relation with his or her behaviour when it is directed at the same target and when it involves the same action' (Ajzen and Fishbein, 1977: 912).

Of course changing attitudes and beliefs beg the question as to where they come from. The question concerns the origins of social attitudes – where they come from and, to a lesser extent, how they are maintained. How is it that some people are in favour of nuclear disarmament, others against it, while still others do not seem to have an opinion either way? Are these attitudes a result of personality characteristics (authoritarian personalities tend to be against nuclear disarmament); upbringing, education, or social class (working-class, less well-educated conservative people are less likely to approve of disarmament); exposure to or choice of media (tabloid more than quality newspaper readers are likely to be against disarmament); or some other factor? Three important issues mean that the answer to this question is far from straightforward. First of all, factors that lead to the adoption of an attitude often differ from those which maintain it. Secondly, each set or group of attitudes may be maintained by different factors. Thus, personality factors may relate to racial attitudes, while social class factors relate to attitudes towards health. Thirdly, these different factors are themselves interrelated and confounded, and hence are difficult to tease apart.

It is the custom in some surveys to break the respondents down by age, sex and class because these factors are thought to represent major determinants of social attitudes. There is, however, considerable doubt as to whether these three classic, but frequently insensitive demographic variables are the major or only correlates of attitudes. Recent work on psychographic or life-style determinants suggest that there may well be many other and more sensitive determinants of young people's social attitudes.

Finally, many organizations are interested in measuring attitudes, often either because they wish to influence how young people think or because those attitudes provide indications of how young people behave. Once again this is a complicated issue and there are a number of theoretical approaches to attitude change – learning theory, social judgement theory, consistency theory, functional theories and so on. Some of the researchers interested in attitude change and communication focus on the characteristics of the *communicator* who is trying to encourage people to change their opinions. Other researchers have focused on the characteristics of the *communication* (message and appeal); still others on the characteristics of the *recipients* (i.e. persuasibility) and others on the frequency of exposure. We already know something of which factors lead to attitude change under which circumstances and with which group. Indeed, there is a whole commercial industry built on the study of these factors. But what emerges from all this work is that seemingly straightforward and simple questions often have rather complicated answers.

What determines the extent of young people's knowledge

It has been quite clear from the previous chapters that the extent of knowledge that young people have about the society in which they live is highly variable. Whereas some young people appear very well informed about the nature and workings of the major institutions of society, others are relatively ignorant. Yet what is more commonly the case is the phenomenon where young people are very well informed about some aspects of society, say religion, but extremely ignorant about other areas like class. This of course begs the question as to the determinants of young people's attitudes and knowledge. Piaget proposed a format for development:

Development = Physical maturation + Experience with the physical environment + Social Experience + Equilibration.

Essentially the possible factors that determine the extent and type of knowledge young people have of society are threefold: genetic, primary socialization factors and secondary socialization factors.

Genetic determinants of attitudes, knowledge and interests certainly attract considerable controversy. For some people it is as scientifically improbable as it is morally repugnant that people 'inherit' social beliefs, while for others it is completely self-evident that, just as genetic, factors determine abilities, preferences and traits, so they determine social knowledge. According to Neale, Rushton and Fulker (1986) twin studies have demonstrated heritabilities of about 50 per cent on pencil-and-paper tests of aggression, altruism, anxiety, dominance, extraversion, intelligence, locus of control, political attitudes, sexuality, values and vocational interests. Recent work in Great Britain and North America has confirmed these findings which suggest to some analysts that to a significant degree social beliefs and attitudes are inherited.

More work has however gone into the primary socialization factors – such as parents' education, class and beliefs – that may affect young people's beliefs and understanding. Results from numerous studies are inevitably equivocal because they do not demonstrate consistent effects of parental education, class, etc. However, this is to be expected for at least four reasons. Firstly, depending on the beliefs and knowledge one is trying to predict, it is not surprising that primary socialization factors operate in different ways. Thus, for instance, parents may powerfully influence religious and sexual knowledge but not political and economic understanding. Secondly, primary socialization factors interact with numerous other factors and unless these are known or specified, it is difficult to comprehend the effect of the former factors. Thirdly, the way these factors are measured differs from study to study and country to country, and comparisons are highly problematic. Finally, it may well be that primary socialization factors influence young people's understanding at some ages much more than others. For instance parents' views, lifestyles and knowledge may closely relate to the understanding of their children from say 8–12 years, but not so closely thereafter.

Finally, secondary socialization factors influence young people's beliefs and understanding. These include schooling, the mass media and organizations that recruit young people. The evidence that these secondary socialization factors play an extremely important role in shaping the way young people perceive the world is legion, as all chapters have attested.

Two important questions remain to be answered concerning the major determinants of young people's knowledge and understanding of society. The first is, which of these factors is most important – that is, are primary socializing factors more important than secondary? Indeed, how are these factors related? Some will agree that genetic factors 'drive' or determine the others, while other theorists would place most stress on the role of institutions in shaping young people's understanding.

Secondly, it may be that these different factors come into play at different times. That is, at different ages these various factors may have quite different impacts. For instance, genetic factors might have more influence early in the child's life and secondary socialization factors later.

The answer to either of these important questions is both complex and yet fundamental. Glib simplistic answers will not do and considerable research needs to be done to answer them.

The growth of understanding: stage-wise theories

The idea that human development occurs through a number of specifiable and prescribed and sequential stages or phases is a popular lay and academic view. Both Freud and Piaget conceived their ideas within such a framework, which suggested that development consists of a number of clearly defined stages through which the child has to pass in sequence because the attainment of one stage is dependent on the completion of the previous one.

Within each chapter examined in this book there have been attempts to describe various stages in the development of full understanding of certain concepts. Frequently rather different stage-wise models compete in the description of a phenomena. Yet there are a number of characteristics common to all stage-wise theories:

A stage is a structured whole in a state of equilibrium.

Each stage derives from the previous stage, incorporates but transforms the previous one but prepares for the next.

Stages follow in an invariant sequence.

Stages are universal to all humans at all times in all countries.

Each stage has a stage from coming-into-being, to being.

All stage-wise theories appear to have a number of implicit assumptions: that the sequence of development is fixed, that there is an ideal end-of-state towards which the child and adolescent inevitably progresses and that some behaviours are sufficiently different from previous abilities that we can identify a child or adolescent as being in or out of a stage. Non-stage theories do not see people progressing inevitably to a single final stage since environmental forces are given more power to create a diversity of developmental responses. At the one end of the stage–non-stage continuum is the view that most of a young person's time is spent in one of several specific stages with short, relatively abrupt transitions between stages. As the length of time spent in a stage is perceived to be shortened and the time in transition is lengthened, one moves along the continuum until all the time is seen as spent in transition, and development is seen as continuous and non-stage. Since a non-stage theory does not necessarily dictate any specific end state or single developmental sequence, the study of individual differences assumes more importance.

However, rather than portray the stage–non-stage approach to development as another manifestation of the famous heredity–environment, nature–nurture maturation learning debate, most would argue that this is a false dichotomy and a non-issue. Most researchers would be interactionists, at an intermediate point on the extreme or strict stage vs. non-stage (or process) approach. A second assumption that most would agree with is that the young play an active part in their own development. That is, young people construct an interpretation of the information that they selectively attend to, based on their previous experience, maturation and indeed momentary needs. The moderate novelty principle applies here which states that young people attend to and learn most from events that are mildly discrepant from (as opposed to very different from or identical to) their current level of conceptions about the social world.

The socialization of understanding

Late childhood and adolescence has been portrayed in many ways: a period of turbulence, doubt, growing awareness, liberation, experimentation, etc. Essentially adolescence is a period of adaptations and adjustments. These include:

adjusting to a new body image, that of a sexually mature adult;

adapting to increased cognitive powers, intellectual abilities and new powers of awareness;

adjusting to increased cognitive demands at school, particularly for abstract thought;

expanding verbal repertoire to acquire the relevant language skills for relating to more complex problems and tasks;

developing a personal sense of identity, recognizing their own uniqueness;

establishing adult vocational goals and a realistic plan as to how to achieve them;

establishing emotional and psychological independence from parents;

developing stable, happy and productive sexual and peer relationships;

managing one's own sexuality including incorporating sex-role concepts into the self-concept;

adopting an integrated functional value or moral system that can be articulated, which guides behaviour;

developing increased impulse control and reduced aggression.

Many of these adaptations involve developing a view about and an understanding of the workings of society. The chapters of this book have attempted to define and describe some of the most important facets of this understanding that young people have to develop. Studies reported in these chapters have been inspired by widely different theoretical perspectives. Miller (1989) has suggested that there are at least six major theoretical traditions in developmental psychology: Piagetian cognitive-stage theory; Freudian and neo-Freudian psychoanalytic theory; social-learning theory; information-processing theory; ethological theory; and, finally, perceptive-development theory. Each has informed research into young people's understanding of society, though it is probably time to say that stage-wise, social-learning and information-processing theories have done most. Each has its shortcomings and limitations but they also share weaknesses in common: a general failure to include all relevant psychological (and non-psychological) influences, low ecological validity for many of the tests and a poor ability to *explain* the course of development that has been described.

But it is important that research in the area of young people's understanding of society is indeed theory driven. A good theory in this area recognizes the central role of cognition in development; provides a way of integrating facts; should be wide ranging; and should recognize that to a great extent young people teach themselves. Most importantly, any description of how young people come to understand must provide an adequate account of the mechanism of development. Further, the social, in social cognition, should not be underplayed, ignored or downgraded as in the past. Knowledge of the social world comes from social experience.

References

Adelson, J. and O'Neil, R. (1966). Growth of political ideas in adolescence: The sense of community. *Journal of Personality and Social Psychology*, 4, 295–306.

Adelson, J., Green, B. and O'Neil, R. (1969). Growth of the idea of law in adolescence. *Developmental Psychology*, 1, 327–32.

Ajzen, I. and Fishbein, M. (1977). Attitude–behaviour relations: A theoretical analysis and review of empirical research. *Psychological Bulletin*, 84, 888–918.

Alhibai, Y. (1987). The child racists. *New Society*, 4 December, 13–15.

Almond, G. and Verba, S. (1973). *The Civic Culture: Political Attitudes and Democracy in Five Nations*. Princeton: Princeton University Press.

Archer, J. and Lloyd, B. (1985). *Sex and Gender*. Cambridge: Cambridge University Press.

Bagley, C. and Verma, G. (1973). Inter-ethnic attitudes and behaviour in British multi-racial schools. In L. C. Bagley and G. Verma (eds) *Race and Education Across Cultures*. London: Heinemann.

Bagley, C., Wilson, G. and Boshier, R. (1970). The conservatism scale: A factor-structure comparison of English, Dutch and New Zealand samples. *Journal of Social Psychology*, 81, 267–8.

Banks, M. and Jackson, P. (1982). Unemployment and risk of minor psychiatric disorder in young people: Cross-sectional and longitudinal evidence. *Psychological Medicine*, 12, 789–98.

Banks, M. and Ullah, P. (1987). Political attitudes and voting among unemployed and employed youth. *Journal of Adolescence*, 10, 201–16.

Barratt, D. (1986). *Media Sociology*. London: Tavistock.

Beaglehole, E. (1932). *Property: A Study of Social Psychology*. New York: Macmillan.

Bem, S. (1981). Gender schema theory: A cognitive account of sex typing. *Psychological Review*, 88, 354–69.

Berger, P. L. and Luckmann, T. (1967). *The Social Construction of Reality*. Harmondsworth: Penguin.

Bernstein, B. (1977). *Class, Codes and Control*, Vol. 3. London: Routledge & Kegan Paul.

Berryman, J. W. (1985). Children's spirituality and religious language. *British Journal of Religious Education*, 7, 120–27.

References

Berti, A. (1988). The development of political understanding in children between 6–15 years old. *Human Relations*, 41, 437–46.

Berti, A. and Bombi, A. (1979). Where does money come from? *Archivio di Psycologia*, 40, 53–77.

Berti, A. and Bombi, A. (1981). The development of the concept of money and its value: A longitudinal study. *Child Development*, 52, 1179–82.

Berti, A., Bombi, A. and de Bein, R. (1986). The development of economic notions: Single sequence and separate acquisitions. *Journal of Economic Psychology*, 7, 415–24.

Berti, A., Bombi, A. and Lis, A (1982). The child's conception about means of production and their owners. *European Journal of Social Psychology*, 12, 221–39.

Black, A. W. (1978). Religious socialisation. In F. J. Hunt (ed.) *Socialisation in Australia*. Melbourne: Australia International Press.

Black, J. (1976). Issues, problems and pitfalls in assessing sex differences. *Merrill-Palmer Quarterly*, 22, 283–308.

Blaikie, N. W. H. (1978). Religious groups and world views. In F. W. Hunt (ed.) *Socialisation in Australia*. Melbourne: Australia International Press.

Black, J. (1976). Issues, problems and pitfalls in assessing sex differences. *Merrill-Palmer Quarterly*, 22, 283–308.

Blumler, J. (1974). Does mass political ignorance matter? *Teaching Politics*, 3, 59–65.

Borgen, W. and Young, R. (1982). Career perceptions of children and adolescents. *Journal of Vocational Behaviour*, 21, 37–49.

Borus, M. (1982). Willingness to work among youth. *Journal of Human Resources*, 17, 581–93.

Bowles, A. and Gintis, H. (1976). *Schooling in Capitalist America*. New York: Basic Books.

Brand, C. (1981). Personality and political attitudes. In R. Lynn (ed.) *Dimensions of Personality*. Oxford: Pergamon.

Breakwell, G. and Fife-Schaw, C. (1987). Young people's attitudes toward new technology: Source and structure. In J. Lewko (ed.) *How Children and Adolescents View the World of Work*. San Francisco: Jossey-Bass, pp.51–67.

Brown, L. and Lalljee, M. (1981). Young persons' conceptions of criminal events. *Journal of Moral Education*, 10, 105–12.

Bruner, J. and Goodman, C. (1947). Value and need as organising factors in perception. *Journal of Abnormal and Social Psychology*, 42, 33–42.

Bruner, J. and Haste, H. (eds) (1987). *Making Sense: The Child's Construction of the World*. London: Methuen.

Burris, V. (1983). Stages in the development of economic concepts. *Human Relations*, 9, 791–812.

Capps, D. (1984). Erickson's life-cycle theory: Religious dimensions. *Religious Studies Review*, 10, 120–27.

Cavalli-Sforza, L., Feldman, H., Cher, K. and Dombusch, S. (1982). Theory and observation in cultural transmission. *Science*, 218, 19–27.

Cherry, N. and Gear, N. (1987). Young people's perceptions of their vocational guidance needs: I. priorities and pre-occupations. *British Journal of Guidance and Counselling*, 15, 59–73.

Cochrane, R. and Billig, M. (1982). Extremism of the culture. *New Society*, 7 May, 291–3.

Coles, R. (1977). *Children of Crisis*, Vol. 5. Boston: Little Brown.

Coles, R.W. (1986). *The Political Life of Children*. Boston: Atlantic Monthly Press.

Collins, W. A. and Korac, N. (1982). Recent progress in the study of effects of television viewing on social development. *International Journal of Behavioral Development*, 5, 171–93.

Connell, R. (1971). *The Child's Construction of Politics*. Carlton: Melbourne University Press.

Connell, R. W. (1977). *Ruling Class, Ruling Culture*. Melbourne: Cambridge University Press.

Connell, R. W., Ashenden, D. J., Kessler, S. and Dowsett, G. W. (1982). *Making the Difference: Schools, Families and Social Division*. Sydney: Allen & Unwin.

Corsaro, W. (1979). Friendship in nursery school. In S. Asher and J. Gottman (eds) *The Development of Friendship*. New York: Cambridge University Press.

Cummings, S. and Taebel, V. (1978). The economic socialization of children: A neo-Marxist analysis. *Social Problems*, 26, 198–210.

Dahlin, B. (1988). Conceptions of religion among Swedish teenagers: A phenomenographical study. *Religious Education*, 83, 611–21.

Damon, W. (1977). *The Social World of the Child*. San Francisco: Jossey-Bass.

Danziger, K. (1958). Children's earliest conception of economic relationships. *Journal of Social Psychology*, 47, 231–40.

Darcy, J. (1978). Education about unemployment: A reflective element. *Oxford Review of Education*, 4, 289–94.

Davey, A. (1983). *Learning to be Prejudiced*. London: Arnold.

Davey, A. G. and Mullin, P. N. (1980). Ethnic identification and preference of British primary school children. *Journal of Child Psychology and Psychiatry*, 21, 241–54.

Davey, A. G. and Mullin, P. N. (1982). Inter-ethnic friendship in British primary schools. *Educational Research*, 24, 83–92.

Davis, K. and Taylor, T. (1979). *Kids and Cash: Solving a Parent's Dilemma*. La Jolla: Oak Tree.

Dawson, J. (1975). Socio-economic differences in size – Judgements of discs and coins by Chinese primary VI children in Hong Kong. *Perceptual and Motor Skills*, 41, 107–10.

Dayton, C. (1981). The young person's job search: Insights from a study. *Journal of Counselling Psychology*, 28, 321–33.

Dearden, J. (1974). Sex-linked differences of political behaviour: An investigation of their possible innate origins. *Social Science Information*, 43, 19–45.

Dennis, J. and McCrone, D. (1970). The adult development of political party identification in Western democracies. *Comparative Political Studies*, 3, 243–63.

Department of Education and Science (1983). *Young People in the 80s*. London: H. M. S. O.

De Vogler, K. and Ebersole, P. (1983). Young adolescents' meaning in life. *Psychological Reports*, 52, 427–31.

Dobson, C. (1980). Sources of sixth form stress. *Journal of Adolescence*, 3, 65–75.

References

Doring, A. (1984). Beliefs about the employed and unemployed held by senior high school students in Queensland. *Australian Journal of Education*, 28, 78–88.

Dowse, R. and Hughes, J. (1971). Girls, boys and politics. *British Journal of Sociology*, 22, 53–7.

Dunphy, D. C. (1978). Peer group socialisation. In F. J. Hunt (ed.) *Socialisation in Australia*. Melbourne: Australian International Press.

Durkin, K. (1985). *Television, Sex Roles and Children*. Milton Keynes: Open University Press.

Ekehammar, B. (1985). Sex differences in socio-political attitudes revisited. *Educational Studies*, 11, 3–9.

Ekehammar, B. and Sidanius, J. (1979). Political perception dimensions based on negative similarities. *Perceptual and Motor Skills*, 49, 19–26.

Ekehammar, B. and Sidanius, J. (1982). Sex differences in socio-political attitudes: A replication and extension. *British Journal of Social Psychology*, 21, 249–58.

Elkind, D. (1964). Age changes in the meaning of religious identity. *Review of Religious Research*, 5, 36–40.

Elkind, D. (1970). The origins of religion in the child. *Review of Religious Research*, 12, 35–42.

Emler, N. and Dickinson, J. (1985). Children's representation of economic inequalities: The effects of social class. *British Journal of Developmental Psychology*, 3, 191–8.

Emler, N. and Hogan, R. (1981). Developing attitudes to law and justice: An integrative review. In S. S. Brehom and F. X. Gibbons (eds) *Developmental Social Psychology*. New York: Oxford University Press.

Enright, R., Levy, V., Harris, D. and Lapsley, D. (1987). Do economic conditions influence how theorists view adolescents? *Journal of Youth and Adolescence*, 16, 541–59.

Evans, G. and Poole, M. (1987). Adolescent concerns: A classification for life skill areas. *Australian Journal of Education*, 31, 55–72.

Eysenck, H. (1951). Primary social attitudes as related to social class and political party. *British Journal of Sociology*, 11, 198–209.

Eysenck, H. (1978). *Psychology is about People*. Harmondsworth: Penguin.

Falchikov, N. (1986). Images of adolescence: An investigation into the accuracy of the image of adolescence constructed by British newspapers. *Journal of Adolescence*, 9, 167–80.

Farrington, D., Gallagher, B., Morley, L., St Ledger, R. and West, D. (1986). Unemployment, school leaving and crime. *British Journal of Criminology*, 26, 335–56.

Faulkner, C. W. (1980). Religious socialization. In D. H. Smith (ed.) *Participation in Social and Political Activities*. San Francisco: Jossey-Bass.

Feagin, H. (1972). Poverty: We still believe that God helps them who help themselves. *Psychology Today*, 6, 101–29.

Feather, N. (1974). Explanations of poverty in Australian and American samples: The person, society and fate? *Australian Journal of Psychology*, 26, 119–26.

Feather, N. (1977). Generation and sex differences in conservatism. *Australian Psychologist*, 12, 76–82.

Feather, N. (1983). Causal attributions and beliefs about work and unemployment among adolescents in State and Independent Secondary Schools. *Australian Journal of Psychology*, 35, 211–32.

Figueroa, P. M. E. and Swart, L. T. (1986). Teachers' and pupils' racist and ethnocentric frames of reference: A case study. *New Community*, 13, 40–51.

Flanagan, J. (1973). The first 15 years of project TALENT: Implications for career guidance. *Vocational Guidance Quarterly*, 22, 8–14.

Forliti, J. and Benson, P. (1986). Young adolescents: A national study. *Religious Education*, 81, 199–224.

Fowler, J. 1983). Stages of faith. *Psychology Today*, November, 56–62.

Fox, K. (1978). What children bring to school: The beginnings of economic education. *Social Education*, 10, 478–81.

Francis, L. (1979). The child's attitude towards religion: A review of research. *Educational Research*, 21, 103–8.

Francis, L. (1987). The decline in attitudes towards religion among 8–15 year-olds. *Educational Studies*, 13, 125–34.

Freud, S. (1910). Leonardo da Vinci and a memory of his childhood. *Standard Edition of the Complete Psychological Works of Sigmund Freud*, vol. 11. London: Hogarth Press and the Institute of Psycho-Analysis.

Freud, S. (1913). Totem and taboo. *S.E.*, vol. 13.

Furby, L. (1978a). Possession in humans: An exploratory study of its meaning and motivation. *Social Behaviour and Personality*, 6, 49–65.

Furby, L. (1978b). Possessions: Toward a theory of their meaning and function throughout the life cycle. In P. Baltes (ed.) *Life-span Development and Behaviour*, Vol. 1. New York: Academic Press.

Furby, L. (1978c). Sharing: Decisions and moral judgements about letting others use one's possessions. *Psychological Reports*, 43, 595–609.

Furby, L. (1979). Inequalities in personal possessions: Explanations for and judgements about unequal distribution. *Human Development*, 22, 180–202.

Furby, L. (1980a). Collective possession and ownership: A study of its judged feasibility and desirability. *Social Behaviour and Personality*, 8, 165–84.

Furby, L. (1980b). The origins and early development of possessive behaviour. *Political Psychology*, 2, 30–42.

Furnham, A. (1982a). The perception of poverty among adolescents. *Journal of Adolescence*, 5, 135–47.

Furnham, A. (1982b). Why are the poor always with us? Explanations of poverty in Britain. *British Journal of Social Psychology*, 21, 311–22.

Furnham, A. (1984a). Getting a job – school leavers' perceptions of employment prospects. *British Journal of Educational Psychology*, 54, 293–305.

Furnham, A. (1984b). The protestant ethic: A review of the literature. *Journal of Adolescence*, 8, 109–24.

Furnham, A. (1985a). Adolescents' socio-political attitudes: A study of sex and national differences. *Political Psychology*, 6, 621–36.

Furnham, A. (1985b). Youth unemployment: A review of the literature. *Journal of Adolescence*, 5, 109–24.

Furnham, A. (1986). The structure of economic beliefs. *Personality and Individual Differences*, 8, 253–60.

References

Furnham, A. (1987a). School children's perception of economic justice: A cross-cultural comparison. *Journal of Economic Psychology*, 8, 457–67.

Furnham, A. (1987b). The determinants and structure of adolescents' beliefs about the economy. *Journal of Adolescence*, 10, 353–71.

Furnham, A. (1988). *Lay Theories: Everyday Understanding of Problems in the Social Sciences*. Oxford: Pergamon.

Furnham, A. (1989). School children's conceptions of economics: Prices, wages, investments and strikes. *Journal of Economic Psychology*, 9, 467–79.

Furnham, A. (1990). *The Protestant Work Ethic*. London: Routledge.

Furnham, A. and Gunter, B. (1983). Political knowledge and awareness in adolescence. *Journal of Adolescence*, 6, 373–85.

Furnham, A. and Gunter, B. (1987). Young people's political knowledge. *Educational Studies*, 13, 91–104.

Furnham, A. and Gunter, B. (1989). *The Anatomy of Adolescence: Young People's Social Attitudes in Britain*. London: Routledge.

Furnham, A., Johnson, C. and Rawles, R. (1985). The determinants of beliefs in human nature. *Personality and Individual Differences*, 6, 675–84.

Furnham, A. and Jones, S. (1987). Children's views regarding possessions and their theft. *Journal of Moral Education*, 16, 18–30.

Furnham, A. and Lewis, A. (1986). *The Economic Mind: The Social Psychology of Economic Behaviour*. Brighton: Wheatsheaf.

Furnham, A. and Radley, S. (1989). Sex differences in the perception of male and female body shapes. *Personality and Individual Differences*, 10, 653–62.

Furnham, A. and Schofield, S. (1986). Sex-role stereotyping in British radio advertisements. *British Journal of Social Psychology*, 25, 165–71.

Furnham, A. and Singh, A. (1986). Memory for information about sex differences. *Sex Roles*, 15, 479–86.

Furnham, A. and Thomas, P. (1984a). Adults' perception of the economic socialization of children. *Journal of Adolescence*, 7, 217–31.

Furnham, A. and Thomas, P. (1984b). Pocket money: A study of economic education. *Developmental Psychology*, 2, 205–31.

Furnham, A. and Weissman, D. (1986). Estimating the value of British coins: A development and cross-cultural perspective. Unpublished paper.

Furth, H. (1980). *The World of Grown-Ups*. New York: Elsevier.

Furth, H. and McConville, K. (1981). Adolescent understanding of compromise in political and social areas. *Merrill-Palmer Quarterly*, 27, 413–27.

Gilchrist, L. D. and Schinke, S. P. (1987). Adolescent pregnancy and marriage. In V. B. van Hasselt and M. Hersen (eds) *Handbook of Adolescent Psychology*. New York: Pergamon.

Ginzberg, E. (1972). Toward a theory of occupational choice: A restatement. *Vocational Guidance Quarterly*, 20, 169–76.

Goldman, R. J. (1964). Researches in religious thinking. *Educational Research*, 6, 139–55.

Goldman, R. and Goldman, J. (1982). *Children's Sexual Thinking*. London: Routledge & Kegan Paul.

Gordon, S. and Gilgun, J. F. (1987). Adolescent sexuality. In V. B. van Hasselt and M. Hersen (eds) *Handbook of Adolescent Psychology*. New York: Pergamon.

Greenberg, B. G. and Reeves, B. (1976). Children and the perceived reality of television. *Journal of Social Issues*, 32, 86–97.

Greenberger, E., Steinberg, L. and Vaux, S. (1981). Adolescents who work: Health and behavioural consequences of job stress. *Developmental Psychology*, 17, 691–703.

Greenfield, P. M. (1984). *Mind and Media*. London: Fontana.

Greenstein, F. (1961). Sex-related political differences in childhood. *Journal of Political Studies*, 21, 353–71.

Greer, J. E. (1984a). Fifty years of the psychology of religion in religious education (Part I). *British Journal of Religious Education*, 6, 93–8.

Greer, J. E. (1984b). Fifty years of the psychology of religion in religious education (Part II). *British Journal of Religious Education*, 7, 23–8.

Gurney, R. (1981). Leaving school, facing unemployment, and making attributions about the causes of unemployment. *Journal of Vocational Behaviour*, 18, 79–91.

Haire, M. and Morrison, F. (1957). School children's perception of labour and management. *Journal of Social Psychology*, 46, 179–97.

Haldane, I. (1978). Who and what is religious broadcasting for? *Independent Broadcasting*, 2, 13–6.

Hamilton, S. and Crouter, A. (1980). Work and growth: A review of research on the impact of work experience on adolescent development. *Journal of Youth and Adolescence*, 9, 323–34.

Hammarstrom, A., Janlert, U. and Theorell, T. (1988). Youth unemployment and ill health: Results from a 2-year follow-up study. *Social Science and Medicine*, 26, 1025–33.

Hargreaves, D. and Colley, A. (1987). *The Psychology of Sex Roles*. London: Hemisphere.

Harms, E. (1944). The development of religious experience in children. *American Journal of Sociology*, 50, 112–22.

Haste, H. (1987). Growing into rules. In J. Bruner and H. Haste (eds) *Making Sense*. London: Methuen.

Havighurst, R. (1972). *Developmental Tasks and Education*. New York: Daniel McKay.

Heald, G. and Wybrow, R. (1986). *The Gallup Survey of Britain*. London: Croom Helm.

Heller, D. (1986). *The Children's God*. Chicago: Chicago University Press.

Helmreich, R., Spence, J. and Gibson, R. (1982). Sex-role attitudes: 1972–1980. *Personality and Social Psychology Bulletin*, 8, 656–63.

Henshall, C. and McGuire, J. (1986). Gender development. In M. Richards and P. Light (eds) *Children of Social Worlds*. Cambridge: Polity Press.

Hess, R. D. and Torney, J. (1967). *The Development of Political Attitudes in Children*. Chicago: Aldine.

Heywood, D. (1986). Piaget and faith development: A true marriage of minds? *British Journal of Religious Education*, 8, 72–8.

Himmelfarb, H. S. (1979). Agents of religious socialisation among American Jews. *Sociological Quarterly*, 20, 477–94.

References

Himmelweit, H., Halsey, A. and Oppenheim, A. (1951). The views of adolescents on some aspects of the social class structure. *British Journal of Sociology*, 2, 148–72.

Himmelweit, H. and Swift, B. (1971). *Social and Personality Factors in the Development of Adult Attitudes Towards Self and Society*. SSRC Report.

Himmelweit, H., Humphreys, P., Jaeger, M. and Katz, M. (1981). *How Voters Decide*. London: Academic Press.

Hitchcock, J., Munroe, R. and Munroe, R. (1976). Coins and countries: The value-size hypothesis. *Journal of Social Psychology*, 100, 307–8.

Hoffman, L. W. (1977). Changes in family roles, socialization and sex differences. *American Psychologist*, 32, 644–57.

Hogan, R. and Mills, C. (1976). Legal socialization. *Human Development*, 19, 261–76.

Holland, J. (1959). A theory of vocational choice. *Journal of Counselling Psychology*, 6, 35–45.

Hood, E., Lindsay, W. and Brooks, N. (1982). Interview training with adolescents. *Behaviour Research and Therapy*, 20, 581–92.

Husen, T. (1987). Young adults in modern society: Changing status and values. *Oxford Review of Education*, 13, 165–76.

Hyman, H. (1959). *Political Socialization: A Study in the Psychology of Political Behaviour*. New York: Free Press.

Ingels, S. and O'Brien, M. (1985). The effects of economics instruction in early adolescence. *Theory and Research in Social Education*, 4, 279–94.

Insel, P. and Wilson, A. (1971). Measuring social attitudes in children. *British Journal of Social and Clinical Psychology*, 10, 84–6.

Irving, K. and Siegal, M. (1983). Mitigating circumstances in children's perceptions of criminal justice. *British Journal of Developmental Psychology*, 1, 179–88.

Itzin, C. (1986). Media images of women: The social construction of ageism and sexism. In S. Wilkinson (ed.) *Feminist Social Psychology*. Milton Keynes: Open University Press.

Jackson, P., Stafford, E., Banks, M. and Warr, P. (1983). Unemployment and psychological distress in young people: The moderating role of employment commitment. *Journal of Applied Psychology*, 68, 525–35.

Jackson, R. (1972). The development of political concepts in young children. *Educational Research*, 14, 51–5.

Jahoda, G. (1979). The construction of economic reality by some Glaswegian children. *European Journal of Social Psychology*, 9, 115–27.

Jahoda, G. (1981). The development of thinking about economic institutions: The bank. *Cahiers de Psychologie Cognitive*, 1, 55–78.

Jahoda, G. (1983). European 'lag' in the development of an economic concept: A study in Zimbabwe. *British Journal of Developmental Psychology*, 1, 110–20.

Jahoda, G. (1984). The development of thinking about an socio-economic systems. In H. Tajfel (ed.) *The Social Dimension*, Vol. 1. Cambridge: Cambridge University Press.

Jahoda, G. and Woerdenbagch, A. (1982). The development of ideas about an economic institution: A cross-national replication. *British Journal of Social Psychology*, 21, 337–8.

Jaros, D. and Grant, L. (1974). *Political Behaviour: Choices and Perspective*. Oxford: Blackwell.

Jennings, M. and Niemi, R. (1971). The division of political labour between fathers and mothers. *American Political Science Review*, 65, 64–82.

Jones, P. (1985). Qualifications and labour-market outcomes among 16-year-old school-leavers. *British Journal of Guidance and Counselling*, 13, 275–91.

Jowell, R. and Airey, C. (eds) (1984). *British Social Attitudes*. Aldershot: Gower.

Juhasz, A. M. and Sonnenshein-Schneider, M. (1987). Adolescent sexuality: Values, morality and decision making. *Adolescence*, 22, 579–90.

Katz, P. (1976). The acquisition of racial attitudes in children. In P. A. Katz (ed.) *Towards the Elimination of Racism*. New York: Pergamon.

Katz, P. A. (1983). Developmental foundations of gender and racial attitudes. In R. L. Leahy (ed.) *The Child's Construction of Social Inequality*. New York: Academic Press.

Kourilsky, M. (1977). The kinder-economy: A case study of kindergarten pupils' acquisition of economic concepts. *Elementary School Journal*, 77, 182–91.

Kourilsky, M. and Campbell, M. (1984). Sex differences in a simulated classroom economy: Children's beliefs about entrepreneurship. *Sex Roles*, 10, 53–66.

Lambert, W., Solomon, R. and Watson, P. (1949). Reinforcement and extinction as factors in size estimation. *Journal of Experimental Psychology*, 39, 637–41.

Lawrence, P. (1965). Children's thinking about religion: A study of concrete operational thinking. *Religious Education*, 60, 111–16.

Lea, S., Tarpy, R. and Webley, P. (1987). *The Individual in the Economy: A Survey of Economic Psychology*. Cambridge: Cambridge University Press.

Leahy, R. (1981). The development of the conception of economic inequality: Descriptions and comparisons of rich and poor people. *Child Development*, 52, 523–32.

Leahy, R. L. (ed.) (1983). *The Child's Construction of Social Inequality*. New York: Academic Press.

Leiser, D. (1983). Children's conceptions of economics: The constitution of a cognitive domain. *Journal of Economic Psychology*, 4, 297–317.

Lewis, A. (1983). Public expenditure: Perceptions and preferences. *Journal of Economic Psychology*, 3, 159–67.

Lloyd, B. (1987). Social representations of gender. In J. Bruner and H. Haste (eds) *Making Sense: The Child's Construction of the World*. London: Methuen.

Lonky, E., Reihman, J. and Serlin, R. (1981). Political values and moral judgement in adolescence. *Youth and Society*, 12, 423–41.

Maccoby, E. and Jacklin, C. (1974). *The Psychology of Sex Differences*. Stanford, Ca: Stanford University Press.

McCurdy, H. (1956). Coin perception studies and the concept of schemata. *Psychological Review*, 63, 160–8.

Macdonald, M. (1980). Schooling and the reproduction of class and gender relations. In L. Barton, R. Meigham and S. Walker (eds) *Schooling, Ideology and the Curriculum*. Lewes: Falmer Press.

McGrew, W. (1972). *An Ethological Study of Children's Behaviour*. New York: Academic Press.

McNeal, J. (1987). *Children as Consumers: Insights and Implications*. Lexington: Lexington Books.

References

Makeham, P. (1980). *Youth Unemployment: An Examination of Evidence on Youth Unemployment using National Statistics*. London: Department of Employment.

Manaster, G., Greer, D. and Kleiber, D. (1985). Youth's outlook on the future. *Youth and Society*, 17, 97–112.

Marjoribanks, K. (1981). Sex-related differences in socio-political attitudes: A replication. *Education Studies*, 7, 1–7.

Marjoribanks, K. (1986). A longitudinal study of adolescents' aspirations as assessed by Seginer's Model. *Merrill-Palmer Quarterly*, 32, 211–30.

Mark, T. (1982). A study of religious attitudes, religious behaviour and religious cognition. *Educational Studies*, 8, 209–16.

Marshall, H. and Magruder, L. (1960). Relations between parent money education practices and children's knowledge and use of money. *Child Development*, 31, 253–84.

Meade, R. and Whittaker, J. (1967). A cross-culture study of authoritarianism. *Journal of Social Psychology*, 72, 3–7.

Meadow, M. and Kahoe, D. (1984). *The Psychology of Religion: Religion in Individual Lives*. New York: Harper & Row.

Miller, L. and Horn, T. (1955). Children's concepts regarding debt. *Elementary School Journal*, 56, 406–12.

Miller, P. (1989). *Theories of Developmental Psychology*. New York: Freeman & Co.

Millham, S., Bullock, R. and Hosie, K. (1978). Juvenile unemployment: A concept for re-cycling. *Journal of Adolescence*, 1, 11–24.

Milner, D. (1983). *Children and Race*. London: Ward Lock.

Money, J. and Ehrhardt, A. (1972). *Man and Woman, Boy and Girl*. Baltimore, Md: Johns Hopkins University Press.

Moore, J. (1988). Adolescent spiritual development: Stages and strategies. *Religious Education*, 83, 83–100.

Neale, M., Rushton, J. and Fulker, D. (1986). Heritability of item responses on the Eysenck Personality Questionnaire. *Personality and Individual Differences*, 7, 771–9.

Nelson, E., Eisenberg, N. and Carroll, J. (1982). The structure of adolescents' attitudes towards law and crime. *Journal of Genetic Psychology*, 140, 47–58.

Nelson, R. (1963). Knowledge and interests concerning sixteen occupations among elementary and secondary school students. *Educational and Psychological Measurement*, 23, 741–54.

Nevill, D. and Perrotta, J. (1985). Adolescent perceptions of work and home: Australia, Portugal and the United States. *Journal of Cross-Cultural Psychology*, 16, 483–95.

Newson, J. and Newson, E. (1976). *Seven Year Olds in the Home Environment*. London: George Allen & Unwin.

Ng, S. (1983). Children's ideas about the bank and shop prefit: Development stages and the influence of cognitive contrasts and conflict. *Journal of Economic Psychology*, 4, 209–21.

Nias, D. (1973). Measurements and structure of children's attitudes. In G. Wilson (ed.) *The Psychology of Conservatism*. New York: Academic Press.

Niemi, R. (1973). Political socialization. In J. Knutson (ed.) *Handbook of Political Psychology*. San Francisco: Jossey-Bass.

Nilsson, I. and Ekehammar, B. (1986). Socio-political ideology and field of study. *Educational Studies*, 12, 37–46.

O'Brien, M. and Ingels, S. (1985). *The Development of the Economic Values Inventory*. Chicago: University of Chicago Press.

O'Brien, M. and Ingels, S. (1987). The economic values inventory. *Research in Economic Education*, 18, 7–18.

O'Bryant, S., Durrett, M. and Pennebaker, J. (1980). Sex differences in knowledge of occupational dimensions across four age levels. *Sex Roles*, 6, 331–7.

O'Donnell, M. (1985). *Age and Generation*. London: Tavistock.

Open University (1977). *Media and Society*. Milton Keynes: Open University Press.

Oppenheim, A. and Torney, J. (1974). *The Measurement of Children's Attitudes in Different Nations*. Stockholm: Wiley.

Orum, A. (1974). *The Seeds of Politics: Youth and Politics in America*. New Jersey: Prentice-Hall.

Palonsky, S. (1987). Political socialization in elementary schools. *Elementary School Journal*, 87, 493–505.

Parry, G. (1983). A British version of the Attitudes towards Women Scale. *British Journal of Social Psychology*, 22, 261–3.

Patterson, J. and Locksley, G. (1981). How fifth formers see the unions. *Labour Research*, 11, 23–5.

Patton, W. and Noller, P. (1984). Unemployment and youth: A longitudinal study. *Australian Journal of Psychology*, 36, 399–413.

Pautler, K. and Lewko, J. (1987). Children's and adolescents' views of the work world in times of economic uncertainty. In J. Lewko (ed.) *How Children and Adolescents View the World of Work*. San Francisco: Jossey-Bass, pp. 21–31.

Piaget, J. (1965). *The Child's Conception of the World*. St Albans: Paladin.

Piotrkowski, C. and Stark, E. (1987). Children and adolescents look at their parents' jobs. In J. Lewko (ed.) *How Children and Adolescents View the World of Work*. San Francisco: Jossey-Bass, pp. 4–19.

Pollis, H. and Gray, T. (1973). Change-making strategies in children and adults. *Journal of Psychology*, 84, 173–9.

Poole, M. (1978). Identifying early school learning. *Australian Journal of Education*, 22, 13–24.

Poole, M. (1983). *Youth: Expectations and Transitions*. London: Routledge & Kegan Paul.

Porteous, M. and Colston, N. (1980). How adolescents are reported in the British Press. *Journal of Adolescence*, 3, 197–207.

Potvin, R. H. (1977). Adolescent God images. *Review of Religious Research*, 19, 43–53.

Potvin, R. H. and Lee, C-F. (1982). Adolescent religion: A developmental approach. *Sociological Analysis*, 43, 131–44.

Raelin, J. (1981). A comparative study of later work experience among full-time, part-time and unemployed male youth. *Journal of Vocational Behaviour*, 19, 315–27.

References

Raelin, J. (1983). Youth permanent part-time employment as a labour market alternative to full-time work: A longitudinal analysis. *Journal of Occupational Behaviour*, 4, 179–91.

Rice, F. (1984). *The Adolescent: Development, Relationships and Culture*. Boston: Allyn & Bacon.

Rizzuto, A.-M. (1974). Object relations and the formation of the image of God. *British Journal of Medical Psychology*, 47, 83–99.

Roberts, R. and Dolan, J. (1989). Children's perception of 'work' – an exploratory study. *Educational Review*, 41, 19–28.

Rosenfield, D. and Stephan, W. G. (1981). Intergroup relations among children. In S. S. Brehm, S. M. Kassin and F. X. Gibbons (eds) *Developmental Social Psychology*. New York: Oxford University Press.

Rosenthal, D. A. (1987). Ethnic identity development in adolescents. In J. S. Phinney and M. J. Rotheram (eds) *Children's Ethnic Socialization*. Beverly Hills, CA: Sage.

Ruggiero, M. and Steinberg, L. (1981). The empirical study of teenager work: A behavioural code for the assessment of adolescent job environments. *Journal of Vocational Behaviour*, 19, 163–74.

Sampson, S. N. (1978). Socialisation into sex roles. In F. W. Hunt (ed.) *Socialisation in Australia*. Melbourne: Australia International Press.

Sanford, N. (1973). The roots of prejudice: Emotional dynamics. In P. Watson (ed.) *Psychology and Race*. Harmondsworth: Penguin.

Santilli, N. and Furth, H. (1987). Adolescent work perception: A developmental approach. In J. Lewko (ed.) *How Children and Adolescents View the World of Work*. San Francisco: Jossey-Bass.

Shapiro, D. and Crowley, J. (1982). Aspirations and expectations of youth in the United States. Part 2 Employment Activity. *Youth and Society*, 14, 33–58.

Shaver, J., Hoffman, H. and Richards, H. (1971). The authoritarianism of American and German teacher education students. *Journal of Social Psychology*, 84, 303–4.

Sidanius, J. and Ekehammar, B. (1980). Sex-related differences in socio-political ideology. *Scandinavian Journal of Psychology*, 21, 17–26.

Sidanius, J., Ekehammar, B. and Ross, M. (1979). Comparison of socio-political attitudes between two democratic societies. *International Journal of Psychology*, 14, 225–40.

Siegal, M. (1981). Children's perception of adult economic needs. *Child Development*, 52, 379–82.

Siegal, M. and Shwalb, D. (1985). Economic justice in adolescence: An Australian–Japanese comparison. Journal of Economic Psychology, 6, 313–26.

Simmons, C. and Wade, W. (1984). *I Like to Say What I Think: A Study of the Attitudes, Values and Beliefs of Young People Today*. London: Kogan Page.

Simmons, R. G. and Rosenberg, M. (1971). Functions of children's perceptions of the stratification system. *American Sociological Review*, 36, 235–49.

Slee, N. (1986). Goldman yet again. *British Journal of Religious Education*, 8, 84–92.

Smith, H., Fuller, R. and Forrest, D. (1975). Coin value and perceived size: A longitudinal study. *Perceptual and Motor Skills*, 41, 227–32.

Stacey, B. G. (1978). *Political Socialization in Western Society*. London: Edward Arnold.

Stacey, B. (1982). Economic socialization in the pre-adult years. *British Journal of Social Psychology*, 21, 159–73.

Stafford, E., Jackson, P. and Banks, M. (1980). Employment, work involvement and mental health in less qualified young people. *Journal of Occupational Psychology*, 53, 291–304.

Stern, A. J. and Searing, D. D. (1976). The stratification beliefs of English and American adolescents. *British Journal of Psychology*, 6, 177–201.

Stradling, R. (1977). *The Political Awareness of the School Leaver*. London: Hansard Society.

Strauss, A. (1952). The development and transformation of monetary meanings in the child. *American Sociological Review*, 17, 275–86.

Strayer, F. and Strayer, J. (1976). An ethological analysis of social agonism and dominance relations among pre-school children. *Child Development*, 47, 980–9.

Sultana, R. (1988). Schooling tomorrow's worker: Trade union education in secondary schools. *New Zealand Journal of Industrial Relations*, 13, 3–20.

Super, D. (1957). *The Psychology of Careers*. New York: Harper & Row.

Super, D. (1963). Self-concepts in vocational development. In D. Syser (ed.) *Careers Development: Self-concept Theory*. New York: College Entrance Examination Board.

Sutton, R. (1962). Behaviour in the attainment of economic concepts. *Journal of Psychology*, 53, 37–46.

Svennevig, M., Haldane, I., Spiers, S. and Gunter, B. (1988). *Godwatching: Viewers, Religion and Television*. London: Wiley.

Taft, R. (1978). Ethnic groups. In F. J. Hunt (ed.) *Socialisation in Australia*. Melbourne: Australian International Press.

Tajfel, H. (1977). Value and the perception of magnitude. *Psychological Review*, 67, 192–204.

Tajfel, H. (1982). Social psychology of intergroup relations. *Annual Review of Psychology*, 33, 1–39.

Tan, H. and Stacey, B. (1981). The understanding of socio-economic concepts in Malaysian Chinese school children. *Child Study Journal*, 11, 33–49.

Tapp, J. L. and Levine, F. J. (eds) (1977). *Law, Justice and the Individual in Society*. New York: Holt, Rinehart & Winston.

Taylor, M. (1985). The roles of occupational knowledge and vocational self-concept crystallization in students' school-to-work transition. *Journal of Counselling Psychology*, 32, 539–50.

Taylor, S. (1982). Schooling and social reproduction. *Australian Journal of Education*, 26, 144–54.

Torney, J. V. (1977). Socialization of attitudes toward the legal system. In J. L. Tapp and F. J. Levine (eds) *Law, Justice and the Individual in Society*. New York: Holt, Rinehart & Winston.

Torney-Purta, J. (1983). The development of views about the role of social institutions in redressing inequality and promoting human rights. In R. L. Leahy (ed.) *The Child's Construction of Social Inequality*. New York: Academic Press.

References

Tremaine, L., Sehan, C. and Busch, J. (1982). Children's occupational sex-typing. *Sex Roles*, 8, 691–710.

Turiel, E. (1983). *The Development of Social Knowledge*. Cambridge: Cambridge University Press.

Vaughan, G. (1978). Social change and intergroup preferences in New Zealand. *European Journal of Social Psychology*, 8, 297–314.

Vaughan, G. (1987). A social psychological model of ethnic identity development. In J. S. Phinney and N. J. Rotheram (eds) *Children's Ethnic Socialization*. Beverly Hills, CA: Sage.

Viney, L. (1983). Psychological reactions of young people to unemployment. *Youth and Society*, 14, 457–74.

Walls Ltd. (1983). *Pocket Money Monitor*. Surrey: Birds Eye, Walls Ltd.

Warr, P., Banks, M. and Ullah, P. (1985). The experience of unemployment among black and white urban teenagers. *British Journal of Psychology*, 76, 75–87.

Watts, A. (1978). The implications for school-leavers: Unemployment for careers education in schools. *Journal of Curriculum Studies*, 3, 233–50.

Webley, P. and Wrigley, V. (1983). The development of conceptions of unemployment among adolescents. *Journal of Adolescence*, 6, 317–20.

Williams, J., Daws, J., Best, D., Tilquin, C., Wesley, F. and Bjerke, T. (1979). Sex-trait stereotypes in France, Germany and Norway. *Journal of Cross-Cultural Psychology*, 10, 133–6.

Williams, J. E. and Best, D. (1982). *Measuring Sex Stereotypes: A Thirty Nation Study*. Beverly Hills: Sage.

Williams, J. E. and Morland, J. K. (1976). *Race, Color and the Young Child*. Chapel Hill, NC: University of North Carolina Press.

Wilson, A. (1981). Mixed race children: An exploratory study of racial categorization and identity. *New Community*, 9, 36–43.

Wilson, G. (ed.) (1973). *The Psychology of Conservatism*. London: Academic Press.

Wilson, W. C. (1963). Development of ethnic attitudes in adolescence. *Child Development*, 34, 247–56.

Winocur, S. and Siegal, M. (1982). Adolescents' judgements of economic arrangements. *International Journal of Behavioural Development*, 5, 357–65.

Witryol, S. and Wentworth, N. (1983). A paired comparison scale of children's preference for monetary and material rewards used in investigations of incentive effects. *Journal of Genetic Psychology*, 142, 17–23.

Wober, M. (1980). *Television and Teenagers' Political Awareness*. London: IBA Report.

Wober, M. and Gunter, B. (1988). *Television and Social Control*. Aldershot: Avebury.

Young, R. (1983). Career development of adolescents: An ecological perspective. *Journal of Youth and Adolescence*, 12, 401–10.

Youniss, J. and Volpe, J. (1978). A relational analysis of children's friendships. In W. Damon (ed.) *Social Cognition*. Washington: Jossey-Bass.

Name index

Name index

Piaget, J. 4, 16, 44, 192. 205
Piatrkowski, C. 79, 205
Pollis, H. 36, 205
Poole, M. 68–9, 78, 85, 101, 198, 205
Porteous, M. 1–2, 205
Potvin, R. H. 114, 125–7, 205

Radley, S. 106, 200
Raelin, J. 72, 80, 205
Rawles, R. 20, 200
Reeves, B. 152, 200
Reihman, J. 19, 203
Rice, F. 2, 206
Richards, H. 21, 206
Rizzuto, A. M. 114, 119, 206
Roberts, R. 66, 206
Rosenberg, M. 179–80, 206
Rosenfield, D. 139, 149, 206
Rosenthal, D. A. 134, 139, 206
Ross, M. 21, 206
Ruggiero, M. 80, 206
Rushton, J. 191, 204

Sampson, S. 100, 206
Sanford, N. 147, 206
Santilli, N. 66, 206
Schinke, S. P. 107, 200
Schofield, S. 104, 200
Searing, D. D. 163, 180, 184, 207
Sehan, C. 79, 207
Serlin, R. 19, 203
Shapiro, D. 67, 206
Shaver, J. 21, 206
Shwalb, D. 49, 206
Sidanius, J. 20, 22, 188, 198, 206
Siegal, M. 46–9, 202, 206, 208
Simmons, C. 17, 206
Simmons, R. G. 179–80, 206
Singh, A. 92, 200
Slee, N. 123, 206
Smith, H. 37, 206
Solomon, R. 37, 203
Sonnenshein-Schneider, M. 107, 203
Spence, J. 97, 201
Spiers, S. 114, 207
Stacey, B. G. 32, 40, 57–60, 175, 180, 207
Stafford, E. 72–3 202, 207
Stark, E. 79, 205

Steinberg, L. 80, 201, 206
Stephan, W. G. 139, 149, 206
Stern, A. J. 163, 180, 184, 207
Stradling, R. 24–7, 207
Strauss, A. 57, 207
Strayer, F. 46, 207
Strayer, J. 46, 207
Sultana, R. 86, 207
Super, D. 83, 207
Sutton, R. 37, 57, 207
Svennevig, M. 114, 207
Swart, L. T. 149, 152, 198
Swift, B. 23, 202

Taebel, V. 57, 197
Taft, R. 149, 207
Tajfel, H. 37, 141, 150, 207
Tan, H. 40, 207
Tapp, J. L. 157–60, 162, 165, 207
Tarpy, R. 35, 65, 203
Taylor, M. 79, 207
Taylor, S. 103, 207
Taylor, T. 35, 61, 197
Theorell, T. 72–3, 201
Thomas, P. 35, 55, 62–3, 200
Torney-(Purta), J. V. 20–1, 32–3, 161–5, 201, 207
Tremaine, L. 79, 207
Turiel, E. 12, 208

Ullah, P. 72–3, 75, 195, 208

Vaughan, G. 136–41, 208
Vaux, S. 80, 201
Verba, S. 20, 195
Verma, G. 142–3, 195
Viney, L. 73, 208
Volpe, J. 12–13, 208

Wade, W. 17, 206
Walls, Ltd. 60, 208
Warr, P. 72–3, 202, 208
Watson, P. 37, 203
Watts, A. 72, 76, 208
Webley, P. 35, 65, 75, 203, 208
Weissman, D. 37, 200
Wentworth, N. 36, 208
Whittaker, J. 21, 204
Williams, J. E. 88, 135–9, 147–9, 208
Wilson, A. 22, 140, 202, 208

Subject index

For Product Safety Concerns and Information please contact our EU
representative GPSR@taylorandfrancis.com
Taylor & Francis Verlag GmbH, Kaufingerstraße 24, 80331 München, Germany

www.ingramcontent.com/pod-product-compliance
Lightning Source LLC
Chambersburg PA
CBHW070410270326
41926CB00014B/2776

*9 7 8 1 1 3 8 6 4 2 1 2 6 *